Palestinian Judaism in
the Time of Jesus Christ

Palestinian Judaism in the Time of Jesus Christ

BY JOSEPH BONSIRVEN, S.J.

Translated from the French by William Wolf

Holt, Rinehart and Winston New York Chicago San Francisco

Introduction

The Purpose of this Book

As historians of the origins of Christianity the commentators of the New Testament are today convinced that they
cannot accomplish their task without being acquainted with
the Jewish milieu in which Christianity arose and began
to develop. After all, we know that those Jews who came
to believe in Christ grafted their new faith to the old one
and wished to implant it into Holy Scripture. They accepted and understood their new faith, therefore, according to the authorized commentaries they had heard and in
the light of the traditions they had received. This greater
awareness of the Jewish background of the New Testament
helps to explain the considerable work which has been
done on this subject in recent decades. After many centuries of nearly systematic disregard and disrespect we follow

the tracks of Buxtorf, Selden, Surenhusius, and many other scholars in the sixteenth, seventeenth, and eighteenth centuries, who dealt with rabbinical literature with so much zeal and ability.

In this book we will limit ourselves to a study of Palestinian Judaism, neglecting the culture which originated in Alexandria. This does not mean that the latter is not of great interest. But we no longer live at a time—which was not so long ago—when one believed that the faith of St. Paul or St. John could be explained by the influence of Philo. Even the Epistle to the Hebrews, which certainly contains quotations from Philo, is theologically independent of the doctrines of that great Jewish philosopher.[1] He will not be completely ignored, however, and there will be at least occasional references to Alexandrian Judaism.

The Jews of Palestine were divided into various sects: Pharisees, Sadducees, Essenes, popular and apocalyptic groups. But in spite of differences, some superficial and others profound and essential, these sects were united by a common fund of beliefs and practices derived directly from the Bible and from revered and universally accepted traditions. It is with this common fund that we will deal in this book.

Sources

But can we reconstruct Judaism at the time of the beginning of Christianity with sufficient accuracy? We believe that the many documents which are at our disposal and which we shall utilize provide direct testimonies tending to converge and to corroborate each other and to guarantee a real certainty.

[1] See my *Saint Paul—Épître aux Hebreux: introduction, traduction et commentaire* (Paris, 1943), pp. 148-55.

In the Gospels and in other parts of the New Testament we find indications, not very numerous but contemporary, whose polemical intentions do not prevent us from recognizing direct evidence. As far as the morals and doctrines of the Jews of Palestine and of the Diaspora are concerned, the books of Philo, who lived from about 20 B.C. to between A.D. 40 and 50, provide considerable evidence which can readily be separated from his personal philosophy. And Josephus, born in Jerusalem in A.D. 37 or 38 and raised among priests and Pharisees, knew from his own experience this Judaism which we wish to reconstruct. In his treatment of beliefs and practices one can easily point out both the distortions caused by his apologetic intentions and by his concern for the feelings of his Greco-Roman readers as in those formulations in which he traces Pharisaism and Sadduceeism back to philosophical schools like Stoicism and Pythagoreanism.

The rabbinic literature—Talmud, Targum, and Midrash—is another important and extensive source. We have known Christian scholars who treated these books with distrust and suspicion and refused to draw on them because of their supposedly recent and uncertain date or their childish credulity. Such a feeling can be partly explained by the forbidding and inaccessible character of such documents. The Jews, on the other hand, as well as many Christians,[2] think that these books ought not to be neglected, for "in them we find beautiful remains of the ancient traditions of the Jewish people," remains which give expression to normative Judaism and represent the line of the catholic tradition of Judaism.[3] But how are we to exploit this *mare magnum* which goes back to the most various

[2] See Bossuet, *Discourse on Universal History*, II, xxi.
[3] G. F. Moore, *Judaism in the First Centuries of the Christian Era* (Cambridge, Mass., 1927; 3 vols.), I, 126.

and often uncertain dates and produces divergent or contradictory evidence?

Let us first distinguish between the different categories.

Among the books edited toward the end of the second or the beginning of the third century we have, first of all, the legal works—Megillat Taanit (a list of days on which one must not fast), the Mishnah ("repetition"), and the Tosefta ("addition," or "supplement"), the last two being a Jewish code of law in six sections and fifty-two tractates. There are also the largely legal commentaries on the last four books of Moses—*Mekilta on Exodus, Sifra on Leviticus,* and *Sifre on Numbers* and *Deuteronomy.* Finally we might mention the *Seder Olam,* a kind of chronicle of Jewish history.

The Targum, or Aramaic paraphrase of the Bible, contains ancient parts; but since it was edited at a rather recent date, it is wise to use it with reservation, especially in connection with the prophets and the books of wisdom.

The Talmud comprises the Mishnah and the Gemara. The latter is supposedly a commentary on the Mishnah, but actually includes passages of morality, piety, edification, historical tradition and legend, and medical lore—in other words, all the knowledge of talmudic times. The Palestinian Talmud (*Yerushalmi*) was edited in Palestine up to the fifth century; its Babylonian counterpart (*Babli,* or "Talmud" par excellence, also called *Shass,* meaning "six sections") was compiled in Babylonia up to the seventh century.

We also have a vast number of Midrashim, homiletic commentaries on biblical books, written—or rather compiled—between the fifth and the eleventh centuries. They are addresses made in the synagogue, whose points of departure were the readings of the Pentateuch and other biblical passages. Examples include the *Pesikta de Rav Kahana,* the *Pesikta Rabbati,* the *Midrash Tanhuma* or *Yelammdenu.*

There is the *Midrash Rabbah*, a detailed explanation of the five books of Moses and the five *megillot* books read on certain feasts or at certain periods (the Canticle of Canticles, Ruth, Lamentations, Ecclesiastes, and Esther); there is the *Midrash Haggadol* on the Pentateuch, the *Shocher Tob* on Psalms, and other Midrashim on different subjects and of various origins.

We wish to deal only with those statements attributed by name to certain rabbis of the first two centuries and with anonymous sentences called *baraitot,* believed to precede the third century. These statements may well belong to the time to which they have been assigned, since those attributed to a certain rabbi are often corroborated by an entire chain of reporters—"according to Rabbi 'X,' Rabbi 'Y' said"—or else they are identically quoted in different works. As a rule we do not refer to texts dated later than the second century, although we do not believe that Judaism shows a real evolution in matters relating to doctrine. By virtue of this principle, we believe that statements made by second-century rabbis reflect the thought of the preceding century.

Nevertheless, we should not forget that in Israel, at least on certain subjects, no universal and fixed dogma was ever imposed. Therefore, we must be careful not to present the statement of an isolated rabbi as the expression of a commonly accepted doctrine. We must also take into account the ironical, exaggerated, and paradoxical character of many sayings; we are in the Orient, and we often hear the words of a popular preacher.

To the rabbinical documents we should also add the official prayers, since many of them, at least in their germinal form, are older than the Christian era.

Another extensive Jewish source is the pseudepigrapha —in the Catholic vocabulary, the Old Testament Apocrypha—which vary greatly as to date and origin. We shall use: *The Psalms of Solomon* (about 50 B.C.), *4 Ezra* and *2 Baruch* (both toward the end of the first century A.D.), all three bearing the mark of an authentic Pharisaic spirit. From the same milieu, though more pietistic in tone, come *The Assumption of Moses* and *The Apocalypse of Moses* (the middle of the first century A.D.), and *The Testament of the Twelve Patriarchs* (second century B.C.). It is difficult to characterize *The Book of Jubilees* (same time) and the Ethiopian *Book of Enoch,* each a compilation of pieces reflecting different tendencies. This new series of writings spreads out from the second century B.C. to the first century A.D. One must also mention *The Letter of Aristeas* (second or first century B.C.), a certain number of fragments of *The Sibylline Oracles* (these go back to various dates), *4 Maccabees* (first century B.C.), and the Slavonic, or Second, *Book of Enoch* (possibly a little older). These four are of Judeo-Greek origin, but they do give information concerning universal Judaism.

Thus we shall part company with those rabbis who do not admit the evidence of these works because they had often been forbidden by official authorities and because they emerged from groups whose orthodoxy was minimal. We also differ from some Christian historians who used other texts they considered more easily accessible and older than the rabbinic writings and who felt these writings represented the thought of the common people.

Other sources of information are Jewish inscriptions and the opinions of Jews expressed by secular Greek or Roman authors as well as by the Fathers of the Church.

Finally, the Old Testament contains indications of the greatest importance not only in Ecclesiasticus (The Book of Sirach), The Book of Wisdom and Machabees—books so close to the time we are studying—but also in the older

books read and studied tirelessly by faithful Jews in order
to foster their religion.

Method

The seven groups of documents which we can use, therefore, are the Old Testament, the New Testament, Philo,
Josephus, the rabbinical writings, the Apocrypha, and the
inscriptions and opinions of ancient authors. When a doctrine of a religious attitude is corroborated by these different witnesses or by an overwhelming majority of them—for
example, by the rabbis who continue the biblical tradition
and are in agreement with the Apocrypha—one ought to
recognize that unquestionable elements of first-century
Palestinian Judaism have been located.

Since we wish to present the living reality of Jewish religion, we shall not be satisfied with exposing only that which
today might be considered its dogmatic theology—the beliefs which animate and inspire conduct—but will also try
to point out the principles and instructions which regu-
lated moral and religious life and which, in the eyes of
Israel, were of supreme importance.

Contents

Introduction   v

The Purpose of the Book
Sources
Method

I   God   3

Existence of God
Anthropomorphism and Excessive Respect
God in Himself
God as Creator
Divine Providence
Omnipotence
Omniscience, Foreknowledge, and Predestination
God's Goodness, Mercy, and Justice
Transcendence or Immanence? Love or Fear?

II   Angels   33

Good Angels
Demonology

III   The People of God—Israel and the
       Nations   42

       The Chosen People
       The People of God, the God of Israel
       Israel's Duties and Qualities
       The Nations
       The Community of Israel: Nation-Religion

IV   The Torah   79

       The Torah and Moses
       The Written and the Oral Law
       The Torah and Life

V   Man and General Ethics   98

       Man
       Sin and Evil Nature
       The Motives for Moral Action
       Sin and Expiation

VI   Religious Life   119

       The Temple and Its Liturgy
       The Synagogues, Private Worship, and Personal Religion
       Religious Practices: Consecration of the Individual
          and of Life

VII   Special Ethics   144

       Duties of Justice
       Duties of Charity
       Relations With Gentiles
       Individual Perfection

Contents

VIII   Life After Death   163

Judgment After Death
The World to Come

IX   Messianism   172

Preliminaries for Redemption
The Person of the Messiah
The Establishment of the Messianic Kingdom
The Days of the Messiah

X   General Eschatology   226

Resurrection
Judgment
Eternal Reward and Punishment

Conclusion   252

Bibliography   261

Editor's Note   In general, references to biblical books and personalities, within the text, follow the Douay-Confraternity edition of Scripture. In quotations from Jewish sources, names of Biblical books have usually been made to conform to the Douay-Confraternity Bible; however, the spelling of the names of biblical personalities often remains in its Hebrew form. With pseudepigraphal works, names have not necessarily been changed to agree with Douay-Confraternity spellings, but have been left in the form in which they are most readily accessible in English (especially in regard to works cited from the edition of R. H. Charles). Thus, the pseudepigraphal works of Esdras are referred to as *4 Ezra,* and so forth.

Palestinian Judaism in
the Time of Jesus Christ

Chapter One
God

"Hear, O Israel, the Lord our God, the Lord is One." This daily prayer, which is at the same time a confession of faith, expresses the very soul of every fervent Israelite. It belongs to a people who has received the divine mission to be the trustee and the missionary of ethical monotheism. How many Jews have died as martyrs with this sacred formula on their lips, stretching out the last syllable of the last word *Ehad* (One), thus affirming their faith in the One God! It is therefore not surprising that the idea of God, the Creator, Providence, is the light illuminating the whole of Jewish thought. The king who, according to *The Letter of Aristeas,* asked some Jewish scholars to discourse before him remarked: "Everything they say has its point of departure in God. In this lies their superiority." The principal function of the rabbi, as both scholar and preacher, was to teach his people about God.[1]

[1] See Schlatter, *Jochanan ben Zakkai* (Gütersloh, 1899), p. 19.

In every type of writing and in every school of thought in the surviving Jewish texts we find, therefore, innumerable statements about God. Nowhere, however, do we find a systematic and complete account of their theodicy. Yet we do not think that an attempt at such a synthesis would be a misrepresentation of their thought. On the contrary, we believe that it would be an authentic representation of their common beliefs, beliefs inspired by their respect for the Holy Scriptures, which they had studied and meditated upon with so much zeal and love.

Existence of God

Like most of the ancients, the Jews could not conceive how one could deny the existence of God. They thought only that one could have mistaken notions about him and that pagans and heretics were in error as to the nature of the One God. The atheists, whom they called Epicureans, were those who rejected Providence, or God's authority. Therefore it was pointless for them to develop arguments to prove a thesis which no one denied. Besides this, the rabbis believed—and this is a tradition found also in Philo and Josephus—that God is known by means of revelation and that only some extraordinary men, like Abraham, were able by themselves to attain the knowledge of God.

In his *Antiquities of the Jews* (I, vii, 1, par. 156), Josephus puts the following proof into the mouth of the chief patriarch: "Since neither the heavenly nor the earthly bodies are able to provide for themselves properly, they act only on orders from above, and therefore He is the only Master to be worshipped and thanked." One can well understand that this historian, living in a Greco-Roman atmosphere, discovered there this philosophical argument and felt the need to present it. Arguments of this kind are attributed to rabbis but appear only in recent collections, and their authenticity is doubtful. Akiba (d. A.D. 135), for example, is said to have answered a heretic who asked him about the Creator of the world: "The world is the work of the Holy One, blessed be He, just as the garment is the work of the weaver. The world testifies to the fact that God has created it, as the house testifies to the work of the mason" (*Midrash Temurah,* near the end). Other rabbinic statements which may be considered proofs for the existence of God were, in reality, meant to provide correct attitudes regarding the nature of a particular divine attribute.

Anthropomorphism and Excessive Respect

The rabbinical statements concerning God show two contradictory tendencies. On the one hand, they not only repeat the many anthropomorphic and anthropopathic expressions of the Old Testament, but they seem to find pleasure in adding to them and in emphasizing style. Thus R. Eliezer the Great (*ca.* A.D. 50) tells us that he heard God moan because of the troubles his children were in (Ber. 3a). R. Yose ben Halafta (*ca.* A.D. 150) reports a prayer addressed by God to himself. We see in these examples inventions of popular preachers who are trying to show how close God is to us. In addition, these statements are evidence of a naïve and trusting piety. But this ought not to lead us to the conclusion that we have here a childish and primitive conception of God. In the transmission of the Hebrew text of the Bible, we find variant readings revealing the intention to eliminate unfortunate expressions. The exegetical tradition tells us that even the ancient scribes made such corrections (*tikkune sofrim*).[2] The Septuagint likewise neutralizes certain Hebrew terms which were shocking to the Greek mind. The Targumin and the rabbis used paraphrases in order to preserve divine transcendence. For example, they would use the passive voice, or they would modify the subject or the direct object attributing certain activities to God—"there is happiness before God," "it was seen before God." They also made some changes in certain stories which seemed to be out of taste. On the other hand, every occasion of scandal is averted by the general principle: Scripture speaks in the language of men.

The respect for God revealed by such practices soon increased, giving way to a tendency to maintain the greatest possible distance between man and the One who rules in heaven. Did they share our surprise in seeing that the Bible calls God by a proper name, YHVH, which seems to put him on the same footing as the Kamosh of the Moabites and the Marduk of the Babylonians? Is that why the rabbis did not wish the holy tetragrammaton to be pronounced distinctly? From the third century on, YHVH is replaced by the priestly *Adonai* (Lord) in public reading of Scripture. After many unfortunate attempts to transcribe the Holy Name, the Greek version renders it *Kyrios* (Lord). In the Aramaic language of the Targum it appears mostly as *Memra* (Word). When the high priest, during the ceremony of Atonement in the Temple, had to pronounce the fearful name during the solemn benedictions, he did it in such a way that nobody could make out the pronunciation. R. Tarfon tells us that he once slipped into the Temple, where, hiding among his fellow priests, he pricked up his ears to hear the holy word. But he found out that the high priest "swallowed" it while the other priests were chanting (T.P. Yoma III, 7, 40d).

The rabbis even came to the point of no longer pro-

2 See my *Exégèse rabbinique, exégèse paulinienne* (Paris, 1939), pp. 119 ff.

nouncing those terms like *El, Elohim,* and *Adonai,* which designated God. These were replaced by abstract terms like the Name, the Place, Glory. This phenomenon can be seen in the statement, "David brought to Jerusalem the ark of the Lord YHVH who dwells above the cherubim, and is called Name" (I Par. 13:6). How strange and baffling it must have been to hear the priest pray in this way to God: "Please, O Name, I have sinned before Thee" (Yoma III, 8), or, "Save, O Name, Thy people" (Ber. IV, 4). God is also called the Heaven (Rule of Heaven), the Power or the Glory, the Elevation of Majesty.

How can we explain these facts? When the Jews made contact with the world of Greek ideas in the third century, they probably started to suppress the proper name for God, which reminded them of idol worship. Later they even grew reluctant to use the other divine names, not out of fear but rather because they became more and more concerned not to mix the sacred with the profane. As a matter of fact, it is about this time that they began to place ever greater insistence on the laws of purity, on ritual, and on keeping sacred objects strictly separate.

God in Himself

The Jews of old had little interest in metaphysics; more interested in the practical, they never worked out a systematic and methodical theodicy. They preferred to think of God in terms of his relations with his creatures rather than to study his very nature and existence. Nevertheless, neither faith nor speculation neglected the loftiest contemplation.

Israel was called upon to testify to the fundamental dogma of monotheism. God created this people for this very purpose, challenging the deepest tendencies of these stiff-necked men. The early history of the chosen nation is a series of infidelities to God, of prostitutions to Baalim and to Ashtoreth. Still, the test of captivity, their resistance to all kinds of persecutions which tried to prevent the re-establishment of the revealed religion, resulted in anchoring the people in monotheism. It was then that Judith's affirmation (8:18) came true: "For we have not followed the sins of our fathers, who forsook their God, and worshipped strange gods."

Popular Judaism, however, does not spend much time in speculation on this fundamental article of faith. It is enough to repeat with Ecclus. 36:5: "They may know thee, as we also have known thee, that there is no God besides thee, O Lord." In the same vein, Josephus reports *(Against Apion,* II, 16, 166 ff., and *Antiquities, passim)* that it is an important point in Jewish doctrine to accept and give worship to only one God. Only in Hellenic Judaism do we find speculations about the God who is One. Usually Judaism expresses God's unity and uniqueness by saying that he alone has created the whole universe (for example, in Ecclus. 16:24-28; 42:15; 43:34). Declarations about God as Creator and King of the universe are, therefore, of the greatest importance.

Monotheism is most often stated in negative terms— in criticism of polytheism and in scornful mockery addressed at idol worship. These attacks are particularly commonplace in the prophetic books, and we see their most complete expression in Jeremias; they occur more frequently in the apocryphal literature than in the writings of the rabbis. The gods of other nations are insulted and given many degrading titles; they are nothing, an abomination, constantly changing. Their origins and natures are explained in similar style: they are demons, the dead who must be mourned, or the inventions of evil angels. Rabbinic documents show that when Jews had discussions with pagans, they would upbraid them for the immorality and the multiplicity of their gods, and for the foolishness of worshiping idols. The unity of God also had to be defended against certain heretics who believed in the existence of two divine powers; nevertheless, God has vouchsafed to appear in different forms, as circumstances demanded. Arguing with a philosopher, Gamaliel (about A.D. 100; see Sanh. 39a) pointed out that the same God who created the mountains also created the winds. Others were to show that the same God gives life and brings about death.

The majesty of God bursts out on every page of the Old Testament, which abounds with terrifying theophanies accompanied by thunder and lightning. Later Jewish literature tries to affirm divine transcendence even more strongly and at the risk of isolating God from the world.[3] This tendency is clearly shown in various titles given to God: Lord of the world, Heaven, Lord of heaven, Glory, Lord of glory, the Great, the Strong, the Almighty, the Exalted One.

God's inaccessible greatness is shown not so much in dwelling on the biblical accounts of his appearances as in describing heaven, the divine abode. Thus we read of different heavens, their treasures, their chambers, the angelic multitude, and the divine throne whose flames blind the onlooker. Since nothing was more appropriate to suggest the incomprehensible heights of divine glory, we find many such descriptions in the Apocrypha.[4] The rabbis are more discreet; to them such subjects were matters of speculation and fit only for a limited group. "You should talk about such things only to wise and in-

[3] Lebreton, *Histoire du dogme de la trinité* (Paris, 1927), I, 143.
[4] Gry, "Séjours et habitats divins d'après les apocryphes," *Revue des sciences philosophiques et théologique* (1910) pp. 694–722.

telligent men" (Hag. 2 and corresponding sections in the Talmuds). Even one's life and reason were in danger when he ventured into the study of the *Merkaba,* the chariot of fire which Ezechiel had contemplated. Only a few chosen ones had been able to endure such revelation.[5]

Thus God is made to appear as beyond human sight and understanding, as far away as possible. This discouraging attitude is corrected, however, by repeated assurances that the Holy One is close to man and dwells among his people.

Philosophic conceptions of God's attributes find their Jewish equivalents in concrete or metaphorical expressions: God is invisible even to the highest angels (R. Joshua ben Hananiah, *ca.* A.D. 100, in a discussion with the Roman Emperor; see Hul. 59b); with him there is neither eating nor drinking; he commands and everything happens according to his good pleasure *(Sifre on Num.,* 28:8); he is the First, the Lord of the world, the Living One of the ages, the Immortal One, Ancient of Days. "Immutable" is a Greek title.

The idea of divine holiness is very popular in Jewish religious thought, always influenced by the brightness of the "thrice Holy One" who appeared to Isaias. The rabbinical title, "the Holy One, blessed be He," appears only toward the end of the second century A.D. By that time the prayers celebrating God's holiness, the *Kaddish* and the *Kedushah,* had long been in use.

To a certain extent, holiness is a definition of God. He is holy in every way—holy in himself and the very principle of all holiness. This holiness is often conceived of in a negative way, such as the exclusion of impurity: "Be ye holy, that is, separated, for I, the Lord, am holy" *(Sifra on Lev.,* 11:44; 20:26). But holiness also has a positive aspect, since

[5] Bacher, *Die Aggada der Tannaiten,* I, *et passim.*

it calls for the practice of the commandments and for good works.

God as Creator

This dogma is one of the poles of Jewish theology and piety. The Bible opens with the double account of creation. Creation is also celebrated by many psalms and characteristic passages in the books of Isaias and Job. Many Jewish authors extol God's creative action, and affirm that everything was made by him. This helps them to show God's unity, his grandeur and universal lordship; it also inculcates the duty of observing his commandments.

"I beseech thee, my son," says the mother of the seven brother-martyrs to her youngest son, "look upon heaven and earth, and all that is in them, and consider that God made them out of nothing, and mankind also" (2 Mach. 7:28). In these words we find the affirmation of the *creatio ex nihilo,* ordinarily encountered in writing influenced by Greek culture. The rabbis expressed it in a more concrete way. A philosopher once said to R. Gamaliel: "Your God is a great painter, but he had fine colors to help him—the tohu and bohu, the wind, the darkness, the waters, and the abyss." The rabbi answered him: "Away with such reasoning! All those that you have mentioned are creatures of God"—and he went on to prove his point with the help of biblical verses (*Gen. Rabbah,* 1:9). We find the same idea in the consecrated formula "God of my fathers . . . who hast made all things with thy word" (Wis. 9:1; Ecclus. 43:34). The main role, played at creation by Wisdom, according to the sapiential books, henceforth devolves on the Torah as God's architect, or instrument. This means that to create is a divine prerogative; God did not have any co-worker, neither among angels nor among men (*Tos. Sanh.*, 8:7). Even if all the creatures of the world united in their efforts, they could produce nothing, not even a fly (*Sifre on Deut.*, 6:5).

Human curiosity would very much like to know how God created everything; the work of creation was the subject of considerable esoteric speculation. Although the rabbis are careful not to give us too many details on this theme, we find numerous and copious cosmogonies in the apocryphal literature. This was only appropriate, since the latter claimed to offer divine revelations concerning the beginning of things and the last days, a knowledge of the incomprehensible divine plan not even shared by the angels. Let us mention just a few of these indeterminate speculations: God produces first the spiritual and invisible model of the visible realities to appear much later; some of these have been created in advance but are being kept in heaven until they can be shown; Zion is in the center of creation; God never ceases to create. In the first benediction of the morning *Shema* one says: "In his goodness he renews every day the work of creation."

Every phase of the account of creation in Genesis is punctuated with the refrain "God saw that it was good." The rabbis are fond of repeating this praise and even apply it to death (R. Meir, *ca.* A.D. 150; see *Gen. Rabbah,* 9:3). Whatever the Merciful One has done is well done and is good (an ancient saying, reported in Ber. 6ob); he has created everything for his own glory (another ancient saying, Yoma 38a). In spite of their numbers, the elements of the universe are perfectly arranged, each in its place (R. Akiba, *Sifra on Lev.*, 11:29). Are we to assume a different tendency in the human organism? (*Sifre on Deut.*, 32:4) Only some apocryphal books, like the Slavonic (or

Second) *Enoch, 4 Ezra,* and *2 Baruch,* trace the evil and corruptible nature of the world back to original sin.

Divine Providence

This is one of the essential articles of Jewish faith. Although only some Hellenist writers call it by that name, all Jewish thinkers believe in it, even when they do not refer to it in so many words. When Josephus points out that the world moves in proper order without a visible guide (*Antiquities,* X, xi, 7, par. 277 ff.), and when the rabbis— and especially the Apocrypha—repeatedly show how God watches over everything, their statements may well have been directed primarily against the Epicureans.

God acts, first of all, on external events: he sends rain, a miracle equal to the whole of creation, and that is why we ought to bless him (there are numerous statements to this effect from at least the first century A.D.); he feeds all men, a greater feat than even the dividing of the waters at the Red Sea or the resurrection of the dead (R. Eleazar ben Azariah, *ca.* A.D. 100; Pes. 118a). He accomplishes what the mightiest of men cannot do: he finds proper mates for men and women (R. Yose ben Halafta, *ca.* A.D. 140, in a discussion with a Roman lady; *Pesikta de Rav Kahana,* 11b ff.). In all this the Creator puts himself at the service of his creatures, according to the very pious opinion of R. Tsaddok (*ca.* A.D. 90); when R. Gamaliel invited his colleagues to a banquet, he wanted to wait on them himself. His guests were surprised to hear one of themselves remark that their host was not greater than Abraham, who had served the angels. It is in this context that R. Tsaddok recalls the example of "the Shekinah (the habitation of Glory, or God), which distributes food at all hours to everyone who comes into the world, according to his need; it satisfies the hunger of all men without distinguishing between the righteous and the idolators" (*Mekilta on Exod.*, 18:12).

In regard to God's action on man's inner life, we find in Judaism two different, if not opposing, views. Those who did not come under the influence of the Pharisees see God at work even in their souls. Philo is convinced of the need for divine graces and of the power of these "virgin daughters." Several apocryphal writers also believe that God gives the just a pure and holy heart—he "circumcises their hearts." God tests and sustains the righteous, giving them wisdom as well as virtue.

Although the Palestinian rabbis admit a certain degree of divine intervention in man's inner life, they wish above all to safeguard man's independence and his freedom of action. Therefore they are distrustful of supposedly external influences which emphasize man's weaknesses and inadequacies. And yet official prayers beseech God to forgive sins, to purify the penitent, and to save man from all his faults and evil inclinations. Some rabbis believe that God helps his creatures through his holy spirit, and is close to them in his Shekinah. But this is more a sign of extraordinary benevolence; ordinarily God limits himself to driving man further on the road that he has already chosen for himself. "I care for those who care for me" (*Sifra on Lev.*, 17:10). "If man defiles himself, one makes him more defiled, and if he sanctifies himself, one makes him more sanctified" (Yoma 39, *baraita;* "one"=God). "If man wishes to obey the commandments, one causes him to obey them, and vice versa" (*Mekilta on Exod.*, 15:26; 19:5). In general, rabbinic thought may well be expressed in the words of Origen's commentary on Jeremias 20:7: "God does not behave like a tyrant but like a king. In the exercise of his rule he does not force but persuades. He wants his creatures to subject themselves voluntarily to the order he has established so that everyone will do what is right, not by force, but because of his own free will."

Omnipotence

The Jews constantly extol this divine attribute, as is evident from the names they give him: Power, the Mighty One, Greatness, Glory, the Peerless One, incomprehensible in his ways and beyond all praise. They like to show the divine power present in creation, which surpasses all human capabilities, and remain aware that the divine ways are very different from ours. Therefore, Jewish teaching emphasizes that we should never doubt God, not even in times of trial and national tribulation. We must rather see in these events exercises of God's justice, and we must remember that the only rule for God's action lies in his own good pleasure (*Tos. Ber.*, iii,7).

God's omnipotence manifests itself also in miracles, which are called powers (a word that reappears in the New Testament), or signs, and which demonstrate God's authority. Nevertheless, on this point we meet with a double attitude. Nobody doubts the reality of the wondrous events mentioned in the Bible, events God multiplies in order to sanctify his great name (*Sifre on Deut.*, 32:3). At the same time, miracles are considered to be in some sense a depreciation of the laws of nature, and it is asserted that when God created the various elements, he already specified the miracles he would perform in their domains (R. Eleazar Hakkappar, *ca.* A.D. 180; *Exod. Rabbah*, 21:5). Moreover, as we mentioned before, quite ordinary activities of providence are considered even more wonderful than real miracles. When even a very great man like Eliezer ben Hyrcanus (ca. A.D. 90; B. M. 59b) performs a miracle in support of his opinion, this feat cannot prevail over authoritative rabbinical decisions. Perhaps miracles were held in low esteem because of the deeds performed by certain wonder-workers. Would this help to explain the way in which the Jews reacted to the miracles of Jesus? Their supernatural character was not contested, but they did not believe in the one who stood behind them.

This mixed judgment in regard to miracles can be seen in two phrases, a benediction extoling "the signs which God has wrought for our fathers" and a declaration of Josephus. After recounting with no reservation the miracles recorded in the Bible, the historian comments: "I am simply reporting what the Bible says; everyone may think what he pleases about such things." These words already herald the doubts which the rabbis of both the Middle Ages and modern times were to express.

Omniscience, Foreknowledge, and Predestination

All these characteristics are elements of divine omnipotence. It is only natural to find these ideas, met so frequently in the Bible, in Jewish literature as well. Thus we read, first of all, that God sees everything, even what is hidden from us—for instance, the blood in our veins, generation, the secrets of the world, the hidden thoughts of our hearts. God is the one who sees but is not seen. In addition there can be no doubt that future events are foreseen by God and that he reveals them to certain privileged souls. Occasionally, Josephus points out how certain prophecies were accomplished.

From these two theses Judaism developed the idea of

predestination. God has foreseen everything, both good and evil, for individuals and nations alike. This idea takes shape either as the heavenly tablets mentioned in several apocryphal books, on which the whole history of the world, along with the laws to be given to man, are inscribed in advance, or as the divine decrees dealing with the fate of man and with the sentences to be pronounced on him according to his merits or defects.

In such a framework, what becomes of human liberty, which the Pharisees defended so vigorously? According to Josephus, the Pharisees finally reconciled freedom of the will and preordained fate, whereas the Essenes placed no restriction on the idea of fate, and the Sadducees completely rejected it. R. Akiba formulated the general principle in these words: "Everything is foreseen, but freedom is still left" (Ab. iii, 17). Freedom is given a large role in many rabbinic statements. "As long as the divine decrees have not been definitely sealed, they can be changed or even retracted by the power of prayer" (R. Gamaliel, *Tos. Eduy.*, i, 14 ff.); whenever God decrees something in advance, he takes into account future merits or failures. The rabbis used this theory to explain to pagans that God is never unjust, either in the choice of those he selects or in the sufferings he inflicts on man. Out of all men he chooses the good, as one would pick good figs out of a basket (R. Yose ben Halafta, *ca.* A.D. 150; *Num. Rabbah* on Pss. 3:2; 65:3).

God's Goodness, Mercy, and Justice

In Exodus 34:6 ff., God manifests himself to Moses as "merciful and compassionate," and reveals the thirteen attributes of divine mercy. The rabbis often remind us of this text, which is an indication that they give primacy to the divine attribute of mercy. They look at mercy under two aspects—that of goodness and grace and that of compassion in passing sentence, opposing strict justice either by correcting it or limiting it.

There are several terms to describe God's attitude toward his creatures. Too often we call it mercy and compassion (like the Hebrew word *hesed*, which is sometimes presented as a divine name), but what is predominant is the sense of gratuitous goodness, of grace and love. Therefore, even when reciting a blessing after a misfortune, God is called "the One who is good and performs good acts." His most beautiful attribute is charity; he grants this to all men, since they are his creatures (*4 Ezra*, viii, 31 ff., xlvii), but he reserves it in a special way to his own people, as is guaranteed in one of the blessings preceding the *Shema*, and in a saying of R. Akiba (Ab. iii, 18). This is a love that is freely given, not based on any merit. It expresses itself in all providential acts and in God's sorrow for the sufferings of men, even when they are being rightly punished. Man's pain seems to touch him personally: "Oh, my head hurts; what a pain I have in my arm" (R. Meir, *ca.* A.D. 150; Sanh. vi, 5). God is even concerned about protecting the honor of his creatures (Sanh. vii, 4). In the biblical law giving permission to leave the battlefield, allowance is made not only for a bridegroom and someone who has just built a home or planted a vineyard, but also for those who are afraid. This provision is made that those who return home before the battle may be considered excused for marital reasons or because they have just built a home (Johanan ben Zakkai, *ca.* A.D. 70; *Sifre on Deut.*, 20:3).

Although the attributes of mercy and justice seem to be in opposition, Judaism tries to reconcile them by pointing

out that they correspond to the two principal divine
names, Yahweh and *Elohim;* this theory is found both
among the early rabbis and in Philo. Another method of
reconciling them is the belief that God forgives the wicked
but tests the righteous. R. Eliezer ben Hyrcanus used to
say: "When we irrigate a garden, we irrigate the whole
thing, but weeding is done on a selective basis" (Sanh. 39).
God shows himself especially patient with sinners, giving
them ample time for conversion; hence man always has at
hand the ransom with which to be redeemed (R. Akiba and
others; *Mekilta on Exod.*, 21:30).

Even before the creation, God wished to combine these
two attributes, as one would mix hot and cold. In his
decisions he inclines sometimes to justice and sometimes to
mercy; if he were guided exclusively by strict justice, not
even the patriarchs could have stood before him (R.
Eliezer, Ar. 17a). Here as elsewhere we notice the growing
tendency to make justice yield to mercy, the result of an
irresistible current of humanism penetrating all Jewish
theology. We have an outstanding testimony to this in the
semantic evolution of the word *tzedakah.* This noun originally meant justice; later it took on the notion of obligation, then alms, and finally charity, so that it could be used
in opposition to *din,* or strict justice.

More and more, divine justice came to be understood
in a restricted sense. God is called the Just One, not only
because he is the source of what is right, but also because
he treats men as a fair judge who takes into consideration
all the demands of retributive justice. The Jewish soul
is, in fact, always dominated and preoccupied by the
thought of judgment. In *4 Ezra,* i–vi, God thought of
judgment when he planned the creation. All hopes are
directed toward "the day" which will witness the triumph
of the just and the humiliation of the wicked. Calamities

are referred to as judgments, and, according to one rabbinic doctrine, God judges the world year by year. He brings his decrees regarding the harvest at the Passover, those concerning the fruit of the trees at Shavuot, and those dealing with water at Sukkot (Tabernacles); on New Year's Day he judges man, and on the Day of Atonement he seals the decree *(Tos. R.H.,* i, 13). Some even say that he judges all men every day and at every moment (R. Yose ben Halafta).

Obviously, God is beyond reproach in his judgments; he weighs both merits and demerits, and his sentences apply an exact talion. Yet even here we find a general tendency to have the principle of indulgence prevail, for God arranges things, at least as far as the righteous are concerned, so that one merit wipes out nine hundred ninety-nine demerits. But to the wicked he is strict and pitiless.

How are we to think of God's justice in the ordinary governing of the world? The problem becomes more obscure, if not insoluble and scandalous, when one considers the trials of the righteous and the tribulations of the chosen people, on one hand, and on the other, the special favors showered on some privileged souls like Abraham. The reply always vindicates the principle of retribution: all predestination takes into account both merits and demerits, even those that belong to the future. If some wicked people are happy in this world, this is to compensate them for their minor merits before they are delivered up to the fire of the eternal Gehenna. Inversely, the righteous have to undergo in this world those sufferings intended to test them, which are called "corrections demanded by love"; in this way they will be punished for their failings so that their lives in the world to come will be entirely happy. This attitude, authentically Jewish in its roots, seems to have been held by Akiba and his school at the

time of the cruel persecutions which accompanied the
Bar Kochba rebellion.[6]

Transcendence or Immanence? Love or Fear?

To give a better definition of the general trends of
Jewish theodicy we must take up a question often discussed in recent years by both critics and apologists of
Jewish thought. Did Judaism so emphasize divine transcendence that God was removed to the farthest reaches of
heaven, and did it thereby lose the sense of God's nearness,
so clearly a mark of the religion of Israel? Do such celebrated texts as these still have meaning?

> For what great nation is there that has gods so close to it as
> the Lord, our God, is to us whenever we call upon him? (Deut.
> 4:7)
> Whom else have I in heaven?
> And when I am with you, the earth delights me not.
> Though my flesh and my heart waste away, God is the Rock
> of my heart and my portion forever . . . .
> But for me, to be near God is my good. . . . (Ps. 72:25 ff.)

This problem of immanence and transcendence is linked
with another and even more baffling question: Is the religion of Israel one of fear or one of love?

The problem of immanence was raised by Christians,
who looked in Jewish theology for something corresponding to their concept of grace, to the doctrine of God's
presence in the depths of our being. They found only
the idea of heavenly assistance, surrounding man from all
sides but without weakening his freedom and spontaneity,
which the Pharisees were so eager to preserve. In order

---

[6] See Wichmann, *Die Leidenstheologie* (Stuttgart, 1930).

to answer the question, therefore, we must go on to ask how the Jews conceived of the divine presence. Did they accept the idea of direct action by God on the soul?

The principle that God's proper residence is heaven and that he cannot depart from it is unchallenged. To justify this unshakable axiom, some rabbis of the first and second centuries offer rather strained interpretations of certain biblical texts. After all, verses like these do seem to contradict each other: "I have spoken to you from heaven" (Exod. 20:22) and "the Lord came down to the top of Mount Sinai" (Exod. 19:20). R. Ishmael ben Elisha solves the difficulty by quoting a third verse: "Out of the heavens he let you hear his voice to discipline you" (Deut. 4:36). R. Akiba considers the last words of the second text, "the top of Mount Sinai," to indicate that the Holy One, blessed be He, lowered the higher heavens onto the top of the mountain and in this way spoke from heaven. This interpretation is supported by the first text and also by the Psalmist: "And he inclined the heavens and came down, with dark clouds under his feet" (Ps. 18:10). Judah Hanasi (ca. A.D. 135–ca. 220) explains the texts according to their intention: "If the sun, which is one among all God's servants, proceeds in its own orbit but also moves outside of it, how much truer will this be of the One who needed only to command and the world came into being" (Mekilta on Exod., 19:20; 20:22, etc.).

This last response affirms another principle, that of the divine immensity; the abstract idea implied here is expressed in concrete form in the rabbinical idea of the Shekinah. This word, derived from a verb meaning "to dwell," refers to God himself, who is thought of as present either in his glory, as was true in the desert, in the meeting tent, or in the Temple, or by his assistance to men through his graciousness and work of sanctification.

Thus we understand R. Gamaliel's answer when a pagan asks him: "Why did the Holy One, blessed be He, reveal himself in the burning bush?" "If he had manifested himself in a locust tree or a fig tree," the rabbi answers, "you would have asked the same question. But the answer is, in order to teach you that no place on earth is without the Shekinah" (*Pesikta de Rav Kahana,* 2b). It is frequently repeated that the Shekinah fills both heaven and earth. Similarly, when an apostate could not understand how the Shekinah could be present in every religious assembly, R. Gamaliel responds: "How does the sun manage to enter the house of an apostate?" The latter protests, "But the sun falls everywhere." Then, R. Gamaliel concludes, "If the sun, which is only one of the innumerable myriads of suns which do the will of the Holy One, blessed be He, exists throughout the whole world, how much truer is this of the Shekinah of the Holy One, blessed be He" (Sanh. 39a). Simeon ben Azzai, a disciple of R. Akiba, justifies God's manifestations in this world: "The Bible says of him: do I not fill the heaven and earth? This shows how much he loves Israel, since he forces his glory—if this may be said—to speak to them on the cover over the Ark, among the cherubim" (*Sifra on Lev.,* 1:1).

These last words imply a certain localization of the Shekinah, mainly to the advantage of Israel. Nevertheless it does not seem to be understood as acting in man's heart, not even according to the beautiful texts we shall quote. The Shekinah accompanies the chosen people constantly, even in their exiles (*Mekilta on Exod.,* 13:21). It is in the midst of those who come together for a religious purpose —for example, ten Israelites, the number required for the recitation of certain prayers, the synagogue congregation, and the court (*Mekilta on Exod.,* 20:24). It even dwells with any two scholars who come together to study the Torah; R. Yose ben Halafta said: "If you wish to see the face of the Shekinah in this world, study the Torah in Palestine" (*Midrash on Ps.* 105: 1). In addition, the Shekinah joins every faithful Israelite; we are assured by Hillel the Elder (d. *ca.* A.D. 10): "My steps lead me to the place where my heart desires to go. If you come to my house, I shall come to yours; if you do not come, I will not come, either, as is said in Exodus 20:24—'In whatever place I choose for the remembrance of my name I will come to you and bless you' " (*Tos. Suk.,* iv, 3). The saying of R. Meir was also well remembered: "Guard my Torah in your heart and let my fear be before your eyes; preserve your mouth from any sin and I shall be with you in every place" (Ber. 17a). Another ancient and well-received expression declares that making a proselyte means to introduce him under the wings of the Shekinah. It was also thought that every sin puts the Shekinah to flight.

Christian faith considers the Holy Spirit the interior agent of our divinization. We thus remain in the general line of biblical literature, especially of the prophetic books, where God is shown laying hold, by means of his Spirit, on all those whom he wishes to make the instruments of his action.

In the early years of Christianity, Judaism seems to have minimized the traditional concepts. First, it replaces the spirit of holiness with a number of inferior spirits ruling over the powers and elements of the world. More important, it attributes only external functions to the intervention of the Holy Spirit. The spirit of prophecy, a fairly frequent title, inspires the prophets and allows them to predict the future, to read the secrets of the heart, and to compose the holy books.

Certain texts, however, do attribute to the Spirit a more inward activity. For instance, there are maxims about

the ladder of virtues which go back to R. Phinehas ben
Jair (*ca.* A.D. 170) or even further: "Purity leads to separation, separation to holiness, holiness to humility, and
humility to the fear of God; fear of God leads to piety,
piety to the Holy Spirit, and the Holy Spirit to the resurrection of the dead" (Sotah ix, 15). These terms remind us
of Isaias and also are related to certain statements of St.
Paul; they represent the Holy Spirit as an interior state,
like the virtues which lead up to it. Hillel, and Samuel
the Lesser said that there were men so holy that the Holy
Spirit should rest on them (*Tos. Sotah,* xiii, 3). Another
Rabbi said: "The Holy Spirit should reside in that man
who clings to the Shekinah. What prevents this? It is your
sins that separate you from God, according to Isaias
59:2" (R. Eleazer ben Azariah, *Sifre on Deut.,* 18:12). "The
Shekinah causes the Holy Spirit to rest on the Israelites,
and the Holy Spirit makes them charitable" (*Mekilta on
Exod.,* 12:36; 14:13). This indwelling and interior action
of the Holy Spirit are even more evident in the Apocrypha:
the Messiah will possess the spirit of wisdom and intelligence (*The Psalms of Solomon,* xviii, 42). And there are
many sources for the idea that the righteous are already
possessed by the Holy Spirit.

In all this we hear a true echo of the prophets. But to
what degree can this Holy Spirit be identified with God? Is
it only a power sent by him, or a personification of one of his
attributes?

In Christianity the mystery of the Holy Trinity provides
us at once and correlatively with two benefits: a more profound knowledge of God's nature, and the most intimate
possible divine presence and immanence. Since the Son proceeds from the Father as a distinct person, he can be sent to
men to make them participants in the divine nature. We
also affirm the mission of the Holy Spirit. This revelation

was prepared in the Old Testament; what did Judaism retain of it?

Its general approach is characterized by its special attitude toward wisdom. In the sapiential books, wisdom is described as "already becoming distinct from God, a hypostasis, or, at least, tending toward such a term."[7] In the literature on which we are drawing, wisdom is usually replaced by Torah. It is even reduced to mere knowledge, though in terms of sacred science as opposed to secular knowledge (Ab. iii, 9, 13, 17, 18). In this context wisdom is no longer a divine attribute but simply a property of human intelligence.

Although at first sight the Holy Spirit would seem to be favored, it does not really appear as a person, in spite of the personal activities which seem to be attributed to it. It is hardly more than a divine instrument.

The Shekinah is sometimes treated like a person, but a careful analysis of the texts shows that it is rather a designation of God, with emphasis on a presence of grace or a manifestation of glory.

Some scholars think that the *Memra* represents a personification. But it is only an expression which the Targumin use to replace the divine name, in order to avoid apparent anthropomorphism. Nor can we discover more of a genuine hypostasis in the expression, "the glory of the Lord," or in the giant angel Metatron, who is later introduced as a helper near God's throne, or as YHVH in miniature.

It is clear that Judaism did not follow the growing trend of the Old Testament, where hypostases were distinguished in God to give a better description of his rich nature and of the immanence of his action in human beings. Instead of this, Judaism increases abstract terms, an empty and emphatic style. In this way, divine qualities and attributes ap-

[7] Lebreton, I, 125.

pear personified, but in fact this remains a matter of style; metaphysics has been replaced by pious rhetoric.

This attitude may be explained by two tendencies. First, there is an excessive respect for God, through which he is removed from man and his personal and concrete character is obscured. Therefore, great care is taken to avoid any apparent anthropomorphism, which in turn leads to even more abstract names for God. In addition there is a growing tendency to give greater emphasis to the legal rather than the prophetic spirit. The Old Testament insights in regard to wisdom and the spirit of God are an anticipation and a preparation of the Christian revelation. They could be perceived only by those whose minds were sufficiently open to the supernatural and who were ready to limit their own freedom before the Lord of all intelligence, who understood that we must lose ourselves in order to save ourselves.

St. Paul seems to have been the first to describe the difference between the two Testaments by saying that the Old Testament describes the fear of slaves; the New Testament, the love of servants (Rom. 8:15). Since then, unfortunately, simplifications have been adopted which have tended to harden and generalize that opposition.

In fact, the Israelites understood the fear of God in different ways: first, as terror before majesty, whose nearness signifies death; then, as a reverence which contains both submission and devotion and represents a truly religious attitude. Thus we read that the fear of God is one of the spirits the Messiah will possess and that he will delight in it (Isa. 11:2 ff.). "The fear of the Lord is the beginning of wisdom" (Prov. 1:7); that man is called happy "who fears the Lord" (Ps. 111:1). The same feelings are expressed in the Apocrypha.

We find a new outlook with the rabbis. They use two expressions: the fear of sin and the fear of God (or of Heaven), the first giving greater emphasis to ethical dimension. In line with biblical thinking, they ultimately identify the fear of God with religion. It is in this sense that, long before Christ, Antigonos of Socho concluded his invitation to serve God selflessly: "And may the fear of the Heavens be upon you" (Ab. i, 3). R. Hanina ben Dosa (before A.D. 70) places such fear above the knowledge of the Law, since it means putting the Law into practice (Ab. iii, 9). Similarly R. Hanina ben Hama (*ca.* A.D. 225) and R. Simeon ben Yohai (*ca.* A.D. 150) repeat the saying: "Everything is in the hand of God [predetermined] except the fear of God; therefore, this is God's only treasure" (Meg. 25a). We have seen that according to R. Phinehas ben Jair, the fear of God leads to piety which in turn leads to the Holy Spirit. Finally R. Judah ben Tema (*ca.* A.D. 100) places it on the same level as the love of God: "Love and fear the Heaven" (Ab. R. N. xli, 14).

Others, however, consider the fear of God an inferior attitude. For instance, of the four categories of those who call on God—those who avoid sin, the proselytes of justice, the penitents, and those "who fear the Heaven"—it is the last who are on the lowest level; they have not yet entered into Israel (*Mekilta on Exod.*, 22:20) Philo declares that to serve God out of fear is a self-interested piety which attributes human passions to God (*De Abrahamo*, 25). After the year 70 we find the rabbis discussing whether Job served God out of fear or love, the former being considered a self-interested worship, perhaps even containing an element of revolt against God. Agreement was not reached, but some rabbis suggested a compromise: the fear of Job, like that of Abraham, was an aspect of his love (Sotah v, 5 and 31a).

Several rabbis even declare that serving God out of fear is not only an inferior attitude, but also sinful. Thus R. Eliezer assures us that if proselytes are visited by heavenly sufferings, it is because their conversion was based on fear instead of love (Yeb. 48b). Therefore, the truly righteous serve God from love, as did Abraham. "Whatever you do, do it from love. In this way you imitate God and fulfill the commandment: 'You shall love the Lord your God with all your heart' " (*Sifre on Deut.*, 6:5; 11:13). This leads to the duty of absolute disinterestedness in our love of God. "Maybe you will say to yourself: I shall study the Torah in order to become rich, or in order to become a rabbi, or so as to get a reward. No! For it is written: To love God means whatever you do, do it out of love" (*Sifre on Deut.*, 11:13). Love should extend even to the point of martyrdom. This is the way R. Akiba, who gave his life for faith in one God, understood the commandment "You shall love the Lord, your God . . . with all your soul, meaning: even if he takes away your soul" (Ber. 61b). When Israel is questioned concerning the tortures he has undergone, he answers that it is because he had observed the divine commandments in spite of persecution. He then adds: "I was wounded in the house of my dear ones" (Zach. 13:6)—as if to say: "This is what I got for being loved by my Father in Heaven" (*Mekilta on Exod.*, 20:6). The righteous, therefore, call the trials sent them by God "the corrections of love."

It may be said, then, that the predominant trend in Judaism is to see in God a God of love. When we consider the intimate ties which link him to his people Israel, this is only a natural tendency.

The Bible instills in Israel the firm belief that it is the people with whom God wants to be united and whom he wants to call by his name, to the exclusion of other nations. It is the people he has chosen and whom he owns. Therefore every Israelite has a limitless confidence in God. This trust does not eliminate the sense of justice, which obliges the people to observe all commandments, but rather inspires them to entrust themselves completely to their Father in heaven. This state of mind is expressed in the two-fold way in which the Jews have addressed God ever since the first Christian century: *Avinu Malkenu,* "our Father, our King."

In Psalms and in other biblical books it is frequently said that God rules. He is called "King" and even "the King of kings." But in a special sense he is "the King of Israel, King of Mount Zion." His kingship is most strikingly manifested among his chosen people, for they recognize his dominion. One of the reasons why God delivered them from Egyptian bondage was to estabish his kingdom with them. Israel is very well aware of its mission. It is because of it that the Jews are so eager to accept "the yoke of the Rule of Heaven," which consists in praising the Lord in prayers and serving him by fulfilling his commandments. It is in this way that God is "our King." This name should not give us the feeling of timid servility; it is primarily the expression of perfect loyalty. Whatever sense of distance and intimidation there might be in *Malkenu* is tempered and corrected by the other term preceding and introducing it—*Avinu,* "our Father."

Again it is the Bible which teaches and accustoms Israel to call God its Father: at the beginning as a collective name because he has created the nation, because he preserves it and overwhelms it with good things. But later, Father is also an individual term—the righteous consider themselves to be God's children. Their enemies make fun of this pious at-titude (Wis. 2:16 ff.; 5:5; 14:3). The Apocrypha uses the term Father infrequently, and mostly in the manner of Hel-lenistic Judaism: God is the Father of all things because he is their Creator. The rabbis, on the other hand, make use of this term with affection, and we find it often in prayer: "The Father," "Our Father," "Our Father who art in

Heaven." Most often they give it a national connotation. R. Johanan ben Zakkai (*ca.* A.D. 70) speaks of the "stones of the altar, which establish peace between Israel and their Father who is in Heaven" (*Mekilta on Exod.,* 20, 26). He also blesses "the God of Israel, who has given to our father Abraham a son who can interpret and understand the glory of our Father in Heaven" (*Tos. Hag.* ii, 1). Father in an individual sense is not found so often. Even before the Christian era, Simeon ben Shetah chides the wonder-worker Honi Hameaggel for behaving with God "like a spoiled child who has managed to get everything he wanted from his father" (Tan. 23a). R. Eliezer ben Hyrcanus praises the pious man who abstains from forbidden foods in order to fulfill the wish of his Father in Heaven (*Sifra on Lev.,* 20:26).

To what conclusions are we led by the Jewish theology, piety, and ethics just described? We must first recognize the greatness and purity of Jewish beliefs concerning God. It is a genuine and strict monotheism with a profound sense of divine grandeur; this leads to a very humble adoration, together with a childlike and unlimited trust in the inexhaustible goodness of the Father. It is a belief in the Creator who alone has brought the universe into being, and preserves it with loyalty and love. There is an awareness of the dominion exercised by the Lord and which extends over all things. These convictions inspire a deeply religious sense: an absolute submission which implies a faithful observance of the commandments; a loyalty which would lead, if necessary, even to martyrdom; a worship imbued with both fear and love; a reverence sometimes excessive but coupled with a touching familiarity toward the Father and Spouse of Israel. In spite of their concrete and popular aspects, these convictions and this piety surpass everything that contemporary philosophies have to offer, not only because of their purity but especially because they are not the prerogative of a small elite: they inspire a whole people.

Judaism owes this excellence to the holy books from which it draws its constant nourishment. Nevertheless we believe that it has given a certain deterioriation and distortion to revelation. Of course the deeply felt national particularism of the Jews does not do serious harm to the universalism of traditional monotheism, yet it tends to restrict one's horizon and to lead to the attitude that God is mainly the God of Israel. It is probably under the influence of the legal mind that Jews came to consider God distant and inaccessible and to invent many abstract, forced, and empty terms. But Jewish worship overflows with filial confidence.

The most dangerous tendency seems to be the emphasis on anthropocentric and natural views as opposed to a theocentric and supernatural explanation. The decrees of predestination must foresee merits and demerits; they must conform to the principle of retribution and yet yield to prayer. Such a trend is opposed to the idea that the Creator intervenes through grace in our most inner being. Little by little the doctrine of hypostasis sketched out in the Bible is eliminated. But these are distorting trends rather than formal and brutal deviations. We are still in the presence of that great God who dominates all of the Old Testament and who finds in himself alone, in his own good pleasure, the reasons for his decisions and his acts.

Chapter Two
Angels

Angels appear often in the pages of the Bible, and their existence was part of the belief of Judaism. At the time of Jesus Christ, the Pharisees accepted this belief, but not the Sadducees (Acts 23:8). According to Josephus the names of the angels belonged to the esoteric teachings of the Essenes, and it was forbidden to divulge them (*Wars of the Jews,* II, viii, 7, par. 142). In his own account of the history of Israel, Josephus sometimes retains the appearances of the angels mentioned in Scripture; at other times he conforms to Greek rationalism, either leaving them out or giving them a different form. Philo admits the existence of good and evil angels—the former have no body but a more divine constitution, similar to the heroes of the Greek philosophers (*De Abrahamo,* 23; *De gigantibus,* 4).

In order not to offend the feelings of the Sadducees and not to be accused of polytheism, the tannaitic texts speak of angels with more reservation than do the Apocrypha. But as soon as rabbinic literature widens, we find an increasing number of statements concerning angels. Out of an abundant literature we will mention here only some of the material which is of special relevance for theology.

Good Angels

The good angels are to some degree defined by their names. Certain biblical terms like *Elim, Elohim, ben Elohim,* seem to have been avoided as misleading. Instead, we hear most frequently of angels or messengers who are considered ambassadors of God. Their nature is described by the term "spirits." They are also called "sons of heaven" (since they dwell in God's abode), "holy ones," "hosts," and "heroes."

Philo speaks of the angels as having no body, ἀσώματοι. This idea, rather alien to the Semitic mind, is therefore expressed in a more concrete form: the angels are beings of fire; unlike men and bad angels, they cannot eat, drink, nor multiply (*Enoch,* XV, 4-11; Hag. 16a). Then how are we to explain that they were able to be united with the daughters of men and that they could eat the meal that Abraham served them? We find various answers to this question. Some authors replace the angels with sons of princes or of judges in their commentaries on these stories (*Targum Onkelos* on Gen. 6:1 ff.); others say that the angels changed their nature (*Test. Naphtali,* iii, 5; *Test. Ruben,* v, 7) or that it was a special miracle which made them appear to be eating (Philo, *De Abrahamo,* 23; *Targum Yerushalmi* on Gen. 18:8 and 19:3; Tob. 12:19).

As spiritual beings and inhabitants of heaven, the angels share in the divine attributes. They partake of God's holiness and are called "the holy ones of heaven"; they also share in his wisdom and knowledge and thus are able to reveal divine secrets. Nevertheless, their bodies and wings are described both when they are in heaven and when they appear on earth. They remain creatures—though privileged, of course—either produced before the Creation or formed day by day out of the fiery river emerging from God's throne (R. Joshua ben Hananiah, *Gen. Rabbah,* 78:1), or else proceeding directly from the mouth of God (R. Jonathan, *ca.* A.D. 140; Hag. 14b). These spirits are innumerable; there are millions and millions of them, and they fill the whole world.

The main function of the angels is to surround God, either in heaven or when he appears on earth. Jewish thinking concerning angels is based on what the Bible tells of them. These statements are then embellished, and the various angelic categories are described. We hear of living angels, *animalia,* fiery beings who support the divine throne, the cherubim, seraphim, ophannim, guardians, those who are constantly awake (some have married the daughters of men), powers, principalities, the thrones, the forces, the angels before the divine Face, many-eyed beings, and others. This heavenly host constitutes our family in the life to come which knows no strife (R. Haninah, the deputy high priest, *ca.* A.D. 70; *Sifre on Num.,* 6:26). They are always busy praising God, and many seers have heard their chants. From this group God recruits his messengers, his "angels of service." The presence and the public worship of the angels in heaven reflect on God's greatness; both his transcendence and providence are revealed in the way he employs these agents and instruments of his government.

According to a widespread conception transmitted by the rabbis and apocryphal books, the angels are in charge of the elements of the world—stars, rain, wind, and so forth.

This is more than personification and the use of symbols. In a continuation of the biblical stories, various Jewish books describe how angels intervened in Jewish history. For instance, they are said to have had an important role in the promulgation of the Law; this tradition is also mentioned by St. Stephen and St. Paul (Acts 7:38 and Gal. 3:19, respectively). The angels help God in passing judgment, too: they inscribe man's actions in the heavenly book, summon or defend him, and execute God's sentences.

Little by little the idea of guardian angels becomes established, only rarely in the Apocrypha but more frequently among the rabbis. The latter base their opinion on Psalms 34:8 and 91:11; and they begin with the idea that heavenly companions are given to men on certain occasions: in traveling two good angels accompany the righteous, and two of Satan's angels accompany the wicked (R. Eliezer ben Yose, *ca.* A.D. 150; *Tos. Shab.*, xvii, 2 ff.). Likewise, when the Israelite leaves the synagogue on Friday night, he is accompanied by both a good and an evil angel who are to verify whether everything has been properly prepared for the holy day (R. Yose ben Judah, *ca.* A.D. 180; Shab. 119b). Only after the third century do we hear of rabbis who believe that every man has an angel assigned to him. Especially in the Apocrypha we find certain angels who offer God, in the form of a crown, the prayers of the righteous who cry for vengeance.

Repeating and developing biblical precedents, Jewish literature gives us considerable information concerning the archangels, not only the three classical ones but also Uriel (or Phanuel), Raguel, Sarakiel, and Ramiel.

It is generally conceded that Michael is God's vicar, the greatest of the angels; he is the patron of Israel, whom he is to guide and to defend, the chief of all angels and the general of God's armies; he reveals divine mysteries and is the one who formally presents souls to God. Similar functions are also assigned to Gabriel.

In Jewish angelology Metatron is the figure who takes on more and more gigantic proportions. At first he appears as a divine personification, as God himself, who performs the role of *metator,* the one who points out the road. Toward the end of the third century he is a kind of assistant to Yahweh, a Yahweh in miniature who shares his throne, comforts him when he is in mourning, instructs his children, and, as a scribe of the divine court, keeps the record of Israel's merits. The legends around him are probably of late origin.[1] Many titanic angels appear in later Jewish literature.

Such considerable development in speculation about angels must be explained by two factors: the overflow of fantasy—a specialty of the haggadah, which delighted in the marvelous—and the need for a concrete representation of divine intervention in the world which would also safeguard the divinity's transcendence, for Jewish monotheism never allows angels to take the place of God. Let us remember this remark by one commentator: "I shall send rain by myself, not through the agency of an angel or a messenger" (*Sifre on Deut.,* 11:14). Nevertheless we find that Jews in their prayers increasingly ask angels to intercede for them with God, or they even invoke them directly. The Talmud tells of a prayer, probably in use since the fourth century, in which the angels are addressed while going to the bathroom: "Be ye honored, ye holy ones who serve the Most High and give glory to the God of Israel; please stay away from me while I go in here and relieve myself, and then I

[1] His period is described in H. Odeberg, *3 Enoch, or the Hebrew Book of Enoch* (Cambridge, 1928). Odeberg ascribes this book to Rabbi Ishmael ben Elisha (*ca.* A.D. 110), but the work seems to be considerably later. See my articles in *Recherches de science religieuse* (1930), pp. 338 ff.

shall return to you" (Ber. 60b). But this cult is not to extend to worship, since the Law forbids sacrifice to the sun, the moon, the stars, and even Michael, the prince of the great army (*Tos. Hul.*, ii, 18). The prohibition is stated in such terms that one is led to believe that certain Jews did practice this form of idol worship. This would explain why the Jews were sometimes accused of worshiping angels and also why Origen declares that such a charge is unfounded.[2] It also seems likely that when Paul warns the Colossians (2:18-19) of such devotions to the angels, he may have been thinking of Jewish practices.

Demonology

Devils seem to be as numerous as angels; they waylay soul and body, and many timid people are afraid of them.

Originally they were not considered as beings who were evil in themselves but, rather, angels of the same species as the others, appointed to be in charge of an important task. Satan is one of them. These fearful powers appear in the Bible under various names: angels of misfortune, cruel angels, destroying angels. The later Jewish literature has retained those terms, and the rabbis often call these angelic executioners *mazzikin,* meaning destroyers, mischievous beings, evildoers.

One of them, the angel of death, occupies an enormous place in belief and especially in folklore. This terrifying angel with a giant tail, who appears long before the Christian era, always lies in wait to kill men with his poisonous sword. But at the time of the revelation at Sinai God took away all his powers over the Israelites; he could do nothing against Moses, and we are told what difficulty he had in lay-

2 *Contra Celsum* I, 26; V, 6 and 9.

ing hold of King David. This figure, who at first was ranked among the "angels of the Face," was finally identified with Satan or Samael and thus shifted into the category of the evil angels.

Evil angels were usually called "demons," a Greek word corresponding to the Hebrew *shedim*. They were also described as impure or evil spirits. Several traditions inform us concerning the origin of these evil creatures. The oldest one is based on a section in Genesis (6:1 ff.) and is also found in *The Books of Enoch, 2 Enoch, The Books of Jubilees,* in *The Testaments of the Twelve Patriarchs,* and in *2 Baruch.* This widely accepted version is that some angel-guardians came down to earth and had commerce with the daughters of men. Giants emerged from this union and did all kinds of harm to both men and beasts. The sinful angels taught men a knowledge that proved disastrous, since it lead to gross sinfulness among them. Another tradition, derived from the previous one, states that the spirits which emanated from those giants remained on earth to do harm to men and corrupt them. Another—and very different— tradition has it that the demons are angels who revolted against God, either at their own initiation or because they were seduced by one of their leaders. The latter, Satanael, was one of the higher angels, and as a result of the rebellion he became Satan.

The rabbis also teach that the demons were created by God, but, following a tradition of a highly suspicious tendency which makes its appearance at the beginning of the third century, they explain them as incomplete beings— as souls to which God could not add a body, since he was interrupted by the Sabbath (*Gen. Rabbah,* 7:5).

The demons have both angelic and human qualities: they have wings and know the future, but they eat, drink, and multiply (Hag. 16a *baraita*). They are of such great number that if we could see their entire host, covering all of space, we would be utterly terrified. For the demons are the enemies of man; more rarely, even of God. They attack human bodies, wounding them and inflicting sickness and disease. They corrupt souls by teaching them evil and leading them to sin. They are also "satans" (in Greek, *diabolos*), denouncing us before God. But they have no power over the righteous, and on the last day they will be punished and destroyed.

Such beliefs led inevitably to superstition. Thus we hear of many rumors concerning the mischief wrought by demons who lie in wait for their victims, especially at night and in certain places like ruins, cemeteries, and forsaken spots. It would be risking suicide to visit such places or to use certain gestures or attitudes which might attract impure spirits. On the other hand, there is no end of gossip about methods which provide protection from their evil influences: amulets, incantations, and prayers to good angels who have power over spirits of this type.

The Book of Enoch (vi, 7; lxix) has preserved for us the names of the angel princes who induced the sons of God into marrying the daughters of men. We know also the leader who drove the fallen angels to rebellion. This great demon appears under various names: Satan, Belial, Samael, Mastema, Azazel, and Beelzebub. He is always presented as a creature who was originally good but was corrupted through his own fault. God will suppress him at the end of time. From now on, at the request of the angels, it is decided that the evil spirits who caused men to sin will be put in chains. Nevertheless, after arguments by their leader, Mastema, God permits one-tenth of the devils to remain on earth to corrupt man, while the other nine-tenths will be cast into their pit of damnation, and good angels will come to man's rescue *(Jubilees, x, 5-15).*

Satan is the enemy of God, but even more the adversary of man, whose soul he attacks with the help of those spirits who obey him. But he often works alone, both as accuser and tempter. To this category belongs his main misdeed, attributed to him by all traditions—the first sin of Adam and Eve. The ancient serpent had forfeited his privileges and was jealous of the happiness of the first man in Paradise; it grieved him that Adam was served by angels of the heavenly household. His unlimited cunning finally provoked the fatal disobedience. Adam and Eve were punished, but by their repentance they gained forgiveness. Ultimately the throne of the great angel will be given to Adam.[3]

[3] *Apocalypse of Moses*, xv-xxxiv, xxxix; Sanh. 50b (R. Judah ben Tema, *ca.* A.D. 200); *Gen. Rabbah*, 18:10 (R. Joshua ben Korha, *ca.* A.D. 150).

Chapter Three
The People of God –
Israel and the Nations

If God is one of the poles around which Jewish thought turns, Israel is the other, and provides orientation for a large number of different concepts. Here we are dealing with dogma, the *national dogma*. Its attraction and influence can be seen in ethical and religious attitudes, in messianic speculations, in the concept of man (the typical man, who is the object of legislation, being the son of Jacob), and even, to some extent, in theodicy.

The Chosen People

A Jewish theologian, Kaufmann Kohler,[1] sees in the election of Israel "The central point of Jewish theology and the key to an understanding of the nature of Judaism." It is

[1] *Jewish Theology* (New York, 1928), p. 239.

therefore a basic article of faith, which Jews must accept. It must also be retained by Christians, since it is often taught in the Old Testament. In addition, St. Paul calls the election of Israel a divine and irrevocable gift (Rom. 11:2, 28, 29).

For Jewish theologians that election had an eternal importance. It must therefore be based on predestination. Paul declares that God knew the Israelites in advance (Rom. 11:2) with the knowledge of his choice. Jewish scholars go so far as to maintain that the whole universe was created for their sake (*Assumption of Moses*, i, 12; *4 Ezra*, vi, 55, 59; *Sifre on Deut.*, 11:21). The election of Israel finds its first earthly realization in the history of the patriarchs, which represents a blueprint and the first fruits of the history of Israel. According to the Bible, Abraham was chosen and separated from his family that he might "observe the way of the Lord, doing what is good and right" (Gen. 18:19). God makes a covenant with him in which he promises Abraham an everlasting posterity of peoples and kings. The sign of the circumcision was to be the seal of the alliance.

Jewish theology takes up these biblical realities, modifies them, and makes important additions. As far as the history preceding Abraham is concerned, the rabbis show that his election was not entirely gratuitous, but a reward for his merits. As a matter of fact, a frequently recurring tradition —found in the Apocrypha, Philo, Josephus, and the rabbis —tells us that the patriarch is the very example of the just man, who found for himself the basis of truth and righteousness. Although he was born and raised in a pagan family, he discovered the truth of monotheism and smashed the idols of his fathers. Thereupon, Nimrod threw him into a burning furnace, but God saved him. Abraham learned by instinct and put into practice all the laws which were later to be promulgated to the Israelites. He was the first proselyte, and led many others to the recognition of God. He was a source of blessings for those who came in touch with him. God tested him ten times, and he showed his loyalty by overcoming all temptations.

This righteousness of Abraham, as well as that of Isaac and Jacob, produced the "merits of the Fathers"—to which would be added the "merits of the Mothers"—an inexhaustible treasury laid up for the benefit of future generations. We read often that all the benefits which God bestowed upon Israel, especially the liberation from Egyptian bondage, are due to the merits of the Fathers, who are said to plead continually for their children. In its primitive and simple form, this is a biblical theme: In several prayers recorded in the Bible, God is asked to remember Abraham, Isaac, and Jacob, and not to forget his people; frequent mention is also made of the fact that many favors which God did for his people came to them out of consideration for the Patriarchs. But this theme is easily distorted into the belief that merely to belong to the family of Abraham is a guarantee of salvation. John the Baptist denounces this racial conceit: "Do not begin to say, 'We have Abraham for our father'; for I say to you that God is able out of these stones to raise up children to Abraham" (Luke 3:8). These words are an anticipation of Pauline doctrine, in which the true character of the election is established, as against the illusions of the Jews. According to the apostle, the promise given to Abraham is the very beginning of all supernatural graces which God wishes to shower on all his posterity; but what counts is descent by spirit, not by flesh. True children of Abraham are those who imitate and reproduce his faith (Rom. 10:7 ff.).

In contrast, the national particularism of the Jews has caused them to restrict the implications of the divine promises to Abraham. Have they meditated sufficiently on the deepest meaning of the universalist prediction: "Through you all the families of the earth shall be blessed"? Nevertheless, we cannot deny that one of the main reasons for which God chose Israel was his love for the patriarchs; the gratuitousness of the divine election is thus affirmed. The Bible also states frequently that it was for his own good pleasure that God chose such a small nation, which could not boast of any great accomplishment.

But the Jewish mind, very much concerned with the doctrine of retribution and merit, cannot easily give up the idea that the election was just reward not only for the merits of the Fathers, but of Israel too (*Sifre on Deut.*, 11:31). Apart from his own people, God found no nation or land capable of receiving the Torah (R. Simeon ben Yohai, *ca.* A.D. 150, *Sifre on Deut.*, 32:8). God foresaw the future merits of Israel —for example, its acceptance of priesthood and of the Davidic kingship (*Mekilta on Exod.*, 12:6; 15:13). A statement of R. Eleazar ben Azariah is even clearer; he bases his text on words of Moses: "Today you are making this agreement with the Lord; he is to be your God, and . . . you are to be a people peculiarly his own" (Deut. 26:17, 18). The rabbi then comments: "The Holy One, blessed be He, said to the Israelites: You have made of Me a unique object of love in the world, for it is written: 'Hear O Israel! The Lord is our God, the Lord alone!' [Deut. 6:4]. Therefore I shall in turn make of you a unique object of love in the world, as it says: And what people like you, O Israel, a nation unique in the world?" (Hag. 3). Another commentary is even more explicit:

We do not know if it is the Place [God] that has chosen Israel as its possession, or if Israel has chosen the Holy One, blessed be He. It is written: "He has chosen you from all the nations on the face of the earth" (Deut. 7:6). But how can we prove that Jacob has chosen for himself the Holy One, blessed be He? By the saying: "Not like these is the portion of Jacob; he is the creator of all things; Israel is his very own, Lord of hosts is his name."

Jeremias 10:16

Jewish thought apparently tends more and more to the idea of a reciprocal choice, which is a distortion of the biblical concept of election.

This explains the important difference between the biblical attitude to the covenant and the affirmations of Jewish theology. The notion of the covenant plays a great role in the Bible. Despite appearances, including that of the Hebrew word *berith,* the covenant is not a bilateral contract, and the Septuagint uses the Greek word *diathéké,* which means testament rather than treaty. In the Greek translation of both the Old and the New Testaments it is also stated that God has "notified" Israel of the covenant. This helps to indicate that God took the initiative, that he did not leave his people free to refuse the alliance that was offered. God's only commitment was to protect and to reward his people if they were faithful to their promises and kept the commandments. Strangely enough, the theme of the covenant is dealt with more frequently in the Apocrypha than in rabbinical writings. As a matter of fact, the latter speak very rarely about it and offer little commentary on the biblical passages which treat of it. Nevertheless, the alliance is often mentioned: people swear by it, the Israelites are called "the sons of the covenant," and proselytes are said to enter into the covenant. Above all, there is reference to the signs of the covenant— the Sabbath and circumcision—and the word itself is often understood in that sense. Thus the covenant was to become for the Jews, above all, a title of glory, like descent from Abraham, and also an expression of their faith in divine favor.

The People of God, the God of Israel

By virtue of the election, there exist very close ties between God and his people, Israel. We shall now try to find out whether post-biblical Jewish literature represents those ties in the same way as they are described in the Bible.

The expressions Yahweh, the God of Israel, the people of God, appear frequently in Scripture. We still meet with them in the Apocrypha, but not very often in the writings of the rabbis. This can be explained by their reluctance to pronounce the very names for God, and perhaps they preferred to use phrases which show the mutual love between God and Israel. Very likely, it is for the same reason that the expressions, King of Israel and our King, are rare in rabbinic writings.

But there is another characteristic denomination which the rabbis like to repeat: Israel is God's "people of possession" (*am segullah*). On this basis, they maintain that every Israelite is as dear to God as all the nations of the earth (*Sifre on Deut.*, 14:2), and that the Israelites are especially dear to him, although the whole earth is his (*Mekilta on Exod.*, 19:5, 16). The same interpretation is applied to the biblical themes that God has no other nation than Israel (*Mekilta on Exod.*, 15:12, 16), and that Israel is God's inheritance, portion, and property.

The metaphorical or allegorical allusion, which describes the chosen nation as the fiancée and spouse of God, is traditional in the Bible, but this way of speaking is absent from the Apocrypha, and the rabbis use it only with great reserve. Traditional exegesis, however, still explains the Canticle of Canticles in terms of the relations between God and his people. The rabbis like to stress the human aspects, and speak of the Israelites as being God's friends or his favorites.

He loves them like the pupil of his eye, and showers them with blessings.

The Bible speaks of Israel as being God's first-born, as the son whom he has formed; this theme is continued in post-biblical literature. Thus R. Akiba said: "The Israelites are beloved, for they are called sons of the Place. A still greater love has been shown to them, for they bear this name as a consequence of the saying: You are the children of the Lord, your God" (Ab. iii, 14, citing Deut. 14:1). Again, R. Simeon ben Yohai declares that God likes to call them by that name (*Pesikta de Rav Kahana*, 17a). On the other hand, a heathen, Tinius Rufus, once objected to R. Akiba: "Sometimes you are called both sons and slaves. When you do the will of the Place, you are called sons; when you do not, you are slaves. And in our generation you are not doing his will" (B. B. 16a). R. Judah ben Ilai seems to have been of the same opinion: "If you conduct yourselves as sons, you are sons; otherwise, you are not" (*Sifre on Deut.*, 14:1). This concept, which makes sonship depend on moral qualities, appears to have been generally rejected. R. Meier said: "The Israelites are always God's children, whether they irritate him or not, whether they are corrupt or not, whether they are rebellious or not" (*Sifre on Deut.*, 32:5). He goes on to illustrate his statement with a parable:

A boy once rebelled against his father. The father then has the boy's teacher intercede for his return. When the son pleads his shame, the father says, "When a child is ashamed of what he has done, should he not return to his father?" Thus it was at the time of Jeremias (3:14). God invited his children to return, but they answered: "Let us lie down in our shame, and let our disgrace cover us." Then God answered: "My children, if you return, is it not to your father that you are returning? For it is written: I was a Father to Israel."

Deuteronomy Rabbah, 2:16

Another text reconciles both views:

Why is it so important to mention the exodus from Egypt in connection with all the commandments? If it is a parable, to what is it comparable? To a king, whose beloved son had been made prisoner. When he freed him, he did not deliver him as a free man, but as a slave. Thus, when the son did not wish to obey one of his orders, he could say to him: You are my slave. When the king entered a city, he would tell his son to tie his sandals, and to carry the things he needed to go to the baths. Whenever the son protested, the father would take out the deed of deliverance to show that he was only a slave. Similarly, when God delivered the children of his friend Abraham, he did not deliver them as his sons but his slaves, so that when they disobeyed him, he could remind them that they were only slaves. When they arrived in the desert, he gave them various commandments; some of them were easy to fulfill, and some of them were harder: the Sabbath, the marriage laws, the fringes, and the phylacteries. When the Israelites began to protest, God said to them: You are my slaves, and I have liberated you only with the understanding that I will give you my commands and you will fulfill them.

Sifre on Numbers, 15:41

Both love and justice are shown again. The duties imposed on the people correspond with the considerable privileges they are to enjoy.

Among all the nations of the world, only Israel enjoys the divine presence. The first gift Moses demanded of God was to let his Shekinah rest on Israel, but not on other nations (R. Yose ben Halafta, Ber. 7a, commenting on Exod. 33:16). Therefore, God always dwells among the Israelites, even when they sin and are unworthy *(Sifre on Num.,* 5:3).

The union between God and his people leads to extremely close ties, so that "To hate Israel means to hate the One who spoke, and the world was" *(Sifre on Num.,* 10:25). "To rise up against them is to rise up against the Holy One, blessed be He" (*Mekilta on Exod.,* 15:6). To help them and to bless them is to help and to bless the Shekinah (R. Simeon ben Yohai and R. Meier, *Tanhuma Vayehi*). Their wonders and their afflictions are the wonders and afflictions of God, who has wished to share their exile and their deliverance (*Mekilta on Exod.,* 17:15; R. Yose ben Halafta, *Pesikta de Rav Kahana,* 71b).

One was convinced that God took special care of his people. Philo is not afraid to remind Caligula of this truth (*Ad Gaium,* I, 6). God demonstrates this by being their guardian angel (*The Book of Jubilees,* xxxv, 17) or, as in numerous apocryphal texts, by entrusting them to his highest angels (R. Nehemiah, *ca.* A.D. 150; *Exod. Rabbah,* 18:5). God's special providence as defender of his people is presented in the double image of the quartermaster, who proceeds the army and prepares a place for them, and of the active warrior who fights for his people and protects them:

"The angel of God, who had been leading Israel's camp, now moved and went around behind them." R. Judah ben Ilai comments: This verse is full of meaning and explains many another passage. To what is this thing comparable? To a man who was travelling over land, who had his son walk ahead of him. Some robbers came to seize the child and take him prisoner; the father placed the boy behind him. A bear came to attack the child from behind; the father took the child in his arms. When the child became uncomfortable because of the blazing sun, the father covered him with his cloak. The father also saved him from hunger and thirst. This is also the way the Holy One, blessed be He, acted, as it is written: "It was I who taught Ephraim to walk, who took them in my arms. . . . Though I stooped to feed my child, they did not know that I was their healer" (Osee 11: 3-4). The father's action, covering the child with his cloak to protect him from the sun, was also mentioned in the Bible: "He spread a cloud to cover them and fire to give them light by night" (Ps. 104:39). When the boy was hungry, the father gave him bread to eat, in accordance with the text: "I will now rain down bread from heaven for you" (Exod. 16:4).

Mekilta on Exodus, 14:19

Nevertheless, since God is righteous and watches over the observance of the Law, he punishes his people when they sin. Therefore, heathens like Achior in the story of Judith (5: 5-25), and Jews like Philo and the rabbis recognize the principle that only by fulfilling God's will is Israel invincible, powerful, and prosperous; inversely, when God is angry, he brings them defeats and disgraces.

Nevertheless, even then, they will never be annihilated or abandoned by God, any more than Osee abandoned his wife. Moreover, God is close to his people, ready to forgive them if they repent, and to bestow his favors on them again (R. Meier, *Pesikta de Rav Kahana*, 162a, 164). Besides, even when judging his own people, God is more indulgent, and also more patient and merciful in the execution of his sentences (*Sifra on Lev.*, 26:18).

Israel's Duties and Qualities

One reason for the existence of Israel is to make God known among the nations. God is manifested by the miracles with which the history of Israel is interwoven. For this reason God brought them out of Egypt in order to multiply miracles in their behalf. According to R. Akiba, the Davidic proclamation, "Thine, O Lord, is magnificence, and power, and glory, and victory: and to thee is praise" (1 Par. 29:11), refers to events in Israel's holy history (Ber. 58a).

Israel as a nation makes God known by doing justice.

According to a statement by the rabbis of Jamnia, at the beginning of the second century, Israel received the command to sanctify God's name, because of their heroic loyalty to the divine Law and for their readiness to accept martyrdom (T.P. Sheb. IV, i, 35a). God said to the Israelites: "I took you out of Egypt on condition that you would sanctify My name, that I may be God by force" (*Sifra on Lev.*, 24:3). This is the way in which R. Simeon ben Eleazar understands the biblical verse: "He is my God, I praise him; the God of my father, I extol him" (Exod. 15:2):

> When the Israelites do the will of the Place, his name is exalted in the world [examples of Josue and Rahab] . . . but when they do not, his name is profaned, if such a thing may be said. Thus we read in the Bible (Ezech. 36:20-22): But when they came among the nations (wherever they came), they served to profane my holy name, because it was said of them: "These are the people of the Lord, yet they had to leave their land." So I have relented because of my holy name which the house of Israel profaned among the nations where they came. Therefore say to the house of Israel: Thus says the Lord God: Not for your sakes do I act, house of Israel, but for the sake of my holy name, which you profaned among the nations to which you came.
>
> *Mekilta on Exodus,* 15:2

Therefore, R. Simeon ben Yohai (*ca.* A.D. 150) makes God say: "If you are my witnesses, I am God" (*Pesikta de Rav Kahana,* 102b).

Finally, some rabbis of the beginning of the second century called on Israel to embellish and glorify God by their worship and by their obedience to the Law (*Mekilta on Exod.,* 15:2).

Another reason for Israel's existence is in order to accept, study, and observe the Torah. According to St. Paul this is one of their prerogatives and highest distinctions, which nothing can take away from them (Rom. 3:12; 9:4).

Why did God give the Law to Israel alone? Corresponding with the two tendencies in Jewish thinking, there are two answers: gratuitous grace, or a reward for present or future merit.

Therefore, R. Akiba said: "The Israelites are well beloved by God, for he has given them a precious vessel. It was the greatest sign of divine love, for this is the precious vessel which was used in creating the world, as it is written (Prov. 4:2): 'Yes, excellent advice I give you; my teaching do not forsake'" (Ab. iii, 14). In the same sense it is affirmed that the Law was created on behalf of Israel (R. Simeon ben Yohai; *Deut. Rabbah*, 8:7; R. Joshua ben Korha in *Sifre on Deut.*, 11:21). And R. Eleazar Hakkappar (*ca.* A.D. 190) commented, "God said to Israel: My Torah is in your hand, and the time [of the coming of the Messiah] is in mine. The two are necessary to each other: if you need me to bring about the time of the Messiah, I need you to keep my Torah. Just as I must not forget that time, so are you not at liberty to forget the Torah" (*Pesikta Rabbati*, 144b).

In those words we anticipate the other view, which stresses the merits of the nation. If God has chosen Israel, it was because he foresaw that only Israel would be able to receive the Law. God revealed the Torah publicly, at a place accessible to all, and he had it translated into seventy languages, as many as there are nations. He then offered it to each of these nations, but all refused it because the Law condemned the very sins by which they lived or in which their leaders excelled. Only Israel agreed to accept the Law and to observe it.

Israel will never be able to lose the Law, for it was not

given to them under conditions (*Mekilta on Exod.*, 18: 27), like other gifts that were later taken away: the Holy Land, the Temple, and the house of David (*Sifra on Lev.*, 26:44). This assurance is both comforting and exalting; in its exile the nation has only God and the Torah (Bar. 77:15; 85:3). After the destruction of the Temple in A.D. 70, R. Johanan ben Zakkai was eager to promote the study of the Torah; he saw that possession of the Law was the reason for Israel's superiority over other nations, who possess only worldly goods (*Eccles. Rabbah*, 9:6).

Israel is a trustee of the Law, and its merits increase by the study of it. We shall see later that the study of the Law is an important commandment, that all Israelites, young and old, pursue it, and that everyone knows the Torah. It is firmly hoped that the Law will never be forgotten in Israel; this is a problem discussed by the rabbis of the first century (Shab. 138b).

The supreme duty, as well as the highest merit, is to observe the Law. Naturally, no one pretends that every Israelite has always been faithful to it, but the heroic fidelity of the nation is frequently celebrated (see Philo and Josephus). It is also said that the Israelites are as full of commandments —and therefore, of merits—as pomegranates are full of seeds; this is what protects them from Gehenna (Meg. 6a).

Moreover, this loyalty underlines many sayings which mention the benefits which Israel derives from the Torah. These include such spiritual gifts as wisdom and intelligence (R. Judah ben Bathyra, *ca.* A.D. 110; *Sifra on Lev.*, 18:14), holiness (*Mekilta on Exod.*, 22:30), purity, and merits (Mak. iii,15). But there are also material benefits, for the strength of Israel lies in its scholars, without whom they can do nothing (R. Akiba; *Lev. Rabbah*, 11:8); their scribes and teachers are the guardians of the city (R. Judah ben Bava, *ca.* A.D. 180). The commandments protect Israel,

just as the wings protect the dove (R. Yannai, *ca.* A.D. 225;
Shab. 49a); they endow the people with an irresistible
power, and give them strength to subdue other nations
(*Mekilta on Exod.*, 17:11). All this is well illustrated in two
parables ascribed to R. Simeon ben Yohai. In the first, he
says:

A loaf of bread and a rod, tied together, came down from
heaven. The Holy One, blessed be He, said to the Israelites: If
you fulfill the Torah, I give you this bread to eat; if not, here
is a stick to strike you with. This is said in the verse in Isaias,
"If you are willing and obey, you shall eat the good things of
the land; but if you refuse and resist, the sword shall consume
you: for the mouth of the Lord has spoken" (Isa. 1:19-20).

Another tradition has it that the rabbi said:

A book and a sword came down from heaven, tied together.
God said to them: If you obey the law inscribed in this book,
you will be saved; otherwise, you will be chastised by this sword.
And this is demonstrated by the words of Genesis 3:24, "He
drove out the man; and at the east of the garden of Eden he
placed the Cherubin, and the flaming sword, which turned
every way, to guard the way to the tree of life."

Sifre on Deuteronomy, 11:12

The Israelites were charged to sanctify the name of God
in the world, and were therefore pledged to holiness: "Be
holy because I am holy." It is in this sense that the chosen
people is called "holy"; in later literature they are referred
to as "the holy nation," "the holy seed." These terms imply
a present state of holiness as well as an ideal to be pursued.

The ideal is indicated in statements like these: "When
the Israelites are holy, God is their God" (R. Phinehas ben
Jair; *Num. Rabbah,* 9:4). "When you are holy, you are

mine, says the Lord" (R. Ishmael, died 135; *Mekilta on Exod.*, 22:30).

How could it be otherwise, since God himself sanctifies them? R. Akiba said, "Blessed are you, O Israelites, for before whom are you purified and who purifies you? It is your Father in heaven, as it says: "I will sprinkle clean water on you" (Ezech. 36:25). It also says: "Yahweh is Israel's bath of purification" (Yoma viii, 10). "Before the angels of the presence and the angels of sanctification, He hath sanctified Israel, that they should be with Him and with His holy angels" (*The Book of Jubilees*, xv, 27). For this same purpose he has separated them from the nations.

This divine act makes God's people a righteous one. "God has given his children righteousness and justice" (R. Simeon ben Halafta, *ca.* A.D. 200; *Deut. Rabbah*, 3:9). "In thy seed shall all the nations of the earth be blessed" (*The Book of Jubilees*, xxiv, 11). After being duly converted, proselytes give birth to children "in holiness" (Ket. iv, 3). Called upon to sanctify the divine name, Israel pursues its mission even to the point of undergoing martyrdom for its Beloved. R. Akiba said: "In the presence of the nations of the world I will greatly praise Israel, even to the One who spoke, and the world was. The nations ask Israel: Wherein lies the difference between your Beloved and others, that you adjure us thus? (Cant. 5:9) And they themselves provide the answer: Because you are ready to die for him, and now you are being slain for him, as it is said (Cant. 1:3): That is why the maidens [*alamot*] love you—they love you even unto death [*al mout*]. And it is also written (Ps. 44:23): Yet for your sake we are being slain all the day" (*Mekilta on Exod.*, 15:2).

Since Israel possesses holiness, it is decorated with every virtue. According to an often-repeated saying, its distinctive marks are goodness, mercy, modesty, and the practice of charitable deeds.

Whosoever has the following three characteristics is a disciple of Abraham our father, and he who has the opposite ones, is a disciple of wicked Balaam. Generosity, humility, and modesty characterize the disciples of Abraham our father, whereas miserliness, conceit, and pride are the signs of the disciples of wicked Balaam. What is the difference, then, between the disciples of Abraham, our father, and those of Balaam? The former enjoy this world and will possess the world to come, as it says: "On the way of duty I walk, along the paths of justice, granting wealth to those who love me, and filling their treasuries" (Prov. 8:20-21). But Balaam's disciples will go down to hell, into the pit of corruption, as it says (Ps. 55:24): "And you, O God, will bring them down into the pit of destruction; men of blood and deceit will not live out half of their days. But I trust in you, O Lord."

Abot v, 19

The possession of the Holy Spirit is a consequence and symbol of that holiness. Commenting on the exodus from Egypt, the rabbis point out that Israel received the Holy Spirit as a reward for their faith, and were thus enabled to sing the inspired chants. For the same reason, all Israelites are qualified to become prophets, whereas priesthood and kingship became the prerogatives of certain families (*Mekilta on Exod.*, 12:1). Hillel states that if all Israelites are not prophets, they are sons of prophets and thus have sufficient knowledge to decide difficult problems of the Law (Pes. 66a). Maybe this is what Philo had in mind when he defined Israel as the race which sees God and meditates.

Since Israel is holy, righteous, and in possession of all virtues, they are assured of the world to come (R. Simeon ben Yohai, *Mekilta on Exod.*, 20:23). This was the very

purpose of their creation, and proselytes were instructed
accordingly (Yeb. 47a, *baraita*). In this way, the chosen nation adds its own merits to those of the patriarchs. Consequently, God grants it specific favors: the mission of Moses
(*Sifra on Lev.,* 27:34), prophetic revelations (*Mekilta on
Exod.,* 12:2), and liberation from Egyptian bondage (Exod.
14:29).

Nevertheless, Jewish writers recognize and denounce the
faults and the failures of the nation. Many times we read
that committing certain sins led to a suppression of various
laws or to their becoming obsolete (Sotah ix, 16). Are we
to believe that at the end of the first century A.D. a moral
crisis raged in Palestine? It is certain that the rabbis denounce many failings. R. Meier explains that the Law was
given to Israel in order to break their violent character
(Betzah 25b), for are they not a stiff-necked people? R.
Judah ben Bava reports that God complains of his children's constant discontent. Adam, Jacob, and the people
wandering in the desert were all guilty of it, and even
when the Roman rule will be overthrown, they will still
"murmur" (*Pesikta de Rav Kahana,* 130b; *The Book of
Jubilees,* i, 8). R. Nathan (ca. A.D. 160) claims that Israel received nine-tenths of the hypocrisy in the world (*Midrash
Esther,* ed. Buber, 95b).

It is a firm conviction of the Jews that God's nation—and
the Holy Land which it has received as its portion—must be
victorious over all others.

Israel is an eternal people, and it will no more pass away
than the heavens and the earth—both of which, moreover,
have been created for its sake. If one were to object that
heaven and earth will pass away, the answer would be that
this is only in order to be renewed, and that Israel, too, will
be renewed (*The Assumption of Moses,* ii,12; *Sifre on Deut.,*
11:21).

Israel is the incomparable and illustrious nation of a mighty race (*Mekilta on Exod.*, 19:6; Bar. 48:20,24; *The Book of Enoch*, xciii,8). In his book *Against Apion* Josephus establishes the antiquity of his people in many ways, claiming they are five thousand years old. In his description of the war which destroyed the nation, he says:

Whereas the war which the Jews made with the Romans hath been the greatest of all those, not only that have been in our times, but, in a manner, of those that ever were heard of; both of those wherein citics have fought against cities, or nations against nations. . . .

. . . these writers (who have previously written about these wars) . . . have a mind to demonstrate the greatness of the Romans, while they still diminish and lessen the actions of the Jews, as not discerning how it cannot be that those must appear to be great who have only conquered those that were little. . . .

. . . it had come to pass that our city Jerusalem had arrived at a higher degree of felicity than any other city under the Roman government, and yet at last fell into the sorest calamities again. Accordingly, it appears to me that the misfortunes of all men, from the beginning of the world, if they be compared to these of the Jews, are not so considerable as they were.[2]

These protests, expressed even after defeat by a writer who had lost none of his national pride, can help us understand how firmly he was convinced of Israel's superiority. He expressed this at length in his free translation of Balaam's prophecy:

Happy is this people, on whom God bestows the possession of innumerable good things, and grants them his own providence to be their assistant and their guide; so that there is not any nation among mankind but you will be esteemed superior to

[2] *The Life and Works of Flavius Josephus: The Wars of the Jews* (New York: Holt, Rinehart and Winston, 1959), Preface, 1, 3, 4.

them in virtue, and in the earnest prosecution of the best rules of life, and of such as are pure from wickedness, and will leave those rules to your excellent children; and this out of the regard that God bears to you, and the provision of such things for you as may render you happier than any other people under the sun. You shall retain that land to which he hath sent you, and it shall ever be under the command of your children; and both all the earth, as well as the seas, shall be filled with your glory: and you shall be sufficiently numerous to supply the world in general, and every region of it in particular, with inhabitants out of your stock. However, O blessed army! wonder that you are become so many from one father: and truly, the land of Canaan can now hold you, as being yet comparatively few; but know ye that the whole world is proposed to be your place of habitation for ever. The multitude of your posterity also shall live as well in the islands as on the continent, and that more in number than are the stars of heaven. And when you are become so many, God will not relinquish the care of you, but will afford you an abundance of all good things in times of peace, with victory and dominion in times of war. May the children of your enemies have an inclination to fight against you; and may they be so hardy as to come to arms, and to assault you in battle, for they will not return with victory, nor will their return be agreeable to their children and wives. To so great a degree of valour will you be raised by the providence of God, who is able to diminish the affluence of some, and to supply the wants of others.[3]

This declaration is particularly significant since it comes from a Jew who is careful not to offend his Greco-Roman readers. It is true that he places it into the mouth of a false prophet, but he clearly shows a national pride undefeated by the worst catastrophe. In spite of the humiliations suffered by the Jews in subsequent centuries, they were always to maintain this spirit. They applied to themselves the

[3] *Ibid.*, iv, 6, 4.

comparison made by a late second-century rabbi—even though it contradicted the historical circumstances: Israel is a rock, whereas the other nations are but vessels of clay. If the rock falls on the pot, woe to the pot. If the pot falls on the rock, woe to the pot. Whatever happens, woe to the pot! (*Esther Rabbah*, 3:6. The Jews have always celebrated the story of Esther, a triumphal revenging of the past, and foretaste of future triumphs.)

It was, however, easier to speak of Israel's nobility: the queen nation, daughter of kings, the beloved daughter of God's friends, the holy daughter of holy men (*Mekilta on Exod.*, 15:2). The phylacteries worn by the Israelites testify to their nobility and show that God is with them (R. Eliezer ben Hyrcanus; Ber. 6a). Although they have fallen from prosperity, they must be considered as free men, since they are the descendants of Abraham, Isaac, and Jacob (R. Akiba, B. K. viii,6). Several rabbis of the beginning of the second century recommend that Jews anoint and dress themselves in the manner of princes (Shab. 128a). If someone should injure a Jew, payment is to be made, as is required in the case of free men (R. Meier and R. Simeon ben Yohai, *ca.* 150; B. K. viii, 6 and 86a). They are forbidden to sell themselves as slaves, and one must not buy or sell them, especially not to foreigners (R. Johanan ben Zakkai; *Tos. B. K.,* vii, 5). Moreover, the Torah gives the general rule that Jewish slaves must be treated like salaried servants; they must not be asked to do things normally performed by slaves—like carrying the master's clothes to the bath house—nor should they be placed at the disposal of the mob (*Sifra on Lev.*, 25:39). For similar reasons, the priest who subjects an Israelite woman to the ordeal of the bitter waters must be careful not to disfigure her when untying her hair; otherwise, he would offend the glory due to God (R. Johanan ben Baroka, *ca.* A.D. 120; *Sifre on Num.*, 5:18).

According to an authoritative Jewish historian, "The authors of the Aggadah made it a major concern to protect the personalities of the holy ages from unfavorable judgments."[4] Thus Rabbi Akiba is taken to task for recalling the sins of Aaron and Salphahad, even though they were mentioned in the Bible (*Sifre on Num.*, 12:10). Therefore, the history that we read in the apocryphal books is somewhat expurgated, and this process of removing objectionable content increases in Josephus, reaching its height in the writings of the rabbis. On the other hand, the Israelite epic is embellished more and more with marvelous traits and legendary miracles.[5]

This excellence extends necessarily to the land of Palestine, flowing with milk and honey. It cannot be praised enough. Philo declares it to be fertile, in spite of its rocky appearances (*De septennio*, xx, 169). Josephus points out that it is absurd to accuse the Israelites of having wished to invade Egypt, since their own country was much better and more fruitful (*Against Apion*, I, 29, par. 273). The rabbis even claim that the Holy Land is higher than all others (*Sifre on Deut.*, 32:13); its twelve districts, which correspond to the twelve tribes, are distinguished by the special taste of the fruit grown there, and each district has mountains, plains, and valleys. The mountainous regions, however, are also good for agriculture, since their slopes—and even the summit—can be cultivated (*Sifre on Deut.*, 11:10,11). The fertility of the land is extraordinary, the olives are juicy, the grapes enormous (T.P. Peah vii, 4, 20a). This is a foretaste of the abundance of messianic times (Ket. 111b). God shows his glory by driving wild beasts out of the country (*Sifra on Lev.*, 26:6).

But the divine preference for this land is best seen in its

[4] Bacher, *Die Agada der Tannaiten*, I, p. 217; II, p. 34.
[5] *Ibid.*, I, p. 108, 114, 142 ff., 184, 191, 196, 230, 304, 401; II, p. 49, 115 ff.

spiritual wealth: The Shekinah dwells there; Palestine is a pure country, since God has sanctified it. In turn, it purifies its inhabitants, and they will be the first to rise at the messianic resurrection (Ket. 111a). To live there is a guarantee of salvation (R. Meier, T.P. Shab. i, 3), and it is sinful to leave (*Sifre on Deut.*, 13:29, in the name of R. Akiba; Ab. R. N. xxvi, 2).

Inevitably, the highest praises are reserved for Jerusalem, the religious and political center, which is called the navel of the Land and of the whole world. The passionate attachment to Jerusalem is movingly expressed in some pages of *3 Ezra* (x, 7), where the author describes his grief and almost scandalized surprise at the destruction of Zion, *mater nostra*. Those invariable feelings are still active today, and not only in Zionist organizations. They haunt many hearts, and the cry of the Psalmist is still heard: "If I forget thee, O Jerusalem, let my right hand forget its cunning."

Zion is indeed the geographical expression of a religion. Since God has selected it in order to reside in the Temple, it is "the holy City." It is given this title on Jewish coins, as well as in rabbinic and apocryphal literature, and by Philo, Josephus, and the Christians (Matt. 4:5); the Moslems were to use it later. Is it not the world's center and pupil? (*The Book of Jubilees*, viii, 19). Philo states repeatedly that the Jews consider it the universal capital; like Esdras, he calls Zion *mater nostra*. Jews turn toward it from all directions; they always wish to go there to venerate their national and religious home. The Alexandrian philosopher made that pilgrimage, and we are moved by the pages in which the author of *The Letter of Aristeas* reports on his journey to Jerusalem. Already in biblical times the "psalms of ascent" described in a touching way how the pilgrims were inspired. When they returned, they no longer were impressed with the marvels of Rome, Alexandria, and Athens; how could such splendors compare with what their loving hearts had witnessed? Material glory, like that of Herod's temple and its liturgy, had been transfigured by the divine Shekinah.

The Nations

Since Israel was convinced of its own superiority, it could not help but feel distant from other nations, and this attitude included scorn and sometimes hatred. This is not to be explained simply as blind pride, and can be understood from a number of vantage points. Israel saw these "nations of the world" as enemies of God, who provoked him with their idol worship and immorality. Was it not, then, a religious duty to pursue them with a secret hatred? Besides, for many centuries Israel was forced to withstand the attacks of its neighbors, great and small, who had sought conquest and booty, and had subjected Israel to humiliating servitude. Antiochus Epiphanes, the epitome of previous enemies, was still a recent memory. For a brief period, foreign domination had been overcome by the Machabees, and the memory of their feat added greatly to the reawakening of national pride, and made the rule of the Herodians and the Roman procurators more insufferable. For these rulers seemed motivated by one concern: to wound the religious sensibilities of those under their administration, to ruin them by financial demands, and to harass them with constant police interference.

Under these circumstances, we cannot be surprised that the rabbis discovered that the condemnation of other nations was contained in the divine plan. Israel's election came more and more to be seen as a kind of exclusivism directed against other nations. According to R. Simeon ben Yohai, God said to Israel: "To you alone I have given my

name; I am not called the God of idol-worshipers, but the
God of Israel" (*Exod. Rabbah,* 29:3). And when the other
nations, moved by Israel's loyalty to God, wish to join it,
the reply comes: "You have no share in God, for my beloved is mine, and I am his" (R. Akiba, *Mekilta on Exod.,*
15:2, commenting on Cant. 2:16). Such exclusivism ends in
hatred: God hates the nations because they give his name—
the name of the Creator of the universe—to a piece of wood.
They should be able to understand such hatred, since Tinius Rufus is angry when he hears that a dog was given his
name (R. Akiba, *Tanhuma Terumah,* 3). In *4 Ezra* (vi, 56)
the ultimate statement of divine scorn is reported: *Nil esse
et quoniam salivae assimilatae sunt, et quasi stillicidum de
vase similasti abundantiam eorum.*

As a result, God shows partiality in favor of Israel, especially in the matter of rewards:

I will look with favor upon you" (Lev. 26:9). Here is a
parable. A king hired many laborers, and among them was one
who had worked with him for a long time. The workers came
to get their wages, and this man with them. The king said to
him: My son, I will look with favor upon you. The others have
done little work with me and I will give them a small salary, but
I shall pay you a large salary. In like manner Israel claims its
reward before God, and the other nations claim their reward.
And he says to the Israelites: My sons, I will look with favor
upon you. These nations of the world have done little work
with me, and I will give them only a small salary, but I will give
you a large salary. That is why it is said: "I will look with
favor upon you, and I will make you fruitful and numerous, as
I carry out my covenant with you."

Sifra on Leviticus, 26:9

Even in the exercise of justice, God is partial. When he
judges the other nations, the examination is long and piti-

less, going into great detail, but he shows more tolerance for Israel (the school of R. Joshua ben Hananiah, beginning of the second century; *Gen. Rabbah,* 82:8). The portion reserved for other nations is Gehenna (*Sifre on Deut.,* 32: 8); they have no share in the world to come (R. Eliezer; *Tos. Sanh.,* xiii, 2). Israel will be happy to see the other nations severely punished (R. Judah ben Ilai; B. M. 33b).

If God treats those nations in that manner, they deserve it because of their deep and inborn perversion: "Their race was wicked and their malice ingrained" (Wis. 12:10). The right name for gentiles is "sinners." When St. Paul calls them this (Gal. 2:15, Eph. 2:1 ff.), he is only taking up an idea which was current among Jews. He catalogues their abominations on several occasions: sins against nature, avarice, envy, murder, strife, cheating, slander, pride, insolence, sensuousness, lack of filial affection (Rom. 1:28 ff., 1 Cor. 6:9ff.). These accusations are the same that we meet with in Jewish literature. They are all wicked (R. Nehemiah; *Sifre on Deut.,* 32:32), possessed by the spirit of sin (*The Book of Jubilees,* xv, 31). They are especially guilty of the three unforgivable sins of idol worship, debauchery, and murder. As the author of Wisdom assures us (14:12), immorality is an inevitable consequence of idolatry; hence all pagans are possessed by the spirit of voluptuousness (R. Simeon ben Yohai, Yeb. 103a and b). All their women are adulteresses, and all the first-born Egyptians, who were slain in the tenth plague, were the offspring of such sinful practice (*Mekilta on Exod.,* 12:33). One should stay away from them because of their bestiality and sexual perversions (*Tos. Ab. Zarah,* iii, 4). They may also be guilty of shedding innocent blood. R. Jacob (*ca.* 130) reports that he once saw a gentile tie up his father and throw him to the dogs (*Sifre on Deut.,* 12:30). Their physicians, midwives, and barbers cannot be trusted, and one should be on guard in dealing

with them (*Tos. Ab. Zarah,* iii, 3 ff.). Their words and
testimonies cannot be believed (*Tos. Dem.,* v, 2). The disciples of R. Johanan ben Zakkai questioned whether their
alms were meritorious; they were usually considered sinful,
since they were the result of pride and self-interest (B. B.
10b). They were accused of having oppressed Israel and
of trying to lead it into sin. An even graver charge was that
they had rejected the law which had been offered to them,
and did not even observe the seven commandments of
Noah which were revealed to them and to which they were
bound. Ulla of Bira told the following parable in the name
of Simeon ben Yohai:

A man went for a walk with his dog and his donkey. He put
five measures on the back of his donkey and two on his dog. The
donkey walked ahead, but the dog's tongue was hanging out.
Thereupon his master removed one measure from his back and
put it on the donkey's back. But the dog's tongue still drooped.
Then his master said to him, "Your tongue hangs out whether
you have a lot to carry, or little to carry." In like manner, the
other nations could not observe the seven commandments
which they had received, so God took them away from those
nations and gave them to Israel.

Leviticus Rabbah, 13:2

This deep contempt is expressed in various sayings. Since
the gentiles are not men (R. Simeon ben Yohai, Yeb. 61a),
they are referred to (especially the Romans) by the names
of the most detestable animals. Various apocalyptic visions
might be cited, in which the nations are represented as
beasts. If we can rely on an isolated text (*Eccles. Rabbah,*
1:9), R. Meier was the first to call Rome a pig. The Hebrew
word for pig is *hazir,* and eventually Rome will "return"
(which has the same root as pig) the empire to its rightful
owner. Since they are not human, their bones cannot make

anyone impure, any more than those of animals (Yeb. 61a, *baraita*). However, contact with them, their saliva, and even getting close to them, is dangerous. Before the time of Christ, the rabbis had declared that their countries were impure.

This general condemnation is sometimes offset by excuses and even praise, which can be found both in rabbinic writings and in Josephus.

The statement of R. Johanan bar Nappaha should be recalled, especially since he is an important authority of the third century and often reports the opinions of R. Simeon ben Yohai, who had been the victim of stubborn persecution: "Strangers who live outside of Palestine are not idolators, but they follow the customs of their fathers" (Hul. 13b). In addition, a legal commentary declares that "The gentiles are not bound by this law outside of Palestine, and they are permitted to erect altars and to offer sacrifice to Heaven at them" (*Sifra on Lev.*, 17:2). This would suggest that gentiles may sacrifice to the true God, and it is only in such a case that the permission is valid. Others believe that pagans and Jews come together in praying to the one God in order to get rain (R. Joshua ben Hananiah, *Gen. Rabbah*, 13:6).

It is recognized that other nations have virtues. When meeting a gentile scholar, one should say, "Blessed be he who has given of his wisdom to his creatures" (Ber. 58a, *baraita*). R. Simeon ben Gamaliel is said to have thanked God for the beauty of gentile girls (Ab. Zarah 20a). Various rabbis tell of examples of filial piety among gentiles, for which God has rewarded them (Ab. Zarah 23b). Just men can be found among them, but these do not delay in becoming proselytes (R. Samuel ben Nahman, *ca.* 260, T. P. Ber. ii, 8, 5c). But if they are righteous, is it not because they have been faithful to the whole Law? Have they not then practically given up idolatry, and consequently become Jews? It is in this sense that we should understand the following text, which deals with the disputed question of whether gentiles can observe the Law, and if they do, whether they derive any advantage from it:

"Keep, then, my statutes and decrees, for the man who carries them out will find life through them" (Lev. 18:5). R. Jeremiah (or R. Meier) said: How do we know that if a gentile observes the Law, he is like the high priest? We have been taught that the man who carries out the laws will find life through them. We are not told, here is a law for priests, Levites, and Israelites, but here is the Law for man: "I, the Lord, am your God." It is also written, "Open up the gates to let in a nation that is just, one that keeps faith" (Isa. 26:2). This does not mean, let in the priests, the Levites and the Israelites, but let in the righteous and faithful gentile. It is also written, "This gate is the Lord's"; it does not say, priests, Levites and Israelites, but "the just shall enter it" (Ps. 118:20). It is also written, "Exult"; it does not say, priests, Levites and Israelites should exult, but "Exult, you just, in the Lord" (Ps. 33:1). Therefore, the gentile himself, if he observes the Law, is like the high priest.

Sifra on Leviticus, 18:5

The defenders of Judaism like to recall this last statement, which is usually attributed to R. Meier, well known for his hostility to Rome. The idea contained in the statement, in which certain gentiles are incorporated in a kind of spiritual Israel, resembles the way in which Catholic theology sees all those who, although outside the Church, are united with God by his grace; according to the expression of Cardinal Franzelin, they are members of the Church in conscience.

Both in teaching and practice, we find universalist attitudes which mitigate and correct the exclusivism that was previously described. In spite of legal prohibitions, some famous rabbis, like R. Gamaliel, had friendly relations with gentiles, visiting their baths and accepting their invitations. "For the sake of peace" one should help needy gentiles. Strangers are allowed to enter the Temple and to offer certain sacrifices. Daily prayers are offered for pagan rulers. One can answer "Amen" when heathens praise God's name. A tradition going back at least to the third century has it that the seventy bullocks offered during the Feast of Tabernacles are for the atonement of the sins of the seventy nations (Suk. 55b). And this is the blessing that should be given over an idol that has been destroyed: "Blessed be he who has uprooted the idol of this place. May it please thee that all idols be uprooted everywhere, and that the hearts of those who adore them come to adore thee" (T. P. Ber. ix, 2, 13b). Such a wish reflects the belief that the pagans—at least a section of them—will be converted in messianic times.

In addition, various biblical texts, which were much commented on by the rabbis, contained universalist principles: that man has been created in the image of God, that all men are descended from the same Father, that one should love one's neighbor as oneself (a summary, it was understood, of all the commandments). Nevertheless, general theory was not greatly influenced by these remarks, nor was sufficient attention given to the universalist perspectives of certain messianic prophecies, particularly in Isaias.

If Judaism admits proselytes, it is in order to transform them into well-integrated Jews, both religiously and nationally. Latin authors like Tacitus complain that they are taken away from their country and the customs of their fathers. This jealous separatism can be justified by the necessity of preserving, in complete purity, the religion that has been revealed and the people who have been entrusted with its preservation and propagation. But was not such a rigid exclusiveness an insurmountable obstacle to the spread of God's religion, which was meant for all people?

For the Jew of the first century, therefore, men were divided into two categories: loyal Jews; and pagans or disloyal Jews, whose sins had set them apart from the holy nation. The former are beloved and blessed by God, the latter are rejected by him; he curses them, and will never stop punishing them.

The Community of Israel: Nation-Religion

These teachings determine the special idea the Jews had of their own religion and nation. Those two nouns, nation and religion, ought to be written as one—nation-religion—since they stand for one substance, made of two elements. In this lies the special character and originality of Israel. It is a direct result of its genesis and of the idea the Jews had of their mission and the duties it implied.

Since God wished to propagate the true religion—ethical monotheism—throughout the world, he had to embody it in one nation. The purity of the revelation and loyalty to the mission demanded that the nation charged with it should jealously preserve its independence and special character. This necessarily meant the alliance of two contradictory factors: a religion of universalist dynamism, and a nation of particularist tendencies. Will these two factors preserve their identity, or will one of them eventually prevail? Let us look more closely at the reciprocal and correlative reactions of the nation on religion and of religion on the nation.

First, what advantages can the nation derive from religion? Religion gives the nation its *raison d'être* and its power to survive. Israel was created, in order to become the guardian and missionary of the divine revelation. Whenever its national existence is threatened, either by the relaxation of the bond uniting the tribes, or by the danger of being absorbed from without, the return to the religion of Yahweh will re-establish and consolidate it. When the Jews were in Babylonian exile, their attachment to religious traditions guaranteed the preservation of national entity. When many of them returned to Palestine in spite of doubtful prospects, it was for religious reasons. A large number were priests and Levites intent on restoring the Temple; they wanted to learn and practice the Law, even at the cost of heavy sacrifices, like divorcing their foreign wives. If the Machabees were able to succeed in their attempt, which at first seemed foolish and desperate, it was because they relied on the religious zeal of loyal followers. Judas Machabeus exhorted his soldiers to fight for the Temple, the laws, and the institutions.

Religion also helped to enlarge the nation, not by means of conquest and immigration, but through conversion. Whoever adhered completely to the religion of the one God and accepted all its laws, automatically became a Jew, not only religiously, but also nationally. He showed this by giving up his former country in order to offer his allegiance to the Jewish culture and the Jewish land. Roman and Greek authors did not fail to complain about the desertion of such converts. For example, Juvenal writes:

> *Romanas autem soliti contemnere leges,*
> *Judaicum ediscunt et servant ac metuunt jus.*
> *Satires*, xiv, 103-4

This success in proselytizing, which was so irritating to foreigners, explains the increase in the number of Jews just before the coming of Christianity. Philo counts them by

the millions, saying they are as numerous as the Romans;
Strabo declares they can be found everywhere. In addition,
whenever Jews were rulers, they applied the principle,
cuius regio illius religio; thus the Machabees punished their
apostate and impious compatriots, and forced circumcision
on those who through negligence or fear had not been
marked with the sign of the covenant. When the Hasmoneans, some time later, conquered Idumea, Iturea, and the
coastal sections of Palestine, they not only required the payment of tribute, but circumcized the inhabitants in order
to make them authentic Jews. As a consequence, Roman
law considered everyone who was circumcized to be a Jew.

Religion also gave the nation broader perspectives, and
enabled it to expand. Contrary to the convictions of David
and the ancient Israelites, it began to be understood that
one can be a true follower of Yahweh without living in
Palestine, and without making an annual pilgrimage to the
Temple. It is no longer indispensable to speak the holy language, and the Jews of the Diaspora adopted the language
of their hosts, reading and translating their sacred books
into new idioms. The Jewish nation did not even need to
possess an independent and sovereign state. On two occasions the Pharisees asked the Romans to deliver them from
their Hasmonean or Herodian kings; all they required was
a certain religious freedom under Roman rule. Has any
other nation ever profited from the universalism of its religion to expand in this way without limits?

Inevitably, the nation takes on an increasingly religious
form. The ideal to be attained is once more the Israel of the
desert, the religious assembly gathered around the ark and
the altar under the authority of Moses, its political and religious leader. One speaks of *kahal* Israel, a sacral society.
The constitution of the Jewish state is religious; supreme
authority is exercised by the high priest, assisted by an over-

whelmingly priestly aristocracy, and by scholars trained in
religious law.\ Their code is the Torah, and they wish to
see it prevail; we may as well speak of nomocracy as theocracy. Josephus defined the Jewish constitution as theocracy
(*Against Apion,* ii, 16, par. 165), which he considered an
excellent system, since it recognized supreme power in
God alone. The various Jewish communities, both within
and outside of Palestine, grouped around their synagogues
and governed by the heads of these synagogues, were basically religious. The group name preferred by the Jews is
also religious: they are Israel. The word Jew merely designates the member of a nation, and Hebrew designates someone who belongs to a certain race.

This intimate combination and genuine interpenetra-
tion, which make religion and nation a single whole, are
for both an invincible force and a guarantee of survival.
The national bond has the unbreakable solidity of the
sacred; religious life, with its beliefs and practices, becomes
deeply rooted in an ethical element, receiving a spiritual
and material dynamism which becomes all-penetrating. Because of this symbiosis, even the most assimilated Jew can
never give up either his ancient nationality or religion.

Nevertheless, even if the nation has benefited from this
close association, religion is tainted by the particularism
which is its support and instrument. Religion gave the nation its universalist dynamism, but it is weighed down with
the particularism which prevents it from shining forth and
expanding. How could it have been otherwise? Generally
speaking, Jewish religion has become restricted to an ethnic
group. Some modern Jews have a sense of this when they
refuse to engage in any kind of proselytism; they hold that
the religion of Israel should be reserved to the nation and
remain its distinctive mark.

The national character of the religion is evident from the

transformation of the Sabbath, circumcision, and the laws of bodily and dietary purity—originally purely religious—into ethnic rites. All these prescriptions had as their primary purpose to keep Israel in careful seclusion, in order to allow it to keep intact the deposit of revelation. As *The Letter of Aristeas* (139) explains it, "Now our Lawgiver being a wise man and especially endowed by God to understand all things . . . fenced us round with impregnable ramparts and walls of iron, that we might not mingle at all with any of the other nations but remain pure in body and soul, free from all vain imaginations." The transition from the religious to the racial and ethnic domain is already accepted; in fact, there are many Jews, both in earlier times and today, who remain faithful to the observances in order to mark their fidelity to their national group. But this is a renunciation of the universalism of the true religion, making its further expansion impossible. St. Paul understood this well; his untiring fight against those who wanted to impose circumcision and the other Mosaic laws on the new Christians was for the purpose of safeguarding Christian liberty (Gal. 4:31; 5:1-5, 12). This liberty provided an indefinite possibility of expansion and, even more important, guaranteed the purity of supernatural meaning, free of any carnal element.

Judaism deprived itself of the means of expansion at its disposal. Proselytism was ardently attempted, but it could not ultimately be successful, since the convert was required to abandon his original fatherland and adhere completely to the Jewish nation. Through the channel of Hellenism, which was dominant everywhere and had influenced many cultured Jews, Judaism could well have been enriched and continue to develop. Apparently the old religion lost its power of assimilation which in earlier times had allowed it to incorporate so many outside elements. In fact, Judaism retained only material elements of Hellenism, like the language and certain customs; it borrowed nothing from Greek philosophy. The Book of Wisdom clearly shows Alexandrine influence, but merely clothed traditional biblical concepts in Greek terms. Nevertheless, the necessity of repelling Hellenic infiltrations, which threatened authentic revelation, and the excessive xenophobia after the fall of Jerusalem led to the condemnation of any compromise with the foreigner. For the same reason, separatist decrees are strengthened, and ceremonial laws are given greater emphasis; there are additional Sabbath restrictions, more laws on impurity, and contact with foreigners is made more difficult. "The fences around the Law," to use the rabbis' phrase, became higher and more impenetrable; the wall enclosing Israel began to look more like those tall ramparts which surround certain Oriental monasteries and make them inaccessible.

These considerations lead us to a question which has often been asked—for example, by Bossuet—and is of special interest to Christians: Was Judaism at this period already in some way a church? Was it a completely universalist organism, capable of incorporating all other nations? It possessed many characteristics of a church; its religious doctrine was based on monotheism, and was therefore open to all; its worship included more and more prayers and instructions; and it had already had a remarkable expansion, even beyond the confines of the Roman empire. All these elements may be considered catholic in tendency, and should have allowed Israel to spread everywhere and win over all nations. But this universalist dynamism was blocked by congenital restrictions, centering around the national particularism which the Jews did not wish to give up. They considered themselves unique, superior to all other peoples, but ready to take them in on condition they would give up

their own nationality and become full-fledged Jews, religiously as well as nationally. Israel refused to become the
leaven which would be mixed in the mass and help raise it
up, losing itself in order to accomplish its divine mission.

We have a number of examples of this exclusive separatism, which contains both jealousy and pride. When St.
Paul said that God told him in the Temple to visit faraway
nations, his listeners threw themselves on him and cried
out that he should not be allowed to live (Acts 22:21,23).
The idea of a universal evangelization, although fundamental and in correspondence with the divine plan, was rejected by them. A century later, according to Justin (*Dialogue with Trypho,* cxxiii, 9), the Jews with whom he con-
versed "were astounded to hear me say that we too [the
Gentiles] were children of God."

The idea of a church, therefore, does not explain the essence and development of Judaism, for it becomes more
and more an ethnic religious community—a nation-religion.
The three terms—ethnic, religious, and community—are
the integral components of the combination. Judaism is
ethnic, not racial or national. Since they are spread all over
the world, the Jews are an amalgam of the most varied races.
In fact, the term "race" can be applied to them only in the
modern sociological sense, since they have—and are con-
scious of—certain psychological traits which form a special
soul. If the Jews are a nationality, a gathering of individuals
who are aroused by the same aspirations and can in this
way be distinguished from other nationalities, they still are
not—and most of them do not desire to be—a separate and
distinct nation, enjoying real autonomy, obliged to separate
themselves from those nations whose loyal citizens they are
and would like to remain. In spite of this, they constitute a
real community, whose elements are closely linked; originally, this element had a religious character. But today

many Jews are religiously indifferent and have no ties with traditional beliefs and practices. They claim to be united only by racial or national ties, but we have seen how important these two factors are. They consider the ancient religion a national heritage and they excommunicate from both family and community any Jew who is converted to Christianity. This indicates that the basis of their community was and still is religious. It is abundantly clear from the study of earlier periods that Israel is a nation-religion.

The joining of these two forces constitutes a social entity, with the strength and indestructibility of a diamond. History shows this to be an obvious truth. How could Judaism perpetuate itself as a nation and a religion, when it was almost constantly under attack, both by outside enemies who wished to exterminate it and by interior agents of dissolution? We have seen what the nation owed to the religious component to which it was related. On the other hand, religion borrowed a special solidity from the ethnic base in which it was incarnate. This was possible because in Judaism, nation and religion are more intimately associated and more totally assimilated than body and soul.

This strengthens religion but encourages the principle of immobilization, so that religion tends to become more static than dynamic. The facts support this interpretation. Judaism no longer shows the power it formerly had—and which always appears in Christianity—to assimilate all the religious, social, and cultural elements which might enrich it, and at the same time to transform them into its own substance. It has lost most of its ability to expand. Its proselytizing activity, which was formerly so intense—"You traverse sea and land to make one convert" (Matt. 23:15)—has diminished more and more in the course of time. Many even think that it should stop entirely, and are satisfied that Judaism should remain the religion of a race.

Chapter Four
The Torah

Between God and Israel, the two poles of Jewish thought, there is the Torah which connects them. God has entrusted the Torah to his people, and they are pledged to its observance. It thus constitutes both a grace and a duty.

It is perhaps because of these two qualities that the Torah occupies such a large place in the Jewish soul; it is certainly one of the subjects of which the rabbis most gladly speak. Most of the statements contained in the Pirke Abot, a collection of the most memorable sayings of the ancient rabbis, are concerned with the Law, and even more with its study. When the rabbis attempt to find symbolic meaning for the events of Jewish history, they almost always discover symbols for the Law: living water, wood which sweetens water, oil, wine, fire, manna, the victory won through Moses' prayer while he held out his arms to heaven—all these things refer to the Torah.[1] When a Christian surveys this literature and

[1] See *Exégèse rabbinique et exégèse paulinienne*, pp. 207-247.

observes this devotion, he cannot help but feel that the rabbis assign to the Torah the place which Christianity reserves to Christ: The Torah is the mysterious figure which is signified and foretold by all the sacred texts.

Mohammed called the Jews "the people of the Book"; it would be more true to say that they are the people of the Torah. It is the very basis of their religion, since in it they find both the revelation of their beliefs and the promulgation of the laws which are to direct their whole life. Whatever liberal theoreticians of Judaism may say, therefore, Israel is by no means a natural religion, developed by the ethical experiences of a people; it is a positive and revealed religion, which derives its dogmas and laws from God.

But the Jews are the people of the Torah for another reason—they worship this divine being. Already in early times Jewish speculation identified the Law with Wisdom; it saw the Torah as God's architect and laborer, whom he employed in creating the world. According to the rabbis, the Torah had lived close to God for an endless time before creation as his daughter. Both Philo and *The Letter of Aristeas* speak of the divine law. This constantly growing concept will ultimately play an enormous role in the Kabbala in relation to eternal Being. This attitude is also evident in the reverence with which Jews treat the Torah scroll, the manuscript volume written on parchment according to strict and traditional rules, clothed in precious materials, covered with gold and silver, and enclosed in the sacred ark behind the Eternal Light.

The Torah and Moses

First, let us try to determine the exact meaning of that impressive and almost untranslatable word, Torah. The

Septuagint translates it as "law," but many Jewish theologians and historians insist that it means "instruction," "religious teaching," and "divine revelation," since it gives light to the intelligence as well as direction for the will. Although such reflections are partly true, they seem somewhat exaggerated. According to ancient biblical usage, Torah means the practical science conveyed by priests, a specific decision, or the law in general. However, when the rabbis speak of Torah, they are thinking of the totality of divine laws, and the study of the Torah is principally a matter of legal order. Therefore, our translation of Torah emphasizes one of its main objects.

The Torah is one of the entities which God created before the universe, and then kept in reserve. Jewish speculation does not make much of this pre-existence of the Torah, but places the beginning of its history at Sinai; the "gift of the Law" to Moses is a favorite subject for commentators and preachers. What is essential is that after being prepared for its mission by purification through suffering, Israel voluntarily accepted the Torah and promised to observe it faithfully. This promise, "All that the Lord has said, we will heed and do" (Exod. 24:7), is often regarded as Israel's greatest merit and claim to glory. In addition, as mentioned by Josephus (*Antiquities,* III, v, 4, par 89 ff.), the Israelites heard the divine revelation directly. This frequently repeated affirmation contains the essence of Jewish apologetics, to be refined later by Judah Halevi, Maimonides, and Albo: Israel's belief in divine revelation is not based on the testimony of others, but on the direct experience of the whole people, and this experience, which was both seen and heard, has been handed down as a living reality from generation to generation.

What was the substance of the revelation at Sinai? According to all statements and interpretations, its main object was the "Ten Words" (Deut. 4:13; 10:4), as engraved on the tablets. It is also claimed that all the commandments (*six hundred and thirteen*) were given at that time, both the written and the oral law; some insist that the additional laws were inscribed between the lines of the original decalogue; others, that the oral laws were revealed to Moses in the Tabernacle. In one way or another, the Ten Commandments are considered to be the essence or the résumé of all other laws—the *Kephálaia*, as Philo says (*De decalogo*, V, vi, 33). We can see how this history emphasizes the role of Moses: he is our teacher, *Morenu*, the highest religious authority, the first and foremost of the prophets, the figure who stands between God and his people. He is universally recognized as the mediator: *arbiter testamenti illius*, as we read in *The Assumption of Moses* (1, 14). According to Josephus (*Against Apion*, II, 16 and 160), his message is divine. In rabbinic literature he is called *Shaliah*, meaning deputy or emissary (*Sifra on Lev.*, 26:46), and to contradict him is equivalent to contradicting God (*Sifre on Num.*, 12:8). St. Paul also gives him the title of intermediary (Gal. 3:19, 20).

Moses was prepared for this mission by a special predestination: "Accordingly He designed and devised me, and He prepared me before the foundation of the world, that I should be the mediator of His covenant" (*Assumption of Moses*, i, 14; cf. iii, 12). His humility is mentioned several times in the Pentateuch, and the rabbis grant him both wisdom and an extraordinary range of innate knowledge; he thus appears as a supernatural being, superior to the angels (*Sifre on Num.*, 12:7). God spoke to him directly, without an intermediary, person to person; he even allowed Moses to raise objections. God has revealed the whole of the Torah to him, even the minutiae of the scribes. No law can prevail against the Pentateuch, since no student can rise up against his teacher or supplant him. Those Jews who debated with Jesus or with the first Christians held the same view; nobody can oppose that authority which is the principle of eternal life (John 1:46; 5:39, 45-47; 6:31,32; 9:28,29; Matt. 19:7; Mark 12:19; Acts 6:11,14).

The Written and the Oral Law

The Torah of Moses is found in the five books of the Pentateuch, the Torah par excellence. In addition to these books, Jewish tradition possesses other sacred books. What authority do they enjoy in comparison with the Torah of Moses?

Those Scriptures which Jewish tradition has preserved are generally known as the Book, or the Holy Book, Scripture, Holy Scripture, or Holy Scriptures. Already in ancient times they were divided into two categories—the Law and the Prophets, an expression which was in use during the second century before Christ. Jewish literature also contrasts the Torah of Moses with tradition, Kabbala. Only later, probably in the first century, do we find the tripartite division of Torah, Prophets, and Hagiographa, or Holy Writings.

By what criteria were these books considered holy? In the discussions which went on for centuries, and in which the sacred character of such biblical books as the Canticle of Canticles, Ecclesiastes, Ezechiel, and Esther were at stake, the answer that always put an end to the argument was always that these books are the work of prophets or saints who spoke with the Holy Spirit.

Consequently, these books were considered to be the word of God. We do not yet encounter any theory of inspiration except in Philo, who thinks of sacred authors as hierophants, seized by divine inspiration, faithfully producing, like musical instruments, the thoughts and words that someone else puts in their heads. Josephus and the rabbis see in scripture the words of God. Therefore, when the rabbis quote the Bible, beginning with the formula, "It has been said," this should be understood as followed by "in the holy book" or "by God himself." In keeping with this idea of attributing the authorship of the biblical books to the Holy Spirit, a *baraita* lists as authors of the individual books either prophets or other men endowed with the gift of prophecy, since the Holy Spirit was above all the Spirit of prophecy:

Moses wrote his own book, the section on Balaam and the Book of Job; Josue wrote his own book and the last eight verses of the Torah (on the death of Moses); Samuel wrote his own book and the Books of Judges and Ruth; David wrote the Psalms, using compositions of the ten sages—Adam, Melchisedec, Abraham, Moses, Heman, Idithun, Asaph, and the three sons of Core; Jeremias wrote his own book and the book of Kings and Lamentations; Ezechiel and his group wrote Isaias, Proverbs, and the Canticle of Canticles; the men of the Great Synagogue wrote Ezechiel, the Twelve (minor prophets), Daniel and Esther; and Esdras wrote his book and Paralipomenon up to his own time.

Baba Batra 14b, 15a

This is evidence that the biblical canon was already firmly fixed at the time of Christ, and included all the books contained in the Hebrew Bible. As for the deuterocanonical books, they were not only accepted by Alexandrian Judaism, but several of them were highly respected in Palestine. For example, the Ecclesiasticus is quoted frequently by the rabbis, possibly because it was written in Hebrew.

The writings of Moses stood higher than all the other sacred books. Since he was the unique mediator, he has already received everything that the later writers will disclose. Hence, when it was a question of establishing the canonical character of the Book of Esther, it was enough to affirm that its content was implicitly understood or attested to in the Torah (Meg. 7a). Likewise, it was pointed out that Ecclesiastes began and ended with words from the Torah (Shab. 30b). Moreover, the Torah of Moses will never disappear, but the other books of the Bible will disappear.

Josephus and Philo, aware of the skepticism of their readers, who rejected the historicity of pagan mythologies, stress the fact that the Bible does not contain any fables. In order to demonstrate that there are no contradictions in it, the rabbis apply themselves to reconciling those texts which seem to be in positive disagreement.

Moses had already told the priests to adapt the Law to the changing circumstances of time and place, and to teach the Torah in terms of the situation (Deut. 17:8 ff.). Such accommodation of law, and the drawing up of what we think of as rules for public administration, were regularly practiced in Israel; it is from this that the oral law derives. The term "oral law," or "law by means of the mouth," may go back to Hillel. It is still rare in the first century; the New Testament, Josephus, Justin, and Origen speak rather of "traditions"—whether those of the ancients or those of the Pharisees.

The rabbis established the legitimacy of the oral law on the basis of some rather strange exegesis. Hillel justified it in general terms:

> The rabbis tell this story. A gentile came to Shammai and asked him: "How many Torahs do you have?"
> The latter answered, "Two, the written law and the oral law."
> "I will trust you in regard to the written law, but not in regard to the oral law. I will become a proselyte on condition that you teach me only the written law."

Shammai became angry and drove him away. The gentile then went to Hillel, who made him a proselyte. The first day, Hillel taught him the alphabet: aleph, beth, ghimel, daleth. The next day, Hillel taught him the letters in the reverse order, and when the new convert protested, he said, "Do you not have confidence in the way I teach the alphabet? Now trust me with the teaching of the oral law."

Shabbat 31a

The real reason for the existence of the oral law lies in the role which Moses assigned to it: to interpret the written law, to provide details which would help to make its practice more precise. This is what the men of the Great Synagogue, who lived long before the Christian era, called "building a fence around the Law" (Ab. i, 1). Other rabbis assure us that the main purpose of the oral law is to make the Torah more tolerable, to make fewer occasions of sin. It is to make life easier by following the general rule that "No decree should be made which the mass of people cannot accept" (R. Simeon ben Gamaliel; *Tos. Sotah*, xv, 10). In this way certain biblical prescriptions which had become hard or impossible to execute were modified or entirely suppressed. A well-known example is that of the *Prosbol*. According to biblical law, all debts were canceled at the arrival of the sabbatical year; the rich, therefore, refused to lend money which they were sure to lose. Hillel thereupon authorized the creditors to secure, by due court procedure, a document which would enable them to recover their money at any time (Sheb. x, 3 ff.).

Unfortunately, the oral law really did not make the Law easier. The rabbis themselves admitted this when they complained that the "fence" stifled the very root it wished to protect, and thus led to apostasy *(Gen. Rabbah,* 19:4, *baraita)*. We can understand this very well when we go through the rabbinic literature. Laws and restrictions follow one upon another, and become more and more precise, so that

the area of freedom becomes increasingly limited. How was
one to observe the Sabbath rest and all its prohibitions—
even against jumping or clapping one's hands? There was
no solution except what happened: to apply legal fictions in
order to evade the Law.

It is probable that some rabbinical prescriptions are
purely academic exercises, and had no influence on human
conduct. This is certainly true of certain laws which arose
after the year 70, and which dealt with Temple worship,
dues, and court procedures, institutions which had either
been abolished or were no longer active. The oral laws
were made in academies or tribunals, and the majority vote
of accredited rabbis was decisive. When one school or court
differed from another, a decision was probably arrived at by
considering the number and quality of the respective scholars. But how could this last point be determined?

The rabbis did not make their decisions arbitrarily. The
main source of their legislation was the traditions, which
were supposed to go back to the first legislator; for a long
time, this was the only recognized basis for decisions. When
Hillel wanted to justify his opinion on a question concerning the Passover, he found that his colleagues rejected all
his exegetical arguments; he succeeded only by assuring
them that he had gotten his decision from Shemaya and Ab-
talyon (Pes. 66a). This story makes reference to another
source of oral law, biblical exegesis, which is to become
more and more important in rabbinic discussion. Nevertheless, we do not believe that these interpretations, by themselves, led to the establishment of oral laws. When we study
these interpretations closely, we are struck by their arbitrary
and subtle character, and it seems more advisable to assume
that they were invoked only to support a tradition already
in existence.[2]

In principle, the oral law enjoyed the same authority as

[2] See *Exégèse rabbinique et exégèse paulinienne*, pp. 53-63, 252 ff.

the written one. Some rabbis even boasted that the former has even greater authority. In order to give the oral law a more solid foundation, it was traced back to Moses: on Mount Sinai God had shown him the whole Law, including all the decisions of the rabbis, grammatical minutiae, and even all the reflections a pious student will show his teacher. All this has been transmitted to us by Moses through an uninterrupted chain of tradition: "Moses received the Torah at Sinai and transmitted it to Josue; Josue gave it to the seventy elders; the elders to the prophets, and they in turn to the men of the Great Synagogue. . . . Simeon the Just was one of the survivors of the Great Synagogue. . . . Antigonus of Sokho received it from Simeon; from then on the chain is continued by pairs, who pass on the tradition in turn" (Ab. i, 1-10). A controversial decision is called "a *halakhah* given to Moses at Sinai." Who could be taken in by this name, awarded as a scholastic expediency?

It is only in this way that we can understand the disputes over contradictory decisions on the same subject. The rabbinic mentality is seen in these discussions: their stubbornness in wanting their opinion to be accepted, or showing that they are in agreement with the decision of a celebrated rabbi; their subtle and long-winded dialectic, their fine casuistry, their profound knowledge both of the written and the oral law—they know the entire Bible by heart—their worship of this divine Torah.

When we read this literature, we understand better the impression already received from the New Testament and Josephus as regards the overwhelming authority of the rabbis in Judaism. They hold legislative power, giving them an unrivaled influence over the people, even controlling the ritual actions of the high priest. They are called upon to decide complicated cases of morality, they are asked to annul vows, and are encouraged to become directors of con-

science and to govern men's souls. One of the indications of
such control is that a family feast could not be celebrated
without inviting a few rabbis. In this way the rabbi comes to
replace the priest; he is said to deserve more respect than
one's mother and father. How has such a figure obtained
this power, which no constitution prescribes and no ordina-
tion legitimizes? The answer is that he is the teacher and is
seen as the heir of "Moses, our Master."

The Torah and Life

Thc divine Torah should guide our whole life; therefore,
the Israelite's first duty is to study it. Although other religions also expect their faithful to study religious law, this
obligation is nowhere as strict or as broad as in Judaism.

Neither age nor condition, neither wealth nor poverty,
can dispense the Jew from this obligation. The only question that is sometimes raised is whether women are also
bound by it. All others come under thc injunction of R.
Yose, the priest (*ca.* 90): "Be sure you study the Torah, for
it is not your property" (Ab. ii, 12). R. Meier lists the rewards of the man who studies the Torah:

He who studies the Torah merits many rewards, and the
whole world embraces him. He is called God's companion and
beloved; he loves both God and men and makes them happy.
Such study invests him with both humility and fear; it helps
him to be righteous, pious, just and faithful; it kccps him from
sin and helps him to reward. From such a man people will derive counsel, knowledge, intelligence and strength (Prov. 8:14).
The Torah confers leadership and penetration of judgment,
and God will unveil its mysteries to the one who studies it faithfully. He will become an inexhaustible spring and a never-
failing stream. He is modest, patient, and ready to forgive in-

juries. Such study makes him great and raises him above all things.

Abot vi, 1

Other statements make it clear that this obligation of study is above all others; it is a meritorious action, even more than prayer and the works of charity. R. Simeon ben Yohai places the crown of the Torah above those of kingship and priesthood (Ab. iv, 13); the gentle Hillel declares that the man who is ignorant of the Law is incapable of piety (Ab. ii, 6), and other rabbis echo him by saying that the common people, who do not know the Law, live under a curse. Finally, Philo, Seneca, and Origen point out that the Jews are very zealous about the matter of religious instruction, and Josephus even claims: "You may question any of us on any law you wish; he will know the answer better than his own name" (*Against Apion*, II, xviii, par. 178).

Such study calls for a teacher, and therefore R. Simeon ben Gamaliel commands: "Everyone should be the student of a rabbi" (Pes. iv, 5). This instruction could be received in schools of various levels, and could at least be heard in the synagogue by listening to the Sabbath sermons. A story of R. Jochanan ben Baroka and R. Eleazar Hisma going to visit R. Joshua ben Hananiah is instructive:

R. Joshua asked them, "What did you hear that was new today at school?"

"We are your disciples and we drink at your waters." [A disciple should not teach in front of his master.]

"But it is impossible that there was nothing new at school. Who preached the sermon?"

"R. Eleazar ben Azariah."

"On what passage did he comment?"

"On Deuteronomy 31:12—"Assemble the People—men, women, and children.""

"If the men come to learn and the women to listen, why do the children come?"

"To see to it that the one who brings them receives a reward."

Tosefta Sotah, vii, 9

Some rabbis would want people to give all their time to the study of the Torah, even to the point of giving up one's job. But they were probably thinking more of apprentice rabbis than of most Israelites, who had to think about earning their living. They were anticipating an ideal, to be realized in the messianic age, when all would become rabbis and be personally instructed by God.

Since studying is such an important duty and brings such a rich reward, the question arises as to whether knowing the Law is not better than fulfilling it. But no one went so far as to say that knowledge alone was enough; they all agree that the true scholar is the one who accomplishes what he teaches. R. Hanina ben Dosa (*ca.* 70) said: "That man's knowledge will remain firm whose fear of sin is greater than his knowledge; but if his knowledge is greater than his fear of sin, his knowledge will not endure. If a man's deeds are greater than his knowledge, his knowledge will last, but if his knowledge is greater than his actions, his knowledge will not last" (Ab. iii, 9-10). R. Eleazar ben Azariah illustrated the same principles with these parables:

To what can we compare a man whose knowledge is greater than his deeds? To a tree with many branches and puny roots. A wind can come along and uproot it and turn it upside down, as it is written: "He is like a barren bush in the desert that enjoys no change of season, but stands in a lava waste, a salt and empty earth" (Jer. 17:6).

But to what can we compare a man whose deeds are greater than his knowledge? To a tree which has few branches but whose roots are deep and widespread. Even if all the winds of the world came and blew against it, they would not be able to move it from its position, as it is written: "He is like a tree planted beside the waters that stretches out its roots to the stream" (Jer. 17:8).

Abot iii, 17

At the beginning of the second century there was a debate at Lydda as to which of the two activities was the better. It was decided that study was more important because it determines action, and also because the gift of the Law preceded the practice of some commandments by a number of years (Kid. 40b). Others, like R. Eleazar of Modiin, say that "To listen is the principle which contains the whole Torah" (*Mekilta on Exod.*, 15:21).

God took Israel out of Egypt in order to give it his Torah. Similarly, R. Johanan ben Zakkai said that Israel was created for the sake of the Torah—that is, in order to study it (Ab. ii, 8). Correlatively, it is said that the Torah was created for Israel. This means that every man—and especially every Israelite—fulfills his purpose in life by doing God's will as revealed in the Torah. It also means that the Torah was given to Israel to increase its merits and give it a special character. It is unnecessary to cite further texts to establish the fact that for Judaism the whole moral and religious life is purely and simply an application of the Law. In order to please its author, receive the yoke of Heaven, and assure one's salvation, it is necessary and sufficient to keep the whole Law; apart from that, there is no need to be concerned about anything or look for anything else. This is both the feeling of the rabbis and the teaching of the apocrypha. Philo sees in the Law of Moses the image and expression of the eternal law, the natural law, "by which the great city of the world is governed."[3] Josephus often states that

[3] Émile Bréhier, *Les idées philosophiques et religieuses de Philon* (Paris, 1908), pp. 11-23.

the Jews arrange their life according to the laws of Moses, which are far superior to those of other peoples (*Against Apion, passim; Antiquities,* III, viii, 8, par. 213).

According to this theory, the pagans, to whom the Law has not been revealed, do not have to observe it, but should keep the seven commandments of Noah: to abstain from idolatry, murder, theft, eating blood or part of an animal that is still alive, and incest; and to practice justice in judgments and to observe the blessings of God (Sanh. 56ab, *baraita*). We are already familiar with discussions regarding the gentile who observes the Law. The Jews do not claim to dispense pagans from the natural law, but simply from Jewish observances. For the Torah does not simply prescribe the duties of natural law, but also includes some practices which have no real religious meaning.

The Jews were well aware of the difference between the two categories of obligations. The precepts of the natural law were "those that would have to be written down in the Torah if they were not there already" (*Sifra on Lev.,* 18:4); in addition, there were positive laws to which the pagans, Satan, and evil nature raised objections. This attitude betrays the feeling that from the point of view of reason and religious sentiment, it is hard to justify the dietary and clothing laws, or the prohibitions in regard to purity. In Alexandrian Judaism, *The Letter of Aristeas* and Philo tried to prove by symbolic considerations that these laws recall or imply the moral virtues. But Palestinian Judaism, although sometimes hazarding rationalist tendencies, made these regulations part of the divine will:

Once a gentile asked R. Johanan ben Zakkai, "Are you not making use of something like sorcery [in the ceremony of the red heifer]? You take a heifer, slaughter it, and burn it. Then you grind the remains and keep the ashes. Then if one of you has been stained by touching a dead body, you sprinkle him with this two or three times; is this supposed to purify him?"

The rabbi replied with a question, "Did a disturbed spirit [epilepsy] ever enter you?"

"No."

"Did you ever see someone in whom a disturbed spirit had entered?"

"Yes."

"And what did you do?"

"We burned some roots to smoke it out, covered it with water, and the spirit departed."

"Have your ears heard what your lips said? Here too we are dealing with an impure spirit, for it is written: 'I will also take away the prophets and the spirit of uncleanness from the land'" (Zach. 13:2).

When the gentile had gone away, the rabbi's disciples spoke to him, "You got rid of that man too easily; how would you answer us?"

"Believe me, the dead body does not stain nor does the water purify, but it is the decree of the King of kings. As the Holy One says, blessed be He, I have established my decrees and I have ordered my observances, and man may not violate my decree."

Pesikta de Rav Kahana, 40a,b

R. Eleazar ben Azariah gave a different justification for these positive laws: "You should not say, 'I cannot wear mixed materials; I cannot eat pork; there are certain marriages which I cannot make.' What you should say is, 'I could do all these things, but my Father in heaven has forbidden them.' All this is based on Leviticus 20:26—'I, the Lord, am sacred, I, who have set you apart from the other nations to be my own.' This is how we avoid transgression and accept the Rule of Heaven" (*Sifra on Lev.*, 20:26).

It is clear, therefore, that the positive laws are obligatory because they are God's will, and they are reserved for Israel, in order to "set it apart." But this principle gives rise to many difficulties. It is only in the third century that they began to count 613 commandments, and as many positive precepts as bones in the human body (248), and as many prohibitions as days in the solar year. Even at the time of Christ, however, there was a whole host of obligatory laws, and the rabbis were not interested in lightening the burden. All must be kept; to violate one of them was equivalent to rejecting the whole Law and refusing God's yoke (*Sifre on Num.*, 15:22). Therefore, there was no point in making distinctions between hard and easy commandments, between those announcing a prohibition and those that contained a precept. Only women are exempted from those precepts which were to be executed in a specific period.

Moreover, we must recognize the exalted nature of the principle that the commandments must be fulfilled for their own sake. They are to be obeyed "for the sake of Heaven," without any self-interested motive. They are also to be practiced with joy, since only those laws which Israel accepted with joy were considered to have been observed.

This last prescription reveals a mind that is faithful to the Law; joy overcomes the primary difficulty which comes from the great number of commandments. This is the same joy that breaks forth in Psalm 119, whose endless repetitions are loved by all religious minds, but may be boring to someone closed to the supernatural. No believer could refrain from admiring the Torah, which represents the whole of one's life, the perfect reflection of divine revelation, the most certain and direct bond between oneself and God. The pious Jew constantly sang of his joy in practicing that Law, and of the consolation it provided, which made him forget all trials and persecutions. This feeling was coupled with heroic loyalty which even extended to martyrdom; Philo speaks of it as a miracle. But he also tells of Jews who were seduced by Greek sophistry, denied the Law, and fell into a life of corruption (*Vita Mosis,* ii, 3 ff.; *De posteritate Caini,* 33).

Nevertheless, the burden became so heavy that the rabbis themselves tried to make it easier, or to avoid it. This was done by working out such legal fictions as the *Eruv,* a technical term for the provision which alleviates certain Sabbath restrictions. Such devices encouraged people to try to find ways to get around the Law, and one may ask how well idealism and loyalty survived under such circumstances.

But the most annoying consequence of the system of the Torah was that genuinely moral obligations were put on the same level as ritual and external observances. Since the latter were extremely numerous, the Jew could be led to attribute primary importance to them, and to think that eating improperly butchered meat was as serious a sin as slander. This danger threatens every religion which has a profusion of positive laws, along with endless regulations imposed by jurists and liturgists. Pharisaism, the most accurate expression of Palestinian Judaism of this period, did not escape the conviction that one can satisfy one's duties to God by fulfilling external rituals, which may easily be emptied of all love. Such formalism and hypocrisy—which inevitably derive from it—were called in ancient times "the plague of the Pharisees." The abuse of legal learning to the detriment of justice and charity was considered one of the four causes for the ruin of the world (Sotah iii, 4).[4]

Jewish historians are wrong, therefore, to reproach Jesus for condemning this failing of the Pharisees. It was necessary for him to make his criticism, both in order to open the eyes of the masses, who put too much trust in their blind leaders, and to warn against that formalism which is a danger to

[4] See *Judaisme Palestinien,* I, 53 ff., for further texts and the opinions of contemporary scholars.

every religion. Of his long discourse against the scribes and hypocritical Pharisees, let us recall only a few key sentences: "Woe to you, Scribes and Pharisees, hypocrites! because you pay tithes on mint and anise and cummin, and have left undone the weightier matters of the Law, right judgment and mercy and faith . . . you clean the outside of the cup and dish, but within they are full of robbery and uncleanness" (Matt. 23:23,25).

Chapter Five
Man and General Ethics

The doctrines which contain the Jewish theology of man
were developed, for practical ends, in terms of moral directives. They refer either to man in general, or to the Israelite, the only human type for whom rules of conduct can be
formulated.

Man

Jewish anthropology derives its essential concepts from
two biblical realities: Man has been appointed by God to
be the ruler of the universe, and man has been created in
the image of God. Man is the center of creation; his value
is equal to that of the whole world, and everything is sub-
ordinate to him. We also encounter the Greek idea that
man is a kind of microcosm, an epitome of the world (Yose
of Galilee, *ca.* 150; Ab. R. N., xxxi, 3). Such statements show
a tendency to an instinctive anthropocentrism.

In the fact that man was created in the image of God, R. Akiba sees a proof for the belief that God loves his creatures (Ab. iii, 18). Others will find a great moral principle here: Murder is a crime because it weakens or eliminates the image of the King (R. Akiba and Simeon ben Azzai, *Tos. Yeb.*, viii, 4); to commit an outrage against man is to commit an outrage against God (*Tos. Sanh.*, ix, 7). Hillel states that to care for one's body is a duty to God, since man is made in his image (*Lev. Rabbah*, 34:3). Since the first man was the root of all humanity, it follows that all men are equal; no man can say to another, "My father was greater than yours" (Sanh. iv, 5).

At the time of Christ, the Greek dichotomy, which sees in man a being composed of body and soul, made its entry into Jewish thinking. But such a conception seems to have been rejected in the realm of ethics. Josephus sees in the human soul "a spark of divinity within man" (*Wars of the Jews,* III, viii, 5, par. 372). A Jewish prayer, probably going back to the beginning of the second century and recited every morning by the pious Jew, asks God to preserve his imprint in the soul: "My God, you have given me a pure soul. You formed it in me, breathed it in me, and protected it within me. You will take it away from me, and you will give it back in the time to come. As long as this soul is within me, I confess before you: Yahweh, my God and the God of my fathers, Lord of the ages, Master of all souls, blessed be Thou, who restores souls to dead bodies" (Ber. 60b; Nid. 30b).

The schools of Hillel and Shammai were busy for two and a half years with a problem that helps us to see the rather pessimistic ideas of the Jews regarding the meaning of life. "One school said that it would have been better for man not to have been created. The other said that it was better for him to have been created than not to have been created. A vote was taken and it was decided that it would have been better if he had not been created, but now that he had been, he should carefully examine his acts" (Erub. 13b, *baraita*). Only the apocalyptic works, *4 Ezra* and *3 Baruch,* attribute the painful and wicked character of this corruptible world to the corruption caused by man's first sin.

Misogyny is another widespread characteristic in Israel. It is already noticeable in Proverbs and Ecclesiastes; it is even harsher in Ecclesiasticus, and explains many rabbinic sayings. One should not trust a woman's virtue or intelligence, since sin came about through her. They are all more or less given to witchcraft. Men who let themselves be led by women are ridiculed. Every pious Jew repeats the prayer of R. Judah: "Blessed be He who has not made me a woman" (*Tos. Ber.,* vii, 18).

In Jewish thought man's most important prerogative is freedom. This is understood, from an essentially moral point of view, as the freedom to choose between good and evil and to select the path one wants—either that of good, leading to happiness, or of evil, leading to destruction. In this way, man is the artisan of his own destiny. We are often reminded of the saying of R. Haninah ben Hama (*ca.* 225): "Everything is in the hand of Heaven, except the fear of Heaven" (Meg. 25). Is this meant as a denial that divine grace can bring about the fear of God? Such freedom is not limited by God's foreknowledge or predestination: "R. Akiba said that everything is foreseen, but freedom of choice remains" (Ab. iii, 15).

Sin and Evil Nature

From its first pages, the Bible tells of man's sin, which led to death for him and his descendants. Christian dogma affirms not only hereditary death but also hereditary sin; the

Council of Trent stated that Adam had passed on his sin to the whole human race, as well as concupiscence, which leads to sin. It follows that if *liberum arbitrium minime exstinctum in eis esset,* nevertheless it exists *viribus attenuatum et inclinatum.* Does Judaism admit that as a consequence of this first sin there is a weakening and distortion of our freedom?

Post-biblical Jewish literature, especially that of the rabbis, attributes special prerogatives to Adam which raise him above the human level. Under the influence of a jealous Satan, he disobeys God, and is punished. Both Adam and his descendants were deprived of divine gifts—in particular, the fruit of the tree of life. In this way "he destroyed many generations." This first sin is also said to have brought about the withdrawal of material advantages—like a marvelous stature—which will be restored in the messianic age *(The Book of Jubilees; Gen. Rabbah,* 12:5). R. Judah tells us that, just as with Elias, the man who does not sin will not die *(Pesikta de Rav Kahana,* 76a).

Certain documents deal with various spiritual consequences of the first sin. Adam lost glory and justice *(The Apocalypse of Moses,* xx); he discovered concupiscence, and with it, the knowledge of procreation *(The Apocalypse of Moses,* xxi, 5; *2 Baruch,* lvi, 6)—Josephus considers this a benefit *(Antiquities,* I, i, 4, par. 44). According to a rabbinic tradition related by R. bar Nappaha (died 279), but possibly older, the serpent gave Eve an instinct for impurity, which was taken away from the Israelites at Mount Sinai (Yeb. 103b).

The idea that sin was introduced into the world by Adam, and that he has passed it on to all of mankind, is extremely close to the traditional idea of original sin. We see it first in *4 Ezra,* a work that is extremely preoccupied with the problem of sin. Adam, who has the evil disposition that is in every man, has sinned; a sentence of death is immediately pronounced against him and his descendants. He has disobeyed and he and all those who will be born from him have been overcome. The nations that will spring from him have also committed evil. What was good has disappeared and left only what is bad; weakness has become permanent. "O thou Adam, what hast thou done! For though it was thou that sinned, the fall was not thine alone, but ours also who are thy descendants! For how does it profit us that the eternal age is promised to us, whereas we have done the works that bring death" (*4 Ezra*, vii, 118-119).

Henceforth the world is corrupt, and all men are to be accused of sinfulness. Nevertheless, the cause of sin in *4 Ezra* is in the *cor malignum* which is in every man, and some people have kept the commandments and escaped damnation (vii, 45, 48, 92; viii, 2).

2 Baruch shows a very similar attitude. The first sin has brought pride, sexual concupiscence, and the decay of goodness into the world. It is therefore the cause of universal damnation. "O Adam, what hast thou done to all those who are born from thee? And what will be said to the first Eve who hearkened to the serpent? For all this multitude are going to corruption, nor is there any numbering of those whom the fire devours" (xlviii, 42-43).

Nevertheless, everyone is responsible for his own sin. He can imitate Moses as well as Adam: "And justly do they perish who have not loved Thy law, and the torment of judgment shall await those who have not submitted to Thy power. For though Adam first sinned and brought untimely death upon all, yet of those who were born from him, each one of them has prepared for his own soul torment to come, and again each of them has chosen for himself glories to come. . . . But each of us has been the Adam of his own soul" (*2 Baruch*, liv, 14-19).

We see now how close this position is to that of St. Paul, and how it differs from it. The apostle stresses the power of sin (Rom. 12:12 ff.), which was introduced into the world, and the Jews of his time have a similar position. But they do not agree with him that the first sin has made all men sinners. In the texts we have cited, there may well be a protest against Paul's doctrine of original sin. Certain Jewish authors[1] even believe that at a certain time Judaism might have accepted a similar doctrine—the transmission of the original sin to all posterity—had it not been forced into rejecting such views as being Christian. Whatever its merit, this opinion has not won over many disciples.

Perhaps we have something similar in the concept of the *yetzer hara*. The idea and the word for it go back to the centuries before the Christian era and are found in all Jewish circles. Every man carries within himself an interior disposition which leads him to sin. Esdras calls this *cor*, or *cogitamentum malum;* the Testaments call it the will *(diaboulion)* to do evil, and the rabbis call it evil tendency, or evil nature. We have given several translations for the Hebrew expression *yetzer hara* in order to show that it is not something irresistible, but simply tempts man to sin. Thus it might be identified with Satan, or one might say that Belial is behind it; like Satan, it is man's enemy and tries to make him do evil.

This evil nature, the evil "yeast" in man, is a creature of God, and has been present in him since his conception. It grows with him and becomes an integral part of his being, for without it, he would not get married, have children, and acquire wealth. But in spite of its power, man can overcome this drive, and subject it to his good nature. For Jewish

---

[1] I. Levi, *Le péché original dans les anciennes sources juives* (Paris, 1907), pp. 14, 29; J. Loewe, cited in Montefiore, *Rabbinic Literature and Gospel Teachings*, pp. 24f.; M. Guttmann, *Encyclopedia Judaica*, I, col. 773 ff.

speculation has developed a good nature as a counterpart to the evil one. The former seems to have arisen long after the latter, as if to provide a perfect balance and to secure our absolute freedom. But the texts do not describe it as constantly active, or as a violent attack on our free will; it is still left to man to lead his good nature to victory.

For it is generally acknowledged that man can and should fight his evil nature. The just man is the one who overcomes his evil nature, who so subjects it that it is finally absorbed by good. The main weapon which God has given Israel for use against evil inclination is the Torah, and especially the study of it. A teacher of the school of Ishmael (died 135) said: "If the wretched one attacks you, drag him into the school; if it is a stone, it will dissolve, and if it is iron it will break" (Suk. 52b). R. Johanan states in the name of R. Banna (*ca.* 220): "Blessed are you, O Israelites, for when you study the Torah and do deeds of kindness, your evil disposition is in your power, and you are not in its power" (Ab. Zarah 5b).

Although Judaism is convinced of the sufficiency of human freedom, it understands that we can be preserved and delivered from sin only with divine help. This is evident in the prayers that devout Jews recite for this intention, and also in this parable of R. Simai (*ca.* 210):

There was once a very high rock at a crossroads and it was in everyone's way. The king said to them, "Break it into pieces, little by little, and at the proper time I will have it taken away." It is in this way that the Holy One, blessed be He, says to the Israelites: My sons, evil inclination is a big stumbling block, but if you break it little by little, I will take it away, as it says, "I will give you a new heart and place a new spirit within you, taking from your bodies your stony hearts and giving you natural hearts" (Ezech. 36:26).

Yalkut Shimoni on Osee, 14:2, par. 532

This is a representative statement; it leaves the initiative and good works to human activity, but also recognizes the need for divine intervention. As R. Simeon ben Lakish said (*ca.* 250): "In the perpetual battle against evil nature, if the Holy One, blessed be He, did not come to the aid of man, he would not be able to resist" (Suk. 52b). We should underline the word *aid*, which makes it clear that the primary act is man's.

The Motives for Moral Action

The Torah is the rule for man's moral acts. But why is he bound to observe it? The Jewish mind is clearly revealed both in its conception of motives for moral action and in the stress placed on the idea of retribution.

Jewish moral teaching is, above all, religious. It has been revealed in the Torah, which is directed to the whole nation of Israel. Therefore, the reasons for keeping God's commandments are primarily religious, but at the same time they have the particular condition of the chosen people in mind.

We have already seen what a great role the covenant plays in the Bible, together with Israel's obligation to observe the divine precepts. Although this motive is not mentioned frequently in post-biblical literature, we often read: "Great is this commandment, for thirteen covenants were made on its behalf."

Another motive is mentioned more frequently during the period we are studying: Every Israelite ought to promote the kingdom of Heaven and to accept it for himself, not out of fear but love. Ancient prayers concerning God's kingdom, the principle that every blessing should mention it, as well as many statements of the rabbis, show how important this idea was. We are told that R. Gamaliel insisted on reciting the *Shema* on his wedding night, although he was dispensed, because he did not want to delay even for one hour the kingdom of Heaven (Ber. ii, 5, 16a). For the same reason R. Akiba recited the *Shema* while being tortured.

Another biblical motive with an important place in rabbinic literature is Israel's mission "to sanctify the divine Name." This is accomplished by martyrdom, which is sometimes an obligation, although in many cases it ought to be avoided. It is achieved primarily by carefully fulfilling the obligations of justice, so that other men—particularly pagans—will be led to praise the God of Israel. We may illustrate this principle by quoting the fine example set by R. Simeon ben Shetah (before Christ):

> Since he worked with flax, his students wanted to buy him a donkey to make his work easier. After they had got an animal from a Saracen, they found a precious pearl hanging down from its neck. They took the donkey to their master and said, "Your worries are over, for we bought for you a donkey and found this pearl hanging down from his neck."
>
> The master asked, "Does its owner know of this?"
>
> "No."
>
> "Then you must return it. For Simeon ben Shetah is not a barbarian. He prefers to hear a gentile exclaim, 'Blessed be the God of the Jews.' This is a greater reward than any worldly goods."
>
> Talmud Jerusalem, Baba Mezia ii, 5, 8c

The glory of God is a similar motive, but on a higher level. Certain rabbis say that they have done a certain deed, not for their own glory nor that of their family, but rather for the glory of God (R. Eliezer and R. Joshua; Meg. 3a). In the same sense a certain act is said to have been accomplished for God (or in the name of Heaven). Similarily, all the acts of Hillel and other rabbis were done "in the name of Heaven" (Ber. 16a; *Tos. B. K.*, VIII 13.). The following remarks were made in connection with the biblical verse "I will sing to the Lord, for he is gloriously triumphant" (Exod. 15:2):

R. Ishmael said, "How can flesh and blood embellish its Creator? I will glorify him by keeping the commandments; by making a beautiful *sukkah* for him, a beautiful *lulab*, beautiful fringes and a beautiful prayer." R. Yose of Galilee said, "Praise and glorify the Holy One, blessed be He, in the presence of all the nations of the world."

R. Yose of Damascus said, "I will build him a beautiful Temple, since 'to embellish' can only refer to the Temple, as it is written, 'They have devoured Jacob and laid waste his dwelling'" (Ps. 78[79]:8). R. Akiba said, "I will praise and embellish the One who spoke and the world came into being; the nations ask Israel who is its beloved in order that they may join him."

Mekilta on Exodus, 15:2

A similar thought may be found in the advice that "No one should use his face, his hands, or his feet except for the glory of his Creator, as it is written (Prov. 16:4), 'The Lord has made everything for his own ends'" (*Tos. Ber.*, iv, 1). When Paul calls on the Corinthians (1 Cor. 10:31) to do everything for the glory of God, this sounds like an echo of the rabbinic saying just quoted. Philo sums up the prevalent teaching when he states that observing the laws contributes to the glory of the universal cause (*De migratione Abrahami*, 23).

Moreover, the practice of the commandments, especially those concerning charity, is a way of imitating God, and this duty applies to all men. Here is a commentary of Deu-

teronomy 11:22, ". . . following his ways exactly, and holding fast to him":

> How can man ascend on high and hold fast to him? Does it
> not say, "His throne was flames of fire with wheels of burning
> fire"? But this means that you should cling to the sages and to
> their disciples, and this will be counted as if you had ascended
> on high.
> How can flesh and blood be called by the name of the Holy
> One, blessed be He? But this means that just as God is called
> merciful and compassionate, you too should be compassionate
> and merciful, and do deeds of kindness to others. Be like him,
> righteous and pious.
>
> *Sifre on Deuteronomy,* 11:22; Sotah 14a

In spite of such noble statements, we must point out that
our literature more frequently encourages the observance
of the commandments with warnings of sanctions. In the
great daily prayer, "Hear, O Israel!" (Deut. 6:4) the two
motives are combined: "Therefore, you shall love the Lord,
your God, with all your heart, and with all your soul, and
with all your strength. . . . If, then, you truly heed the commandments . . . I shall give the seasonal rain to your land"
(Deut. 6:5; 11:13-14). Indeed, in a theology which considers
the system of retribution as an absolute principle, the two
points of view could hardly be separated from one another.

This principle, the eleventh in Maimonides' Thirteen
Articles of Faith, contains two correlative points: Every act
is followed by a corresponding reward or punishment; whatever happens to man is a result of his good or bad deeds.

The first of these two principles is universally acknowledged. We have innumerable rabbinic statements to the
effect that every commandment implies a statement of
reward, and it is because of the promise of a reward that
man is encouraged to do good deeds. We have the same at-

titude in the Apocrypha. It is even more remarkable that Philo, in spite of his leanings towards Stoicism, follows the same approach; commenting on those biblical passages which specify the blessings and curses connected with the observance of the commandments, he states that they are both just and helpful in arousing hope and shame (*De praemis et poenis*, I, 4, 8-9). We should also ask whether such rewards were regarded as something God owes man, or has agreed to pay in all fairness.

The counterpart of that first principle leads to the conclusion that all sufferings, even death, are punishments for a sin. Therefore, when any misfortune occurs, the Jewish mind looks for the cause; the Gospels have several examples of this conviction (John 9:2; Luke 13:2,4). One even knows the exact fault for which a particular sickness is the punishment; slander, for example, is punished with leprosy (*Sifra on Lev.*, 14:35).

Ordinarily, retribution is given in this world, and it consists therefore of material rewards or sorrows. But the conviction grew that the real sanction and its re-establishment of the moral order is reserved for the world to come. Thus R. Tarfon (*ca.* 110) concluded several moral warnings with these words: "But know that the righteous will receive their reward in the world to come" (Ab. ii, 16). This thought is also clearly expressed in one of the daily prayers found in the Mishnah (Peah i, 1): "These are the things that have no exact measure: the corner of the field which is to be left to the needy, the first fruit, voluntary festival sacrifices, charity, and study. The following things are rewarded in this world, but the main reward is reserved for the world to come: to honor one's parents, to perform works of charity, and to make peace among men. But the study of the Torah is worth as much as all the others."

God judges man not only at the last judgment, but also

daily and annually. The latter occurs on the New Year, when everybody's good and bad deeds are taken into account. If a man can boast of more merits than demerits, he is classified among the righteous; otherwise, he is called wicked. In case of an equal balance, he is called average. But the final decree is not passed until ten days later, on the Day of Atonement; up to that time one can modify the sentence by penitence and good deeds. Thus we see that an arithmetic rule of commutative justice is used. But God's tolerance, especially toward Israel, is also recognized.

The term "measure for measure" is used when it comes to handing out rewards. There is no good deed without its appropriate reward. R. Eleazar ben Azariah states that the Egyptians had been rewarded for what they gave to the Israelites, although this was in their own interest (*Sifre on Deut.*, 23:8). But this prinicple is weakened a little when it is said that the punishment is less than the corresponding sin, so that reward is greater than punishment (*Sifra on Lev.*, 5:18).

The principle of "measure for measure" is completed by that of exact retaliation. When Hillel saw a skull floating on the water, he exclaimed, "You have been drowned because you have drowned others, but those who have drowned you will in turn be drowned" (Ab. ii, 6). Because Joseph buried his father, Moses buried Joseph, and if he had not done so, the Israelites would not have taken care of him (*Tos. Sotah,* iv, 7).

We find the same attitude to a woman who was suspected of having committed adultery (Num. 5:11 ff.). After invoking Isaias 27:8, "Measure by measure, by exile thou didst contend with them" (RSV trans.), R. Meier said: "This applies in all cases, for instance that of the woman suspected of adultery. She was not ashamed, so the priest shows her to all present. She had removed her veil, so the priest bares her

head. . . . She disrobed; therefore the priest puts her to
shame" (*Tos. Sotah.*, iii, 2-4).

Although ordinarily, punishment is thought to refer to
material and exterior things, we also find interior punishment. Ben Azzai said, "Be quick to fulfill even a slight commandment, and avoid transgression. For one commandment leads to another, even as one sin leads to another, and
the reward for one commandment is another commandment, and the consequence for one sin is another sin"
(Ab. iv, 2).

It is also stressed that retribution is made on a strictly individual basis, as had been taught by Jeremias and Ezechiel.
Therefore, if children die on account of their fathers, it is
because they had done the same things (*Sifra on Lev.*, 26:39).
But the idea of solidarity in reward and punishment is maintained. R. Simeon ben Eleazar said: "Happy is the man
who has practiced a commandment, for he has tipped the
balance toward the side of merit, both for himself and the
whole world. But woe to the man who has committed a
transgression, for he has tipped the balance to the side of
debt, both for himself and the world. 'A single slip can ruin
much that is good' (Eccles. 9:18); because of this one sin that
he has committed, he has lost many goods both for himself
and the world" (*Tos. Kid.*, i, 14).

The same holds true for merits. We have already seen
what treasures have been stored up through the merits of
the Patriarchs and of Israel. It was also believed that the
prayers and sufferings of the just could atone for the sins
of others (*Mekilta on Exod.*, 12:1, 22:22).

The last affirmation helps to correct the otherwise rather
rigorous principle of retribution. Another way of making
this idea more flexible was to realize that God often allows
his rewards and judgments to remain unknown, both so
that no law will be neglected and in order to offset unworthy

motives (*Tanhuma bar Abba; Ekeb.*, iv, 3). The maxim of Antigonos of Sokho was often repeated: "Do not act like servants who work for their master on the condition they receive a gift, but be rather like servants who work for their master without considering the gift. And let the fear of heaven be upon you" (Ab. 1, 3). R. Eleazer ben Pedat (died 279), commenting on Psalm 112:1, "Happy the man who fears the Lord, who greatly delights in his commands," emphasizes "*in his commandments,* not in the reward for keeping the commandments" (Ab. Zarah 19a).

Sin and Expiation

Since the Israelite is deeply religious, he is constantly concerned about sin, either to avoid it or to atone for it. Sin may be essentially defined as a violation of the divine will, which the Law has revealed. Originally every violation of a law was considered at least a material sin; we know of the ritual sacrifices for faults committed because of oversight or ignorance. Little by little, Jewish theology decided under what conditions the violation of a law constituted a real sin, requiring reparation for the harm done to one's neighbor and the offense given to God. There developed a more attentive analysis of the human act, anticipating what we call moral theology. An attempt was made to determine the degree of knowledge, intention, and will required for guilt, or how ignorance or oversight might be valid excuses. Casuistry became more subtle, and sometimes overly complex. The element that constitutes the sinful act was seen as a revolt against God and the scorn of his Law, which in practice may even extend to the denial of the Creator.

This notion makes it possible to recognize sin in purely interior acts. Jewish theology, for example, speaks of sinful glances or adultery of the eyes (Nid. 13b, *baraita*), and sins of desire, impurity through bad intention. Hence a man is guilty if he eats lamb while thinking and wishing that he is eating pork (R. Akiba, *Tos. Naz.*, iii, 14). There are also sinful thoughts about sex which lead to nocturnal impurity (Zab. ii, 2). R. Reuben ben Strobilos, a disciple of Akiba, gives a general statement of the conditions that establish guilt: "A man is not guilty of something only if he has committed the act; he is guilty if he has committed it in part; or even if he has not committed it at all, he has planned in his heart to do so; or if he has not planned to do so, he is glad to see it committed by others" (M. K. 18b).

What is the effect of sin? It is considered a defilement, a lack of regard for divine sanctity. It soils the earth and drives away the Shekinah; it corrupts man and develops evil tendencies which never stop growing; at first it is a thin thread, but it becomes a thick cable. It blinds and hardens the heart. It is punished by all kinds of misfortunes and plagues. Would it, then, not be better to be an animal which cannot sin? (*4 Ezra*, vii, 62 ff.) How could sin come into the world? It is universally believed that sin is not God's work. "I swear to you sinners that just as hills and mountains have never and will never become servants, sin has not been sent to earth. Men have made it by themselves, and those who commit it will be cursed" (*The Book of Enoch*, xcviii, 4).

We have already heard what tradition has to say about the origin of sin; it was introduced into the world through the jealousy of Satan, who tempted Adam, and it was subsequently taught to others by the bad angels and their descendants. Nothing can eliminate or diminish man's guilt. Even when we take into consideration his evil nature, his concupiscence, and his ignorance of the Law, he alone is responsible.

Can man avoid sin? According to a few isolated rabbinic statements, some men were without sin. But the generally accepted opinion—especially in the Apocrypha—is that no one has ever been without sin, not even the Patriarchs or Moses. When R. Eliezer claimed that he had never broken a commandment, after teaching that no one was without sin, sufferings were sent to him in order to open his eyes (Sanh. 101a).

Since sin is unavoidable and has such terrible consequences, it is of the greatest importance to know how one can be cleansed of it. The Jewish mind attaches great importance to deliverance from the burden of its sins. In both the Bible and later literature we find a great many penitential prayers, and they occupy an important place in Jewish piety. Jewish doctrine recognizes many ways to atone for sins, and R. Ishmael describes four of them:

If a man has violated a positive commandment and repented, God will surely forgive him, according to Jeremias 3:23; if he has violated a negative commandment and repented, he must wait till the Day of Atonement provides forgiveness, according to Leviticus 16:30; if he has violated a commandment punishable by death, either through the hand of God or through the sentence of a human tribunal, and he has repented, sufferings sent by God will expiate, according to Psalm 88:33; but if he has profaned God's name, then even if he has repented, neither his repentance nor the Day of Atonement can purify him, but repentance and the Day of Atonement expiate one-third of his guilt; sufferings endured for the rest of the year, another third; and the day of death purifies, according to Exodus 23:21.

Tosefta Yom Hakippurim, v, 6 ff.

Let us see first what ritual expiation is mentioned in Mosaic legislation. Leviticus makes sacrifices for sin of primary importance. According to the rabbis, the offering up of the sacrificial animal had to be accompanied by confession and by reparation for the wrong done to another. According to the schools of Hillel and Shammai, other sacrifices also had a purifying value. Those at the New Moon, pilgrimages to Jerusalem, and even the daily sacrifices helped to wash and whiten the sins of Israel (*Pesikta de Rav Kahana*, 61b, reporting an opinion of second-century rabbis). Even those modern Jews who have given up all beliefs and practices want to obtain the great liturgical expiation of the Day of Atonement. Its ritual practices are explained in detail in chapter 16 of Leviticus. It is still observed as a day of fasting, in addition to almost interminable prayers in the synagogue. Those who completely participate in it are thought to have all their sins forgiven. The services leave an indelible impression; there are the confessions of the high priest, clothed in special garments, the various sacrifices, the blood sprinkled on the holy of holies, the cloud of incense, and the sending of the scapegoat into the desert of Azazel. When the latter was pushed off a rock, the red thread hanging in the Temple was said to turn white, as a proof that all sins were remitted (Yoma vi, 8 and corresponding Gemara).

Suffering and death, as we have seen, are means of expiation. The former may consist of the corporal punishment inflicted by a court. Although the culprit is called wicked before this punishment, he is a brother again afterwards, a proof that suffering has purified his sin (R. Hanina ben Gamaliel, *Sifre on Deut.*, 25:3). Sicknesses and other sufferings sent by God are also expiatory. If a righteous person is afflicted, sufferings are called "corrections dictated by love," and they are gladly accepted. Some men are even sad if such sufferings are absent for a prolonged time (*Mekilta on Exod.*, 20:23, reporting a generally accepted doctrine).

Natural death, or even death by capital punishment can also atone; the condemned man, we are told, will have a share in the world to come, provided that he confesses his guilt (Sanh. vi, 2). The doctrine of vicarious atonement through suffering, by death, and especially by martyrdom, seems to have been generally accepted in the Jewish world before Christ (2 Mach. 7:37; *Sifre on Num.*, 25:13).

It has been said that all types of atonement imply penitence. But this word is really not a proper rendition of the Hebrew *teshuvah* or of the corresponding Greek term *metanoia*; "conversion" would be better. Judaism has much to say about this, and it occupies a large place in Christian literature and the Gospels as well. Josephus and Philo also mention it; Philo believes it to be the second degree of perfection. He defines it as escape from shipwreck, a reform of one's entire life, a turning to good. Conversion is the special quality of a courageous soul (*De poenitentia, V*).

Penitence includes several acts. First, there should be a confession of sins, which ought to precede any offering. It is also advisable to confess yearly on the Day of Atonement, together with the high priest, and several more times during one's life (*Tos. Yom Hakkippurim*, v, 14 ff.). To be sincere, it ought to include a detailed admission of all the faults of which one has been guilty, and the promise to sin no more. If these two conditions are not fulfilled, it is false penitence and cannot lead to divine pardon. It would be like a man who wishes to purify himself in a ritual bath, but always keeps a reptile in his hand. In such a case all the waters in the world fail to have the purifying effect (*Tos. Taan.*, 1, 8). In addition, if you have wronged someone, you must repair the damage and try to be reconciled with him. This is expressed in the following way: "God forgives only the sins committed against him; but those committed against a neighbor are pardoned only when you are reconciled with him" (*Sifra on Lev.,* 16:30). Such a sincere and complete confession leads immediately to pardon (*The Psalms of Solomon,* ix, 12; Josephus, *Wars of the Jews,* V, ix, 4, par. 415).

The efficacy of penitence is a commonplace of Jewish literature; it is also one of the foundations of religious life. God is always ready to accept contrition. His hands are spread out among the wings of the angels who support his throne, in order to receive penitents (R. Judah ben Bava; Pes. 119a). God's eagerness in favor of penitents is illustrated in the example of Manasse; the angels reportedly did not want God to forgive him, but in order not to discourage sincere penitents, God made a hole in heaven so that he could hear the prayers of the penitent king (R. Judah ben Illai; Sanh. 103a).

Divine pardon is complete; sins are not only eliminated but they are even changed into merits (R. Simeon bar Yohai; T.P. Peah I, i, 16b). The purified sinners are in some way re-created (*Sifre on Deut.,* 3,29).

Penitence has a considerable place in the history of Israel, since it has provided the people with extraordinary divine favors; it can even hasten the last redemption (*Sifre on Num.,* 11:3; T.P. Taan. I, i, 63d). In the life of individuals, it should also play a major role. R. Eliezer suggests that we repent at least one day before our death—to be safe, we should always do penance and be dressed accordingly (Shab. 123a). In this spirit R. Jacob (*ca.* 120) stated he would prefer an hour of penitence and good deeds in this world to the whole life of the world to come (Ab. iv, 17).

Penitence is open to all, since God gives all sinners the opportunity to repent before he punishes them (*Mekilta on Exod.,* 15:5). But since this doctrine might cause sinners to delay repentance, it is insisted that certain great sinners will never be forgiven, especially those who have lead others to sin (Ab. v, 18). In addition, those who persist in sinning because they rely on divine pardon will not be forgiven (Yoma viii, 9).

Thus the doctrine of penitence constitutes one of the most exalted religious and moral doctrines of Judaism, and it prepared souls to listen to the warning of John the Baptist, which was repeated by Jesus: "Repent, for the kingdom of heaven is at hand."

Chapter Six
Religious Life

We are accustomed today to separate morality from religion; we make a distinction between those obligations which have to do with justice and mercy and those which refer to worship. But this was not the case in Israel; there everything involved religion. Nevertheless, it is proper to deal with religious life and moral life in different chapters. By the former, we mean not only acts connected with public worship, but all other observances, since they play such an extensive role in the life of the Israelite. For instance, forty-three out of the sixty-three books of the Mishnah are devoted to this matter.

We shall not attempt to describe all the practices of the Jewish religion, but only the feelings and ideas which underlie those rites. Let us also remember that, generally speaking, those practices are reserved to *males* as the true members of Israel.

In addition to the public liturgies of the Temple and synagogues, Jewish religion includes many private rites, making up an individual and domestic liturgy which is even more important and also more characteristic of the spirit of Judaism.

The Temple and Its Liturgy

Certain modern historians of Judaism want to make us believe that ever since the development of synagogue worship, Jews have been somewhat disaffected as regards the Temple. But all known facts contradict such an assumption: the attachment for the Temple shown by the Machabean soldiers, the mourning for the Temple ruins after the year 70, the eagerness with which all loyal Jews visit it, the memories which they cherish regarding its wonderful wealth and solemn ceremonies. One only has to read *The Letter of Aristeas* to become convinced of the truth of this statement:

The ministration of the priests is in every way unsurpassed both for its physical endurance and for its orderly and silent service. For they all work spontaneously. . . . The service is carried on without interruption—some provide the wood, others the oil, others the fine wheat flour, others the spices; others again bring the pieces of flesh for the burnt offering, exhibiting a wonderful degree of strength. For they take up with both hands the limbs of a calf . . . and never miss placing them on the proper spot. . . . When [some of them sit down] those who have already rested . . . rise up spontaneously since there is no one to give orders in regard to the arrangement of the sacrifices. The most complete silence reigns, so that one might imagine that there was not a single person present, though there are actually seven hundred men engaged in the work, besides the vast number of those who are occupied in bringing up the sacrifices. Everything is carried out in reverence and in a way worthy of the great God.

We were greatly astonished when we saw Eleazar engaged in the ministration, at the mode of his work and the majesty of his appearance, which was revealed in the robe which he wore and the precious stones upon his person. . . . On his head he wore a tiara, as it is called, and upon this in the middle of his forehead an inimitable turban, the royal diadem full of glory with the name of God inscribed in sacred letters on a plate of gold. . . . Their appearance created such awe and confusion of mind as to make one feel that one had come into the presence of a man who belonged to a different world. I am convinced that anyone who takes part in the spectacle which I have described will be filled with astonishment and indescribable wonder and be profoundly affected in his mind at the thought of the sanctity which is attached to each detail of the service.

The Letter of Aristeas, xcii-xcix

At the time of Jesus the Temple of Jerusalem, restored by Herod and shining with white marble and gold, revealed such unequaled splendor that people were justified in calling it "famous all over the world" (2 Mach. 2:23). The admiration its beauty merited was increased by the many legends told about it: The odor of its spices caused goats to sneeze for many miles around; on the feast of Sukkot it challenged the illumination of the sun, and all of Jerusalem was as bright as daylight; the noise caused by the opening of the Temple gates awakened the whole city. These stories are simply the popular and naïve expression of the love people had for their unique Temple. This love was primarily based on the conviction that the Sanctuary was the dwelling place of the living God, the residence of the Shekinah, and a token of consecration and benediction of Zion and of all Israel

As God's own house, the Temple is a very pure and holy place. If an Israelite wished to enter it, he was required to purify himself thoroughly. This obligation was even stricter for the priests. If one of them dared to perform his priestly service while in a state of impurity, he deserved to have his skull broken with sticks (Sanh. ix, 6). Heathens were not allowed to go beyond the outer sanctuary reserved for them: "Anyone trespassing beyond this barrier has only himself to blame if he is put to death." The Law was explicit: "No one was to ascend the Temple mountain with his cane, pouch or wallet or with dirty shoes. Nor was one allowed to use it as a pathway or to spit in it" (Ber. ix, 5; cf. Mark 11:16).

Because of its holiness, the Temple is able to expiate for the sins of Israel. For this reason it is also called "Lebanon," that which whitens (R. Johanan ben Zakkai, *Sifre on Deut.*, 1:7). Similarly, R. Johanan also sees the altar as guaranteeing peace between the people of Israel and their Father in heaven (*Mekilta on Exod.*, 20:25). Even the robes of the high priest, especially his precious headgear, enjoy the same privelege (*Tos. Pes.*, 6, 5; Philo, *De specialibus legibus*, I; *De victimis*, 7). The idea that by virtue of their consecration, certain objects can produce a spiritual effect comes close to our concept of the sacraments.

We can well understand that the cult of the Temple was extended to the priesthood. Priests, too, were consecrated, both by being anointed with holy oil and by their functions. It is true, however, that at the time of Jesus, the high priests and their relatives, who had important responsibilities in the Temple, were neither highly regarded nor loved. Worldly and greedy, they had sold themselves to Rome and were harsh and contemptuous to the lower clergy and the people. Nevertheless, the high priest seemed to be a kind of sacred mediator between God and his people, and was necessary for the great annual expiation on the Day of Atonement. Moreover, he remained the religious leader, and to a great extent also the political head of the nation; he was, therefore, still revered. The lower clergy seem to have been worthy men, entirely devoted to their priestly and sacrificial functions even unto death, letting themselves be slaughtered at the altar during a siege of the city rather than abandon their service. We can thus understand why even after the year 70 we find the title of priest inscribed on tombstones.

Recalling the profound admiration with which *The Letter of Aristeas* describes the liturgy of sacrifice, we must put aside present-day attitudes and personal feelings if we are to understand the mind of the Jews of those times. Today we look with horror on those slaughters, and would be disgusted with the smell of the offerings. For the people of antiquity, however, sacrifice was the main expression of worship.

In this connection, the generosity of the Jews should be mentioned first. Burnt offerings twice daily, additional sacrifices on Sabbaths and holidays, offerings for sin, and voluntary sacrifices brought in fulfillment of a vow—this represented the annual destruction of considerable livestock and of a large amount of flour, oil, and wine.

Why were the Israelites so anxious to offer sacrifices? Was this desire based on genuinely religious feelings? The prophets had frequently reminded the people that God did not need the blood of bullocks and of heifers, and Israel remembered that lesson well. It was then taught that God wanted these sacrifices, not for himself, but because of compassion for his children; they allow him to grant grace and forgiveness (*Sifre on Num.*, 28:8). That is why sacrifices may be called "paracletes" (R. Eliezer, T.P. Taan. I, i, 63c).

But how can sacrifices have power of atonement? We re-

call the expiatory character of the altar; it is said to consecrate whatever is offered on it (Zeb. ix, 1, 7). Jewish theology
attaches a great significance to the various rites, and long
after the destruction of the altar the rabbis continue to
argue about their virtues. Both the believer who brings the
sacrifice and the priest who actually offers it should have
precise intentions. They must observe the prescribed rituals
for the immolation of the animal and the offering up and
burning of its parts; otherwise the sacrifice is invalid. A
supernatural virtue is even attributed to material actions,
but we must not believe that a gross ritualism smothered
all deeply religious feeling. Philo writes that if the sacrifice
is to fulfill its purifying function, he who offers it must be
possessed of a pure spirit and his life must be full of good
deeds (*De victimis*, v, 7; *De sacrificantibus*, 3). There is a
little of this thought in the apocryphal books, but it is
less frequent among the rabbis. However, R. Simeon ben
Yohai declares that God does not like sacrifices made possible by theft or those offered by sinners (Suk. 29b on Mal.
1:13).

In addition, the liturgy of sacrifice gives more and more
place to prayer. In the Temple, the priests and Levites chant
the Psalms and recite the Decalogue, the *Shema* ("Hear O
Israel, your Lord is One") , and various benedictions which
ask for God's blessings, both temporal and spiritual. The
faithful take part in the ceremonies by responding to the
invocations of the priests, genuflecting, and performing acts
of genuine and interior worship. The apostles find it only
natural to go up to the Temple at the time of sacrifice, and
Paul pays for the offerings of the Nazarites and purifies himself so that he can offer sacrifice with them.

Jewish piety attaches considerable importance to those
festivals which make up the liturgical calendar. Let us try
to describe the feelings which underlie these holidays.

First we have the Festivals of Pilgrimage, called *regalim*: Passover; the Feast of Weeks (Pentecost); Sukkot, the Feast of Tabernacles. On these occasions many Jews flocked to Jerusalem. Such pilgrimages refreshed their piety, their admiration for the Temple and its liturgy, and their pride in belonging to God's chosen people. These were joyful festivals, characterized by songs and by merry meals to which one had to contribute the "second tithe." Originally, they had been connected with agriculture, and this character was still evident in the blessings asked of God, the offerings of sheaves and first fruit, and the pouring of libations. On these days God is said to decide on the yield of the harvest, the fruit of the trees, and how much rain is to be expected in the coming year *(Tos. R. H.,* i,13). There is an analogy between the ritual offerings and the favors requested; the material symbols used in those rites clearly correspond to invisible realities. These festivals also had a national significance from early times, re-emphasizing again the basic character of Judaism as a religion-nation. Passover recalled the liberation from Egyptian bondage and was therefore the feast of freedom and independence. The Feast of Weeks commemorated the giving of the Law at Sinai. The Feast of Tabernacles, with its huts and green branches, recalled the wanderings in the desert and the creation of the nation.

Other festivals seem to have only national significance. Hanukkah celebrates the victory of the Machabees and the recovery of an unexpected liberty (Josephus, *Antiquities,* XII, vii, 7, par. 323 ff.). The festival of Purim joyfully relives Esther's bloody triumph over Aman. Both these days stirred up the jealous patriotism of a people that was continually crushed, but always sure to be resurrected! Such feelings were further heightened by the fast for the Ninth of Ab, a day of mourning for both Temples, destroyed on the same day.

Two other festivals were intended to call the faithful to repentance, to awaken the sense of sin and the longing for purification. First comes the New Year, Rosh Hashanah, when God begins to judge men; he is asked to keep Israel in remembrance (R. H. i, 2). The same day is also considered the birthday of the universe, and the kingship of God is celebrated. The other festival is the Day of Atonement, Yom Kippur, called by Philo the holiest of the festivals, also referred to as *the* day, *Yoma*, like the tractate which deals with it. Convinced of the wickedness of sin and as- sured of forgiveness, the faithful Israelites observed the entire day in strictest fashion; eating and drinking was for- bidden, as well as washing and anointing oneself, wearing leather shoes, and having sexual relations. They listened to the confessions of the high priest, attended the solemn sacri- fices offered by the supreme celebrant after several acts of self-purification, and watched the scapegoat sent away into the wilderness carrying away all their sins. But even that day was not without joy; it was the occasion when the maidens of Jerusalem, attired in white, went out to dance in the vineyards in the hope of finding future husbands (Taan. iv, 8 and 30b, *baraita*).

The Synagogues,
Private Worship, and Personal Religion

At the time of Jesus there were already numerous syna- gogues, and every village had one of its own. Such sanctu- aries reminded the worshipers of the Temple, but did not supplant it.

In certain respects synagogue worship meant a religious revolution, the creation of a liturgy which was not con- cerned with sacrifices. For this new way of worship the

whole world owes Judaism a debt of gratitude. Those synagogue assemblies satisfied the essential needs of the Jewish
soul—prayer and the study of Scripture. Synagogue liturgy
gave emphasis to prayer, psalms, and formulas originally
used in the Temple, and developed them further. Religious
instruction is given through the Torah and the reading of
the Prophets, as well as by homilies following the reading.
This simplified worship first took place on Sabbaths and
festivals, but was later extended to two weekdays. Since no
priests were needed for such a service, it helped to encourage
the use of laymen, especially Pharisaic rabbis, in the per-
formance of religious functions.

Thus the development of the synagogue cult represents
two movements: It paves the way for a more interior religion, and it adds to the influence of Pharisaism. There
was even a more important historical consequence: The
spread of synagogues everywhere—along with the form of
worship connected with them—made for a greater cohesion
of Jews throughout the world, and made it easier for the
Jewish religion to survive after the destruction of the
Temple.

We have already mentioned the great importance of the
individual liturgy as used in the home. The vitality of
Judaism in individual hearts and families is a reflection of
the intensity and the regularity of that liturgy. Let us look
at it now in greater detail.

The Jews have often been called the people of prayer.
The Old Testament contains magnificent prayer formulas
which have inspired and fostered Christian piety to this
very day. In post-biblical literature, too, we find many
prayers in which there is an echo—although sometimes
weakened and deformed—of the biblical supplications.
Since the character of a religion is seen best in its prayers,
it is important to examine Jewish prayer more closely.

Rabbinical writings include a complete doctrine in regard to prayer, made up of directives which are more moral and spiritual than legal. These should be briefly considered before studying Jewish prayer itself.

The need for prayer is taught through practice as well as through formal laws. Its value is sometimes affirmed in excessive terms. Thus we are told that it replaces sacrifice and is more important; it represents the highest form of worship. Certain rabbis consider prayer more important than good deeds or even the study of the Torah—but this is a minority opinion. A Jew's daily life should be framed by prayer. To begin the day without reciting the morning prayer is to be impious. The best place for prayer is the Temple or the synagogue, and the best time is that of public supplications, for then one can join the community. This is the origin of the custom of praying two or three times a day, at the time of the morning and evening sacrifices, and also at *Neilah,* when the Temple gates are closed. The pious Jew also prays before and after his meals, and in this way fulfills the "seven times a day" of Psalm 118:164. All the important events of the day are sanctified by blessings—eating, drinking, seeing something remarkable, getting important news, meeting a friend after a long interval. Special formulas have been devised for all these occasions. All this is in accord with the ideal of R. Meier—to perform one hundred blessings or good deeds every day (Men. 43b on Deut. 10:12).

In order to pray, one must select a clean place, adopt an appropriate posture, maintain strict attention, and direct one's intention and devotion to God. The general belief is that every genuine prayer is heard by God. Marvelous stories are told of miracle workers, "men of deed," whose prayers brought rain at exactly the right time and even cured people living far away (see esp. Taan. iii and its

Gemara). These men were professionals, who knew by various signs—for example, when prayers seemed to stream from their lips—that they had been heard on high (*Tos. Ber.*, iii, 3). Their stories may be legends or superstitions, but such wonders have their counterpart in warnings against vain, conditional, or calculating prayers, which are deemed sinful because they fail to respect divine sovereignty.

It is more just—and more interesting—to consider Jewish prayer itself in the forms it has created, beginning with the public prayer of the Temple and of the synagogue. In the morning one first recited the Decalogue, a declaration accepting "the yoke of the commandments." Then came the *Shema*, the great official prayer; its recitation was an acknowledgment of "the yoke of the kingdom of Heaven." It contains three biblical texts—Deuteronomy 6:4-9; 11:12-21; Numbers 15:37-41. They state the obligation to serve God and the promised reward for the fulfillment of the commandments. It is not so much a prayer as a confession of faith, and is characteristic of Jewish piety both in the sentiments it expresses and the use of God's words. Many believing Israelites insist on reciting the *Shema* at the time of their death. Thus we are told that when R. Akiba was tortured to death by the Romans, he prolonged the last syllable of the word *ehad* (one) as a proclamation of divine unity.

Even at the time of the Temple liturgy, the *Shema* was already framed with blessings. Unfortunately it is impossible to extract the original kernel from the very extensive texts now in use. But we can give the essential parts. The morning is begun by giving thanks to the Creator:

Blessed be Thou, O Lord, our God, King of the universe, Who formest the light and createst darkness, Who makest peace and createst everything, Who in Thy mercy givest light to the earth and to its inhabitants, and Who in Thy goodness renewest every day continually the work of creation. . . . Who hast made the heavenly luminaries. Blessed be Thou, O God, Who makest the luminaries.

The second benediction thanks God for the revelation and the election of Israel:

With an everlasting love Thou hast loved us, and with great and abundant mercy Thou hast had pity on us, our Father and King. . . . Thou hast chosen us from among other nations and tongues, and with love Thou has joined us to Thy great name, our King, so that we may praise Thee, celebrate Thy unity and fear and love Thy name. Blessed be Thou, O God, Who out of love hast chosen thy people Israel.

The third of the morning benedictions follows the *Shema.* It is the benediction of redemption and is the oldest of the three:

True, firm, established, enduring, right, faithful and beloved is this word unto us forever. . . . Thou hast been the help of our fathers for all times. Thou hast been shield and salvation for them and for their children after them through all generations. Blessed be Thou, God, Redeemer of Israel.

The evening *Shema* is framed by four benedictions. The first three are similar to those recited in the morning; the last prays for divine help during the night. It has a less official character, and we shall not quote it.

The great official prayer, the *Tefillah,* the supreme prayer, was in great part already used in the Temple. It is also called *Shemoneh Esreh,* because it was originally composed of eighteen benedictions. R. Gamaliel gave it its present form at the end of the first century, partly to exclude Jewish Christians. Since it is extremely representative of Judaism, we reproduce it at length, in its Palestinian version.[1] In the synagogues the Babylonian form is recited, which is more developed and has been somewhat expurgated.

God, open my lips, and my mouth shall pronounce Thy praise.

1. Blessed be Thou, O God, the God of our fathers, the God of Abraham, Isaac and Jacob, the great God, strong and terrible, most exalted One, Creator of heaven and earth, our shield and the shield of our fathers, our trust in every generation. Blessed be Thou, O God, the shield of Abraham.

2. Thou art strong, humiliating those who exalt themselves and pronouncing judgment against the oppressors, Thou livest forever, bringing the dead back to life. Thou causest the wind to blow and the dew to fall, Thou supportest the living and revivest the dead, and on a sudden Thou wilt bring us salvation. Blessed be Thou, O God, Who bringeth the dead back to life.

3. Thou art holy, and Thy name is awe-inspiring. There is no God besides Thee. Blessed be Thou, O God, the Holy God.

4. Favor us with the knowledge which comes from Thee, and with the intelligence and understanding which comes from Thy Torah. Blessed be Thou, O God, Who favorest us with knowledge.

5. Cause us to return unto Thee, O God, and we shall return. Renew our days as before. Blessed be Thou, O God, Who delightest in our conversion.

6. Forgive us, O Father, for we have sinned against Thee, wipe out and remove our iniquities from before Thine eyes, for great is Thy mercy. Blessed be Thou, O God, Who forgivest abundantly.

7. Look upon our distress and fight for us, redeem us because of Thy name. Blessed be Thou, O God, Redeemer of Israel.

8. Cure us, O God, of the wounds of our hearts, or sorrow and longing. Remove them from us and heal our sicknesses. Blessed be Thou, Who healest the sicknesses of Thy people Israel.

[1] According to Dalman, *Die Worte Jesu*, appendix.

9. Bless this year, O our God, in our behalf, so that it shall be good for all kinds of harvests, and let us see soon the time of our redemption. Send dew and rain to the earth, and feed the earth with the treasures of Thy goodness and blessings. Blessed be Thou, O God, Who blessest the years.

10. Sound the great trumpet for our freedom, and raise the standard for the calling together of our exiles. Blessed be Thou, O God, Who gatherest in the scattered members of Thy people Israel.

11. Restore our judges and our counselors as at the beginning. And be Thou alone Ruler over us. Blessed be Thou, O God, Who lovest justice.

12. Let there be no hope for renegades, and wipe out the kingdom of pride speedily in our days, and may all Nazarenes and heretics perish instantly, may their names be erased from the Book of Life and not be inscribed with those of the righteous. Blessed be Thou, O God, Who humblest the proud.

13. Mayest Thou have mercy on those who are converted to justice, and give us ample reward together with those who do Thy will. Blessed be Thou, O God, the trust of the righteous.

14. Have mercy on Thy people Israel, on Thy city Jerusalem, on Zion the dwelling place of Thy glory, on Thy Temple, and on the kingship of the House of David, Thy truly anointed one. Blessed be Thou, O God, the God of David, Who buildest Jerusalem.

15. Hear, O God, the voice of our prayer and have pity on us, because Thou art a God full of grace and mercy. Blessed be Thou, O God, Who hearest prayer.

16. Be gracious unto us and dwell in Zion, and may Thy servants serve Thee in Jerusalem. Blessed be Thou, O God, Whom we serve with reverence.

17. We thank Thee, our God and God of our fathers, for all Thy kindnesses, for Thy love and mercy which Thou hast bestowed upon us and upon our fathers. When we stumble, Thy love supporteth us. Blessed be Thou, O God, Who lovest to be gracious.

18. Send Thy peace to Thy people Israel and to Thy city and

Thy portion, and bless us all together. Blessed be Thou, O God, Who makest peace.

We also transcribe what we believe to have been the original form of the *Kaddish,* a prayer repeated several times during the synagogue service. Its first part used to be said in Aramaic at the conclusion of the homily. Pious Jews still recite this prayer in memory of their deceased parents:

May His great name be magnified and sanctified in the world which He hath created according to His wish. May He bring about His kingship [may he bring redemption to fulfillment, Show us His Messiah, and ransom His people] in our own lifetime, and in that of all Israel, soon and speedily. Say ye all: Amen. May His great name be blessed for ever and ever.

In the public worship, whether in the Temple or the synagogue, Psalms were chanted or recited, setting the tone for the aspirations and sentiments of popular piety. We cannot establish with certainty exactly which Psalms were used in that way. The *Hallel*—Psalms 112-117—was said several times during the year, and the Psalms of Ascent—119-133—at the time of the pilgrimage. After the daily sacrifice the Levites used to sing the following Psalms, one on each day of the week: 23, 47, 81, 93, 80, 92, 91.

The blessings with meals had probably already found their form:

Blessed be Thou, O God, King of the universe, Who feedest the whole world.

We thank Thee, O God, for having given to our forefathers a pleasant, extensive land, and for having taken us out of Egypt. ... We thank Thee, O God, for this land and for this meal.

Have mercy, our God, on Israel, Thy people, and on Jerusalem, Thy city, and on Zion, the dwelling place of Thy glory, and with the kingship of the House of David, Thy anointed one. . . . And rebuild Jerusalem, the holy city, speedily in our days. Blessed be Thou, O God, Who rebuildest Jerusalem in mercy.

Some of the blessings still being used are of ancient origin, like the following: "Blessed be Thou for not having made me a gentile, a woman or an ignoramus" (*Tos. Ber.*, vii, 18). It would be valuable to see more of the personal prayers of individual rabbis, since they are an authentic expression of their own soul and of the Jews in general.[2]

As a rule every prayer was to begin and end by praising God (the beginning of the first century, Ab. Zarah 7b). It should also mention the kingdom of Heaven (R. Johanan ben Zakkai, Ber. 40b). The importance of giving thanks could not be overstated; one was not supposed to use anything before giving glory to God. The numerous penitential prayers have already been mentioned.

Prayers of petition also occupy a considerable place. In first place come requests for the nation, since prayer should always be collective. But we also have petitions for individual needs, of a worldly rather than a spiritual character.

What is remarkable in these prayers is the tone of filial confidence, and a freedom that sometimes comes close to impudence. Nevertheless, true prayer shows respect as well as unconstraint. We are told that R. Akiba's prayer for rain was heard because he had said: "Our Father, our King, we have no other God besides Thee. Our Father, our King, have mercy on us for Thy own sake" (Taan. 25b). It should also be stated that the Patriarchs and the great events in national history are often mentioned. The latter attest to divine mercy, their memory gives confidence to the faithful

---

[2] The interested reader will find additional examples in *Judaisme Palestinien*, II, pp. 300 ff.

and is a further claim on the God of Israel. Again we have the concept of religion-nation.

People ask today whether and to what extent mysticism may be found in Jewish piety.[3] Let us first define mysticism as an immediate experience of God, especially of the life and supernatural action of God, in the inmost depths of our being. In spite of what is often said on the subject, there is no mysticism in the esoteric speculations of some rabbis, which should be considered preludes to the Kabbala. We cannot believe that the revelations and visions mentioned in the apocalyptic writings, unveiling the secrets of heaven, are anything but a literary form. But it is quite possible that certain pious people were favored with divine words and prophetic revelations. We do not reject a priori the historicity of the story according to which a heavenly voice told John Hyrcanus in the Temple that his sons had won a victory (Josephus, *Antiquities*, XIII, x, 3, 7, par. 282, 299; Sotah 33a). Our documents do not allow us to decide whether in first-century Judaism there were some who enjoyed divine communications of a more interior character and at more frequent intervals. Are we to detect a kind of rapture or ecstasy in Akiba's hours-long prayer, during which he no longer had awareness of outer contingencies and seemed to be lost in God? R. Judah (*ca.* 150) said that "When R. Akiba joined the congregation in prayer, he was brief because of the people. But when he prayed by himself, he would be left in one corner and later be found in another, because of his prostrations and adorations" (*Tos. Ber.,* iii, 5, 7).

What are we to learn from this? In general, Judaism has nearly always been opposed to asceticism, and its desire to safeguard human liberty from interior interventions of

[3] Abelson, *Jewish Mysticism* (London: 1913); Schechter, "Saints and Saintliness," *Studies in Judaism,* series II, pp. 148 ff.

divine grace could hardly prepare souls for the various mystical states.

Religious Practices:
Consecration of the Individual and of Life

Observances are one of the most characteristic aspects of the Jewish religion. Like a tight net, they encompass all the moments and deeds of one's life. This attitude is based on the conviction that God's action extends to all beings. In order to recognize this sovereignty through the consecration of everything it possesses, to guarantee God's protection, the soul wants the whole of existence to be penetrated by religion. For this purpose, outward symbols are required—a demand quite in keeping with the basic tendencies of Judaism. This insistence—that religion should permeate life— necessarily leads to a situation in which customs that are specifically national or necessary for everyday life come to be considered as religious. A kind of secularization of religion takes place. This leads to an ethnic religion, mixed with superstition—a devaluation and a degrading of the religious sense.

Circumcision is the first and foremost of the observances concerning the human body. Whatever its origin and its first meaning may have been, the rabbis see in it only the covenant with God, permitting man to take part in all the activities of the Jewish religion, and assuring him a share in future salvation. The spiritual effect of this bodily sign must be emphasized. Circumcision means the consecration of the human body to God (R. Akiba, *Gen. Rabbah*, 46:4). Since at least one drop of blood must flow, it is a sacrifice to God (Shammaite Law, *Tos. Shab.*, xv, 9). Only those who are circumcised belong to God, and one should not have relations with the uncircumcised; indeed, they are looked upon with a horror which often breaks out in the Old Testament. Circumcision is one of those commandments for which the Israelites have given up their lives, and they clung to it in spite of the decrees of their persecutors. Fathers and mothers would rather suffer martyrdom than not provide their children with that sign of the covenant. Even in our own days we see Jews who have almost completely forsaken their religion insist that circumcision be performed by a surgeon. But this is more of an indication of group attachment than an acceptance of the religion.

God's sovereignty, even over clothing, was seen in the ban on wearing garments in which different materials are woven together. Other practices enjoined include the *tzitzit*, the fringes affixed to the four corners of the outer garment; the *tefillin*, or phylacteries, little boxes containing biblical verses which were tied to the forehead and to the left arm; and the *mezuzah*, another little box with biblical quotations, nailed to the doorpost on the right side of the entrance. All three were intended to remind the people by visible means of the duty to observe the commandments. Increasing insistence on material symbols led to a literal interpretation of the injunction: "Therefore take these words of mine into your heart and soul. Bind them at your wrist as a sign, and let them be a pendant on your forehead" (Deut. 11:18; cf. also 6:8). This cult of the material symbol is also shown in the great care pious Jews take in their religious observances. Their faithfulness was also stimulated by the belief—sometimes bordering on superstition—that the *mezuzah* was a guarantee of divine protection.

The consecration of time was realized by the Sabbath and the holidays with their Sabbatical rest, called "the good days" (Yom Tob, the name of a tractate of the Mishnah). God has set aside the last day of the week and sanctified it, and by observing it, Israel becomes a witness to the Creator (*Mekilta on Exod.*, 31:14), and has a share in divine holiness. The Sabbath is also a sign of the covenant. Moreover, the various obligations connected with this day make clear that it is devoted to God. The first obligation is rest; any activity resembling work is forbidden. Already at the time of Jesus, ancient traditions enforced excessive restrictions which people tried to circumvent by legal fictions. Since this time belonged to God, it excluded everything that could benefit man; nevertheless, the principle "to live by the commandments" permitted relaxation of certain prohibitions in order to preserve life. The consecration was also evident in the piety in which the Temple and synagogue services, with their prayers and instruction, were conducted. Philo sees in the Sabbath the day of national philosophy (*De opificio mundi*, 43). Finally, joy, which is an essential part of Jewish piety, ought to mark this holy day; it was expressed in three meals, in special clothes, and in the home liturgy. Since the Sabbath is a sign of the covenant and of national rite, Jews have given up their lives for it and have insisted on observing it in order to be separated from other nations.

Every day is consecrated by the prayers which mark it out, and by benedictions meant to sanctify all essential deeds: getting up and going to sleep, dressing and undressing, going to the toilet, washing one's hands, taking one's meals, eating certain kinds of food and drinking certain liquids, seeing the ocean or the rainbow, and meeting a friend after a long absence.

In this way all of life's significant moments are consecrated. A boy's birth is marked by circumcision and redemption; his education consists principally of his initiation into the duties of religion; his religious coming of age; his engagement and marriage; severe sicknesses, calling for special prayers; death, preceded by the last confession; and, finally,

the funeral and the mourning periods—all these occasions
are surrounded with blessings. This concern to call on God's
grace in every moment of existence and constantly to discover some kind of a divine intervention opened the door
to superstition. People were convinced that diseases were
caused by impure spirits; fearful of ubiquitous demons,
they naturally took refuge in remedies which resembled
magic, and amulets were worn, supposedly providing some
protection against the attacks of such malevolent creatures.
The official rabbinic doctrine is more to blame for permitting the use of amulets and for accrediting those who made
them. Needless to say, astrology and dream interpretation
were also widely and officially used.

The Israelites were so much concerned with the consecration and sanctification of their lives that they were very careful to avoid anything which could separate them from God.
For the same reason they subjected themselves to individual
privations, and made interior, private sacrifices. This is the
origin of those laws which deal with impurity and purification, and which regulate the use of vows.

The Levitical law treated certain physiological functions
as uncleanliness. Contact—even indirect—with a dead body
or with lepers and certain ritually unclean animals meant
that one had to undergo certain rites of purification. The
sixth section of the Mishnah deals in great detail with such
laws. We also know from the Gospels (Mark 7:2-9) how
scrupulously the Pharisees observed them. Most of these
prescriptions concerned the Temple and its liturgy. Since
defilement and purification were related to divine sanctity,
holiness and sanctification appeared to be a material state.
Indeed, according to R. Phinehas ben Jair's "ladder of virtues," physical purity leads to separation, and this in turn
leads to holiness. In order not to become impure the Jews
tried very hard to avoid all contact with pagans. The laws

of purity encouraged a negative idea of holiness as a separation, and they finally became a form of ethnic particularism. *The Letter of Aristeas* refers to the laws of separation as "inviolable barriers and walls of iron," meant to prevent any mingling with gentiles.

The dietary laws, too, are presented as laws of purity. There are impure animals that must not be eaten, consecrated blood which must not be consumed; there are, therefore, special precautions in the immolation of pure animals. At the time of Jesus Christ, pious Jews observed these laws very carefully. There is the example of old Eleazar, who would rather die than eat, or even seem to eat, of forbidden food (2 Mach. 6:18-31). Josephus tells of his priestly colleagues who, while in Rome, subsisted on figs and nuts, so as not to become defiled (*Wars of the Jews*, VII, viii, 1, par. 264). These laws were irksome because of their particularism and separatism, but were accepted by the Jews as the will of their Father in Heaven. They saw in them a means to participate in divine sanctity, which was also thought of in a negative way and under a material aspect: "For I the Lord am your God; and you shall make and keep yourselves holy, because I am holy. . . . As I am holy, so shall you be holy; as I am separated, you also are to be separated" (*Sifra on Lev.*, 11:44).

Such abstentions readily led to the practice of vows, already provided for in the Mosaic law; they became the subject of long discussions in rabbinic literature—tractate Nedarim. A vow resembles a sacrifice, and the very word which is used for it most frequently, *korban,* is taken from the vocabulary of sacrificial worship. Generally speaking, vows were solemn promises to God to abstain from a particular pleasure or food or from any profit to be derived from a particular individual or his property. A Nazarite's vow, called by Philo "the great vow," meant abstaining from wine for a particular period and from getting a haircut. Like offering a sacrifice, making a vow was intended to please God, whether in time of danger, or in order to obtain a request. R. Akiba believed that such a practice was like a fence around piety (Ab. iii, 13).

But despite all that we hear of vows, can we really see in the historical and legal texts of the time of Jesus a reflection of a great religious movement? Vows were made by practically everybody, and covered practically everything. There were many Nazarites. This suggests that the idea of a vow had become secularized;[4] it was considered a more formal type of solemn promise, but without real religious meaning. Therefore, the law had to specify which formulae were legally valid and to explain under what conditions a father had the right to cancel his children's vows, or a husband those of his wife. The custom according to which a rabbi was authorized to annul certain vows also had to be legitimatized. It seems strange that a human being should be permitted to interfere with God's rights; in justification the rabbis invoked the need of safeguarding men's honor and protecting them from sin, making allowance for their ignorance and thoughtlessness (Ned. v; vi; ix, 2-5). The rabbis look on this task as a sacred act. When R. Gamaliel was asked to cancel a vow, he waited until he had digested the Italian wine he had just drunk; he then alighted from his donkey, clothed himself with his prayer shawl and sat down: it was only then that he canceled the vow.

Such abuses explain why some rabbis condemned any kind of vow. They called Nazarites sinners, because they refrained from drinking wine (R. Eleazar Hakkappar; *Sifre on Num.*, 6:10). In general, however, the attitude of the time was favorable to the practice of vows, provided that they be made with moderation and that nobody pledge all

---

[4] Wendel, *Das israelitisch-juedishche Gelübde* (Berlin, 1931), p. 126.

his goods to *Gaboa* (the Exaltation, or God; *Sifra on Lev.*, 25:25).

In addition to such abstentions, dictated by laws of purity or undertaken in the form of vows, there were also fast days. Some were observed by the whole of Israel, like the Day of Atonement and the anniversaries of national catastrophes. Others were prescribed by a particular congregation in order to avert a threatening danger like drought. Others were adopted voluntarily by an individual, either to atone for a sin, or to obtain some favor, or in a spirit of sacrifice or penitence. The Pharisees, for example, used to fast every Monday and Thursday.

It is precarious to attempt a synthesis of all the features of the religious mentality of Judaism. Nevertheless, it is possible to state that the Jews are an essentially religious people who wish to permeate their whole life with religious gestures. They see in God not only their Father and their King, but also the Holy One, whose holiness must be emulated and reproduced. This encourages both worship—giving homage to the Lord and hoping to obtain favors from him —and observances—trying to sanctify every human being and to consecrate him to God. In order to reach these goals, the Jewish mind likes to use visible rituals. Spiritual realities are thereby translated and established, and this seems to be a way of influencing God. This explains the attachment to the sacrificial liturgy and the large number of observances. Nevertheless, this attitude does not prevent an increasingly powerful tendency to a more inner worship and a more ethical concept of holiness.

The Jewish religion is basically national. The God in whom it trusts is the God of the Fathers and the God of Israel, and the favors asked for are mainly those which have to do with the nation's glory and future. Many rituals and sacrifices are performed in the name of the community of

Israel. The main goal of the observances is to maintain the people of God in holiness and in the proper state of separation. This explains the Jewish attitude toward observances; we must not make the mistake of believing that the Jews suffocate under a tight net of regulations. They gladly accept their laws and their restrictions because they are accustomed to them, but more importantly, because they are happily and proudly determined to preserve the chosen race in all its purity. Nor is the collective character of the Jewish religion opposed to the constant development of individualism.

The progress of individualism goes hand in hand with that of a more interior worship. The latter finds its expression in synagogue worship and in the increasing authority of the rabbis. There is neither opposition nor incompatibility between the communal character of Judaism and its individualism, no more than between priests and rabbis. Although the priests were controlled by the Pharisees, they remain the mediators between God and his people. Pious Jews pray and study in the synagogue, but the happiness of God's presence and majesty, the wish to participate in the great national liturgies, and the need to remain in touch with the most authentic organs of sanctification and expiation lead them always back to the Temple.

Chapter Seven
Special Ethics

Let us state again that for Judaism what we call ethical duties form a part of the religious life. There is so much material to choose from on this point that we must limit ourselves to the principal elements.

Duties of Justice

As has often been pointed out, Mosaic law and Jewish ethics are nearly without parallel in their civil and criminal codes. They are both established, not in terms of mankind in general, but for the national community.

We are told (Luke 10:29) that a learned man once asked Jesus: "Who is my neighbor?" The context for that question is the commandment in Leviticus (19:18): "Thou shalt love thy neighbor as thyself." Jewish commentators understood the term "neighbor" as meaning one's racial brother, a member of the same community; they always placed it in opposition to foreigner. For them, mankind consisted of two factions: faithful Israelites—God's friends—were the "neighbors," whereas all "others" (*aherim*) were apostates and pagans, and, therefore, God's enemies. This philological fact shows the key difference between the Christian and the Jewish view of the world. It is also shown by Jesus' own statement (Matt. 5:43): "You have heard that it was said, 'Thou shalt love thy neighbor, and shalt hate thine enemy.'" In spite of the indignation shown by apologists of Judaism, we find this characterization of biblical and rabbinic ethics to be very accurate; it excludes half of mankind from the human sphere and sets up relations of enmity.

Nevertheless, this principle was weakened in many respects. For example, the Mosaic law, supported by the rabbinic codes, commands the Israelite to lighten the burden of his enemy's beast, and the Book of Proverbs (24:17) warns him not to rejoice at his enemy's misfortune. Many rabbinic sentences condemn unfounded hatred, jealousy, and vengeance, at least when directed against "the sons of thy people" (*Sifra on Lev.*, 29:18).

The second characteristic feature of Jewish ethics is the importance given to justice. If we take the Golden Rule as a general statement of our duties toward our neighbor, we can learn a great deal by comparing Jesus' formulation with that found in Jewish sources. When Hillel was asked for a general rule for dealing with one's neighbor, a summary of the Law and the Prophets, he answered with the traditional formula, "Whatever is hateful to thee, do not do to thy fellow man" (Shab. 31a; cf. Tob. 4:15 and *The Letter of Aristeas*, 207). But Jesus gives the rule in positive terms, "Therefore all things whatever you would that men should do to you, even so do you also to them; for this is the Law and the Prophets" (Matt. 7:12; see also Luke 6:31). The first formulation is that of justice, which separates "mine" from "thine," and thus also draws a line dividing men from one another. The second formulation is on the level of love, which unites all people. In one, justice comes first; in the other, charity. We also read that R. Simeon ben Gamaliel considers *din*, rigorous justice, to be one of the three pillars on which the world is built (Ab. i,18). This comes close to the Roman adage *summem jus, summa injuria*. Here again, however, rigid principle is often corrected and softened by other rules and directives. A man should go beyond justice and right; he should not simply insist on his rights, but also listen to the dictates of his heart. Rabbinic adages constantly encourage working for the welfare of mankind and sacrificing individual interests for the sake of peace. We shall also see that the duties of charity play a more and more significant role.

We should not be too surprised, therefore, when we find codes of law in rabbinic literature rather than ethical treatises. Nevertheless, we do find collections of moral maxims, like the tractate Pirke Abot (Sayings of the Fathers), the two tractates of Derekh Eretz (Ways of the Earth, that is, rules of conduct). These contain echoes of the biblical-wisdom literature, as found in Proverbs, Ecclesiastes, and Ecclesiasticus. From the particular form of these compositions it is clear we are not to expect a systematic exposition of ethics. Nor do we find a more methodical approach in the apocryphal books, which are even richer in moral exhortations.

Jewish authors have every reason to be proud of the family ideal which is presented in biblical and post-biblical literature. In this respect Judaism is eminently superior to other ancient civilizations.

To get married is a duty imposed by the divine precept,

"Be faithful and multiply," and it must therefore be fulfilled at an early age. The Law forbids incestuous unions.
A man should choose a wife, not for physical or selfish reasons, or with impure intentions, but in order to contract a
real marriage (Tob. 8:9). A religious ceremony consecrates
the union. The wife is always dependent on her husband, almost to the extent of being his slave. However, the husband
is advised to "love her as his body and to honor her more
than his body" (Yeb. 62b, *baraita*). The husband must not
submit his wife to all of his whims. If it is very easy for him
to divorce her, the fact that he must write a bill of divorce
in a regular legal procedure and must return the dowry
puts a certain limit on his despotism. Theoretically, in certain extreme cases, the wife can demand a divorce. As far as
conjugal relations are concerned, modesty is advised. But
the husband may use his wife in any way he sees fit, and in
certain circumstances anti-conceptional measures are advised.

Jews were known to have many children. Whereas in
pagan circles, letting children die of exposure was a common practice, Judaism considered this to be murder. Children were considered a trust from God. The rare historical
and legal indications which have come down to us show that
parents loved their children very much, doing all they could
to give at least their boys the kind of education which would
make of them true sons of God. Children were expected to
honor their parents at least as much as they would honor
God; if necessary, they should sell everything they owned
and even go begging, in order to support their parents (R.
Simeon ben Yohai; T.P. Peah I, i, 15d).

Slaves and paid employees, even if hired for a limited
time, were also part of the family. The Law states that Hebrew slaves must be treated with so much consideration
that, according to a common saying, "he who acquired a

Hebrew slave, acquired a master" (Kid. 20a, *baraita*). Non-Jewish slaves must also be respected; to kill one of them was punishable by death (*Mekilta on Exod.*, 21:23); if a part of his body was irreparably damaged, the slave had to be given his freedom (Kid. 24a, *baraita*). Legislation tended to restrict or even suppress altogether the purchase of foreign slaves, since their circumcision was required—so that they were made into Israelites (Yeb. 47b). As far as the paid employee was concerned, biblical teaching was that to withhold wages was almost as grave an offense as taking the workman's life (*Sifra on Lev.*, 19:13); rabbinical texts grant him many concessions and advantages.

As for duties towards one's neighbor, we can give only a very general sketch. It is only natural that, in accordance with the Bible, the Jewish Law demands respect for both the person and the goods of one's fellow man. But there are some special and instructive aspects of this teaching. Murder is forbidden because it destroys the image of God which is inherent in man. Manslaughter is not punishable by death, but there must be a clear proof of nonpremeditation. The permission to kill in self-defense is limited to certain extreme cases. Any attack on the health or life of another is a crime, and requires reparation. Scandal is more serious than homicide, since it takes away eternal life (*Sifre on Deut.*, 23:8). A very detailed civil code assures the respect for material goods. Such regulations deal with legally valid business transactions, the obligation to maintain fair prices, prohibition of fraudulent practices and unfair competition. Some of these laws apply only to the Jewish community—for instance, the obligation to return a lost object, to lend money without interest to the needy, and not to raise animals that are likely to destroy the crops.

Prescriptions dealing with the honor of one's fellow man and the necessity of respect for truth reveal very well the

excellence of Jewish ethics. God himself is said to be concerned about the honor of his creatures, and he shows this
in certain laws. Therefore, man must guard the honor of
his neighbor as if it were his own, and he must not humiliate
him, especially in public. It is better to throw oneself into a
fiery furnace than to insult somebody publicly, since losing
one's reputation is more serious than losing blood. To abuse
one's fellow man is forbidden, whether by making fun of
him, by making wounding remarks, or by having a double
or triple tongue (an expression which includes defamation
and calumny as well as any effort to disrupt peaceful relations). Making accusations is a serious offense, especially in
times of persecution. In order to obtain God's pardon for
such sins, reparation must be made by becoming reconciled
with the one who has been offended, compensating him for
the shame which has been inflicted upon him. It is also forbidden to pronounce reckless judgments, for this would be
an attack, however secret, on the honor of another. The just
man always gives his neighbor the benefit of the doubt, in
spite of all contrary appearances. Nevertheless, one must
not fail to correct his neighbor, as prescribed in the Mosaic
law (*Sifra on Lev.*, 19:17). The following story shows some
of the difficulties inherent in this work of charity:

R. Tarfon said: Where can we find in this generation somebody who knows how to accept a reprimand? R. Akiba said:
Where can we find in this generation somebody who knows
how to give a reprimand? R. Johanan ben Nuri added: I call
on heaven and earth to witness that R. Gamaliel took R. Akiba
to task more than five times because of me. I had complaints
against him, and R. Gamaliel reprimanded him. But I also
know that R. Akiba only loved him more for this, as it says
(Prov. 9:8): "Reprove not an arrogant man, lest he hate you;
reprove a wise man, and he will love you."

Sifre on Deuteronomy, 1:1

It is also a duty to speak respectfully to the person with whom we are conversing, and not interrupt him. We should return the salutations of others and try to be the first one to extend greeting. It is said that R. Johanan ben Zakkai never let anyone say *shalom* ahead of him (Ber. 17a). The aged are to be honored by not sitting before they are seated, and by allowing them to start the conversation. We should all have a sense of gratitude: "It is not right to throw a rock into a well where you have just been drinking" (B. K. 92b).

Jewish ethics particularly insists on a respect for truth. Truth is called "the seal of God," and is even one of the divine names. To lie to a man is to lie to God, since he is always a third party with one's neighbor (R. Akiba, *Sifra on Lev.*, 5:21). One must shun whatever resembles deceit, including flattery, excessive compliments, or extending an invitation in the expectation it will be declined. A rabbi's appearance must reflect his standing (R. Gamaliel, Ber. 28a). This implies the duty of absolute sincerity. *The Testaments of the Patriarchs* consider simplicity a virtue that contains all others. Therefore, hypocrisy in any form is frowned upon, including that of the Pharisees, who advise others to be strict but allow themselves certain liberties (R. Joshua ben Hananiah, Sotah iii, 4. 21a). They are said to use their knowledge in order to exploit others. This is what is meant by the expression "the plague of the Pharisees." Such condemnations are very close to those made by Jesus, although some Jews consider them to be unjust.

The laws deal also with duties to the group, above all, to the national community. Solidarity of attitude and sentiment is of the most importance. One must not "separate oneself from the community," especially in times of tribulation (Hillel, Ab. 2, 4; Taan. 11a). One must pray with and for them. The brotherly feeling which tied all Jews together was well known to the pagans: *quanta concordia,* as Cicero complains (*Pro Flacco,* xxviii, 66); *apud eos, fides obstinata, misericordia in promptu,* as Tacitus recognizes (*History,* v, 5). This solidarity must be primarily one of the heart: "All Israelites are surety for one another" (*Sifra on Lev.,* 26:37). If one of them suffers, all suffer (*Mekilta on Exod.,* 19:6) . Social laws also include the respect due to the king and other leaders, and the obligation to assist those who administer justice. The Jews, who had for a long time been subjected to foreign rulers, teach that one must obey the empire, pray for its welfare, and respect its laws. Philo and Josephus praise the loyalty of their fellow Jews, and their devotion and prayers for their emperors. But these general principles do not always prevent rebellions. They cannot subdue the Jewish character, which is neither docile or easily satisfied. This is the explanation for the revolts against the authority of the Roman procurators, which were so frequent in the first century, and the accusations which Greco-Roman authors hurl against the Jews as being seditious, obstinate, and disrespectful to the Emperor. Such attitudes are excused and fully explained by the excessive demands and sufferings of which Palestine was the victim during many decades of the first century.

Duties of Charity

The Mosaic codes declare it to be a duty to help the needy by giving them a share in the harvest of the fields and vineyards, by lending them money, and by giving them charity. Jewish law is no less charitable. It becomes a real obligation to give alms and perform acts of charity, such as, hospitality, education of orphans, redemption of prisoners, attendance at weddings, visiting the sick, assisting at funerals, consoling families in mourning, and saving a man from imminent death and dishonor, even if this should mean the loss of one's own life.

To give to charity is an important duty. Josephus (*Against Apion*, II, xxviii, par. 207) declares it a sin not to assist the needy when one can do so. R. Joshua ben Korcha (*Tos. Peah*, iv, 20) adds: "It is worse than idol worship." The importance of this obligation is based on various considerations. God's mercy is to be emulated; one must show oneself to be a true son of Abraham, and win God's mercy (R. Gamaliel, *Tos. B. K.*, ix, 30). "I need to accumulate an imperishable treasury for the world to come"—this was the answer of King Monobazus to those who accused him of spending too much money on charity (*Tos. Peah*, iv, 18). Giving alms also assures the donor of certain worldly goods, since it helps him conserve his own wealth. A saying which was frequently quoted in Jerusalem about the year 70 had it that R. Johanan ben Zakkai called charity "the salt of riches" (Ket. 66b). Finally, let us remember the observation of R. Eleazar ben Bartota (*ca.* 100): "Giving alms is simply returning God's property back to him" (Ab. iii, 8 on Par. 29:14).

What is the proper manner of dispensing alms? Jewish literature answers this question in a way which reflects the most considerate feelings about the dignity of the poor. We must give charity in a disinterested way, for its own sake (R. Johanan ben Zakkai, B. B. 10b). There are four categories of those who give charity: "The man who gives, but does not want others to do so—his eye is bad as far as others are concerned; the man who wants others to give, but does not do so himself—he is a miser; the pious man is the one who gives charity and wants others to do so, too; the wicked man does not want to give, nor does he wish others to do so" (Ab. v, 13).

The whole merit of giving alms lies in the spirit of charity underlying it (Suk. 49b). One must give it to all who ask

for it, even to swindlers (T.P. Peah viii, 9, and 21b). But it
is better to lend money than to give it outright. The poor
should be supported according to their former way of life.
Hillel is said to have given a horse to a rich man who had become destitute, and on one occasion when his valet failed to
show up, he even ran in front of the rider (*Tos. Peah*, iv,
11). But this is idealistic hyperbole rather than practical
advice. Alms should never hurt the recipient. R. Simeon
ben Yohai considered it better to be thrown alive into a
fiery furnace than to put someone to shame publicly, and
Mar Ukba's feet were burned when he hid in an oven in
order not to be seen giving charity (Ket. 67b).

In the hierarchy of good deeds, the works of charity are
superior to alms. The Catholics speak only of "works of
mercy"; their concept is narrower than the Jewish one. The
one who gives alms give money only, without any consideration for the poor and the living, whereas charity makes
demands on both our goods and our energies; both rich and
poor, living and dead, are to be assisted (*Tos. Peah*, 4, 19).
Even God was shown to have practiced charity: he visited
Abraham when the latter was recovering from circumcision,
he buried Moses, and he attended the wedding of Adam and
Eve (*Sifre on Deut.*, 11:10; *Gen. Rabbah*, 8:15).

Relations With Gentiles

We have already seen that the Jews consider the heathens
to be God's enemies. In addition, both the Mosaic and rabbinical codes are conceived with the Jewish community in
mind. What is to govern relations with gentiles?

The Torah had ordained that no pagan was to be allowed
to remain within Israel, and there were serious attempts to
realize that ideal. It was on this account that Esdras and the

Hasmoneans forced the inhabitants of Palestine to submit to circumcision. However, both within and outside the Holy Land, as long as the Romans were the rulers of Palestine, Jews had to live together with gentiles. How were they to behave? This is what Josephus has to say on this subject: "Our Lawgiver has taken the most appropriate measures to prevent us, on the one hand, from corrupting our national customs, and on the other, from rejecting those who wish to join us. We gladly receive those who desire to submit to our laws. But we are not to mingle intimately with those who come to us only for a limited time" (*Against Apion,* II, xxviii, par. 209 ff.).

This is systematic separatism. The gates open only for real proselytes—to those who wish to live in Israel in complete assimilation, not for "those who come only for a short time." Virtually all gentiles were thus excluded, and they were offended at being considered impure. Such practices led to an almost complete suppression of commercial and social relations with pagans. The Jews did not wish to cooperate with idolatry—reread the directive of St. Paul in 1 Corinthians, chapters 8 to 10—and they were afraid of being victims of their murderous and voluptuous tendencies. Generally speaking, the obligations of justice and charity were prescribed for the benefit of fellow Jews and did not apply to gentiles. It is true that harming the latter was considered a desecration of the holy name, but one was allowed to profit from their errors and even to deceive them (B. K. 113b). One does not have to restore to them any object they may have lost. Foreigners could not understand or accept such an attitude.

God does not love the other nations as much as he loves Israel. You can prove this from the fact that you may keep objects stolen from a pagan, but not those stolen from an Israelite. Once the empire sent out two soldiers to find out what good things the Torah of the Israelites had to offer. They conducted themselves as proselytes and went to Usha to study with R. Gamaliel. They learned the Bible, the Mishnah and the Midrash, as well as legal decisions and moral teachings. When taking their leave, they said, "Your Torah is completely good and praiseworthy, except for one thing: Israelites may keep an object stolen from a pagan, but not one stolen from another Israelite."[1]

Sifre on Deuteronomy, 33:3

These were only principles; fortunately, the need to live together, a deeper understanding of what it means to "sanctify God's name," and the obligations of humanity led to the making of exceptions, both in theory and practice. "In the interest of peace" it was permitted to greet pagans, be charitable toward them, have friendly relations with them, and take part in their festivities, as many rabbis actually did. In Jerusalem a special section in the Temple was reserved to them, and they were allowed to offer sacrifices. Such offerings were brought every day, for the sake—and at the cost—of the emperors. Prayers for their welfare were recited in the synagogues, and some synagogues were even dedicated to pagan kings. According to Josephus (*Against Apion,* II, xiii, 33, par. 144, 237), it was even forbidden to insult pagan gods or to criticize their cult, but apparently not all rabbis felt bound by this decision.

Individual Perfection

We are concerned here with duties toward oneself and with certain virtues which lead to perfection, according to

[1] In other versions of this story, the key line is that Jewish women may not assist gentile women in giving birth or in nursing their children, but they may accept such services; a Jew does not have to pay for damages a vicious animal has caused to a gentile.

the moral ideal preached by the Prophets and the biblical books of wisdom.

According to Philo (*De Decalogo*, 32), the biblical commandment "You shalt not commit adultery" also includes seduction, pederasty, unnatural sexual relations, and generally all forms of immodesty. This is quite in accord with the common Jewish doctrine of his time, which holds that not only adultery and sexual perversions are forbidden—these were already condemned in the Torah—but which abhors every kind of impurity. Such sins pollute the Holy Land and represent a source of innumerable evils. In the following words, addressed to the biblical Joseph, Philo again represents the Jewish tradition:

We, the descendants of the Hebrews, have excellent customs and laws. Other nations allow their young men of fourteen years of age to go to prostitutes and to other women who sell their bodies. But according to our laws, all hetairas are condemned to die. Until there can be legitimate relations, we do not have intercourse with a woman. Both parties enter marriage as virgins, and for us the purpose of marriage is not pleasure but the propagation of children.

De Josepho, 9

Similarly, before Isaac died, he said to his children, "I have never known any woman besides my own wife, lascivious glances did not lead me into fornication. Nor have I ever drunk intoxicating drinks" (*Test. Iss.,* vii, 2). These lines remind us that not only impure acts were condemned, but also sinful looks and evil desires, since it is these that lead to fornication and other sexual disorders (Simeon ben Yohai, *Mekilta on Exod.,* 20:4; *Tos. Mik.,* vi, 5). Such principles are often mentioned by the rabbis and still more strictly insisted upon in the Apocrypha, especially in *The*

Testaments of the Twelve Patriarchs with its strong pietist attitude.

Consequently, the entire conduct of the Israelite had to have a modest stamp. Even in his relations with his own wife, he was to show reserve, and nudity, shamelessness, and indecency were forbidden. Impure and improper language was suppressed.

Pride, arrogance, and anger were also frowned upon. Humility, a virtue which God praised so highly in Moses, was held in high esteem. It includes gentleness, and excludes any arrogance. Hillel was often mentioned as the prototype of such a man. When he died, one man said, "A pious and humble person has passed away" (*Tos. Sotah*, xiii, 3). One of his teachings was often repeated, "When I humble myself, I am elevated, and when I am elevated, I am humbled" (Ab. R. N. xi, 3). Here is one of the stories told about him:

The rabbis teach that men should always be as humble as Hillel, and not violent like Shammai. Once two men made the following bet: The one who would succeed in enraging Hillel was to receive four hundred coins. One of them immediately decided to try. It was a Friday afternoon, and Hillel was washing his head. That man went to his door and exclaimed in a rough manner, "Is Hillel in? Is Hillel in?"

Hillel wrapped himself in his robe and went out to him, saying, "My son, what do you wish?"

"I want to ask you something."

"Ask, my son."

"Why do the Baylonians have round heads?"

"This is an important question, my son. The answer is, that their midwives are not very skilled."

The man went away, but returned a short while later, crying, "Is Hillel in? Is Hillel in?" Again, Hillel went out to meet him and asked him what he wanted. "Why are the Palmyrcans short-sighted?"

"Another important question, my son. The reason for this is that they live in a sandy country."

Again, the man left and came back after some time. Again, Hillel put on his robe and asked the man to state his request.

"Why do the Africans have such large feet?"

"A very important question, my son. It is because they live near channels."

Thereupon his interrogator said, "I have many more questions, but I am afraid to irritate you."

Hillel made himself comfortable in a chair and said, "Now ask me all your questions."

"Are you really that Hillel whom they call the Prince of Israel?"

"Yes."

"I hope there are not many more like you in Israel."

"Why, my son?"

"Because you made me lose four hundred coins."

"You must learn to control yourself. It is better that you lose your money than that I lose my patience."

Shabbat 31a

This story shows that humility was conceived of as being a mixture of patience and gentleness. The other humility, the recognition of one's nothingness before the grandeur of the Creator, seems to have been more infrequent. We do not find many statements like this one, by Levitas of Jabneh (first century), "Be very humble, the hope of man only comes to worms" (Ab. iv, 4). Nevertheless, pride was considered to be incompatible with piety, and above all with wisdom—that is, the knowledge of the Torah (Ben Azzai, *ca.* 110; Ab. R. N. xi, 3). Paganism never understood this attitude, which prepared the way for the apotheosis of humility in Christianity.

Can we find in Judaism an anticipation of Christian asceticism, especially insofar as virginity and voluntary poverty are concerned? In principle, Judaism is opposed to asceticism, especially as the rabbinic tradition becomes predominant. We have already seen that certain rabbis did not like vows. Statements of the third century condemn habitual fasting and abstention from pleasures. He who fasts more than necessary is called a sinner (Taan. 11b). Rab, one of the leaders of the Babylonian School (third century) stated that "Man will have to give an account for all the pleasures he might have enjoyed, but did not" (T. P. Kid. iv, 12, 66b). Others advised: "Be sure to eat and drink, for the world we leave is like a wedding feast" (Er. 54a). "Are there not enough prohibitions in the Torah without adding to them?" (T. P. Ned. ix, 1, 41b) The common doctrine thinks of wealth as being a desirable blessing, and of poverty as a punishment (Ned. 41a), harmful to the intelligence and to the knowledge of God (Er. 41b, *baraita*).

However, some teachings show the opposite tendency, and it will not be easy to reconcile them with those we have just quoted. Fasts were practiced by certain rabbis and by some heroes of the apocalyptic books, but always with a definite goal in mind: to atone for sins, or to keep away an imminent catastrophe. Thus, R. Tsaddok fasted so that Jerusalem might not be destroyed (Git. 65a). *The Testaments of the Twelve Patriarchs* mentions certain righteous people who fasted in order to obtain spiritual favors. The leaders of the community would sometimes prescribe periods of fasting in order to obtain rain. Fasts and prayers were also practiced by groups of the *Maamadot,* nonpriestly Israelites who attended the Temple sacrifice. Rabbinical texts, as well as the Gospels, prove that many Pharisees fasted every Monday and Thursday (Meg. Taan.; Luke 18:12). Moreover, traditional wisdom, faithful to biblical directives, advises a frugal life. Hillel and others insist that a man should take good care of his body, since it was created in the image of God (*Lev. Rabbah,* 24:3), but all rabbis condemn excessive eating. Several warn against eating too much meat, and encourage the avoidance of delicacies (*Tos. Ar.* iv, 25; R. Judah ben Illai, Pes. 114a). An austere way of life is especially necessary for students, and the stories about apprentice rabbis show that they had to undergo many privations. On all sides it is taught that a man should control his passions and moderate his desires (R. Ishmael, *Eccles. Rabbah,* 11:13; *4 Ezra,* xiv, 34). We know also of righteous people who rejoiced when they had to suffer from bodily sicknesses; they saw them as "corrections of love" sent by God, a divine means of trial and purification. This doctrine is generally accepted both in the Apocrypha and rabbinical literature.

Certain pietists of the Apocrypha warn of the dangers inherent in riches. Thus we read in *The Testaments of the Twelve Patriarchs* and in the *Book of Enoch* that the righteous do not like gold, and that miserliness is a source of evil. The Essenes were sworn to poverty. But if some rabbis came to praise poverty, this was due to persecutions and the national defeats in 70 and 135. Destitution was almost universal, and this context helps us to understand R. Akiba's saying, "Poverty is an ornament to Israel, as a red halter looks pretty on a white horse" (*Lev. Rabbah,* 35:3). There is quite a different meaning in the statement by R. Joshua ben Kisma (*ca.* 120): "Real wealth lies in the knowledge of the Torah and in intelligence" (Ab. vi, 9).

Whenever continence is an integral part of a true fast, it has the same religious value as a sacrifice. When the high priest prepared himself for the Day of Atonement, he lived for eight days cloistered in the Temple, away from his wife. It was also said that at Sinai the Israelites separated from their wives (R. Nehemiah, *Gen. Rabbah,* xxxv, ix, 8-9). Therefore, chastity was a favorable condition for intimate contact with God. In addition, Judaism professed high esteem for continence outside of marriage and modesty within it, helping to prepare souls to appreciate the beauty and the spiritual fruitfulness of virginity. Later, the Gospel will state that this ideal cannot be reached by everyone (Matt. 19:11).

We may conclude that if certain rabbis were opposed to asceticism in principle, it was still practiced and respected in certain areas, for example among pietist groups. In addition, the doctrine and conduct of many other rabbis helped to gain acceptance, both theoretically and practically, for a genuine austerity of life. It must also be pointed out that the numerous and detailed observances and prohibitions which marked the individual and social life of Israel were in themselves a form of asceticism.

Of all the teachings of Judaism, nothing is more exalted and beautiful than its ethics; it is loyal to the ideas expressed in the Old Testament and superior to all the ethical doctrines of antiquity.

We have already pointed out how loyal the rabbis were to the letter and the spirit of the Bible. Their only fault may have been that they seemed to depart somewhat from the prophetic ideal when it came to the principles of asceticism and mysticism.

In Judaism, the moral law is an essential part of religion. The one God dictates the rules of conduct, and what he demands above everything else is a holy and righteous life, an effort to emulate divine sanctity.

In theory and practice Jewish morality presents new features which show its excellence. It points to a more warmhearted and finer sense of humanity and a greater appreciation of chastity. It is hard to do justice to Judaism's respect for the dignity of the woman, love of children, humane treatment of slaves, concern for human life, and sense of obligation for the honor and the spiritual life of others. Its teaching of the innumerable and delicate duties of charity, exact justice in regard to the possessions of others and the respect for truth, assistance of needy co-citizens, prohibition of exacting interest on loans, and a rigorous national solidarity make up the ethics of brotherly love. Because of its brotherly concern for the Jewish community, we can well understand why it is so human and charitable. This is also its defect, aggravated by regulations which relegate the stranger to a domain of inequality and inferiority. But even on this point, charity and human kindness impose restraint, and eventually win out.

The laws in regard to the sexual life have no equivalent in ancient civilizations. The pagans had no idea what chastity, purity, and modesty meant. This tendency toward perfection is completed by a profound understanding of humility. Above all, it is amazing to see that these ideas were not simply the teaching of a philosophical school, nor were they restricted to a special elite, but they embodied the rules of conduct professed and followed by an entire people.

Chapter Eight
Life After Death

We agree with Bossuet that on the subject of personal survival the Bible contains only sparks of the truth, and not a clear and definite teaching. There are statements in Ecclesiasticus which reflect the traditional belief: "Who in the nether world can glorify the Most High in place of the living who offer their praise? No more can the dead give praise than those who have never lived. . . . The like cannot be found in men, for not immortal is any son of man. Is anything brighter than the sun? Yet it can be eclipsed. How obscure then the thoughts of flesh and blood!" (17:22 ff.) "More and more, humble your pride; what awaits man is worms" (17:17).

Nevertheless, at the beginning of the first Christian century, many Jewish circles believed that at the time of death, souls are separated from the bodies and brought to judgment. They are then either sent to a place where rewards await them, or to a place of punishment. Thus we see that this doctrine made its appearance shortly before Christianity. As a matter of fact, a comparative study of the apocryphal books shows that eschatological conceptions are diverse and vague up to the first years of our era. It is probably at this time that the teachings which we find in the rabbinic writings become accepted among the Pharisees.

The progress of Jewish thought in this direction was favored by a similar progress in anthropology. There was more and more a conviction that man is composed of body and soul, and that the soul, after leaving the body at death, can enjoy a separate existence. Such views must have been disturbing to those who wished to remain loyal to the traditional concepts in anthropology and religion. The Sadducees rejected the doctrine of resurrection and found it even harder to believe in a happy or unhappy afterlife.

It was therefore unavoidable that there would be a great divergence of opinion in these matters. Many people held on to the ancient idea of the Sheol as the dwelling of the dead. But others began to bring light to the melancholic shadows, either by the hope for a resurrection of the righteous, or by preparing the way for the ideal of a final reward.

Those who share the Greek view concerning the separation of body and soul are quite willing to give up the old concept of the Sheol. They arrive naturally at the idea of immortality, and as a consequence, accept the sanctions of the afterlife. According to Josephus, the Essenes believed that "the immortal and imperishable soul, once detached from the ties of the flesh and thus freed from a long bondage, flies happily upwards" (*Wars of the Jews,* II, vii, 2, par. 154 ff.). The Wisdom of Solomon, accepting the spirituality of the soul, also teaches the immortality and the beatification of the righteous—they are both rewards, just as death and the misfortune of the wicked are the penalty for their sins

(1:12, 16; 2:24 ff.; 3:1 ff., 14; 4:1 ff., 7:10; 5:2, 15; 8:13, 17; 15:2 f.). This book leaves one with the impression of a mixture of Hellenism and a modified Jewish tradition.

In *The Book of Enoch,* xxii (first or second century B.C.), there is a concept of transition. The angel Raphael shows Enoch four holes where the souls of the dead are shut up while awaiting the day of judgment. The fact that the caves are separated suggests a kind of approbation, especially "the source of living water and light" which is present in the dwelling place of the righteous.

The character of transition is also evident from the fact that the Sheol is reserved for the wicked. Possibly under the influence of newly acquired moral notions and demands, the Sheol, Hades, becomes the place of damnation (*The Psalms of Solomon,* xiv, 6; xv, 11; xvi, 2). Thus we arrive naturally at the new concept of the Gehenna, where the wicked are sent to suffer without respite, with the possible exception of the Sabbath.[1] Others believe that the wicked wander in sadness and endure seven kinds of torment as they await the day of judgment (*4 Ezra,* vii, 88 ff), or that they are expelled from the world (R. Nehorai, *ca.* 150, *Kallah Rabbati*).

The place assigned to the righteous has been described in different ways. Here is a summary of the different levels of their happiness:

They shall rest in seven orders. The first order is that they have striven much and painfully to overcome the innate evil thought. . . . The second order is: that they see the round in which the souls of the ungodly wander. . . . The third order is . . . their Fashioner attests that while they were alive they faithfully obeyed the Law. . . . The fourth order is: they understand

[1] I. Lévi, "Le repos Sabbatique des âmes damnés," *Revue des etudes Juives,* xxv (1892), 1 ff., XXVI, 131 ff. R. Johanan ben Zakkai, Ber 28b; R. Eliezer ben Shammua, Sanh. 52a.

the rest which they now enjoy . . . and the glory which awaits them. . . . The fifth order is: they rejoice that they have escaped what is corruptible . . . and they see the straitness and painfulness from which they have been delivered. . . . The sixth order: it is show unto them that their face is destined to shine as the sun. . . . The seventh order is . . . they are hastening to behold the face of Him whom in life they served, and from whom they are destined to receive their reward in glory.

4 Ezra, vii, 90-98

Here we find already a certain state of happiness, but it consists mainly in anticipation. In the same vein, some texts place the righteous either in the vicinity of Abraham (*4 Macc.,* 12, 17; 18, 23), in the Garden of Eden (Ber. 28b), or even into the third heaven, which is not God's own dwelling place (*Apoc. of Moses,* xxxi, 4; xxxvii, 5; xl). Only a few authors "assign to the pure souls the holiest place in heaven, from which, after a long time, they will again enter pure bodies" (Josephus, *Wars of the Jews,* III, viii, 5, par. 374). The parables of *Enoch* (xxxix, 3 ff.) show the couches where the righteous will rest among the angels in heaven, before the face of the Almighty. Rabbis like Eliezer place the treasure of the souls in the seventh heaven, the heaven of God, or even under the divine throne (Shab. 152b).

Judgment After Death

According to all the views mentioned above, man's fate is determined immediately after his death. This is done in various ways. Some hold that the righteous are received and greeted by good angels, and that God then grants them peace and rest. The wicked are received by three groups of evil angels, who expel them from the world, reveal their disgrace and drive them away (*The Testaments of the Twelve*

Patriarchs, Asher, vi, 5 ff.; R. Meier, *Num. Rabbah,* xi, 7).
Here are two statements by R. Johanan ben Zakkai:

R. Eliezer had advised that all men do penitence the day before
they die—and since this was uncertain, to be penitent at all
times. In this connection R. Johanan ben Zakkai told this parable: Once a king invited his servants to a banquet, but without
giving the exact date. The wise servants got ready immediately
and remained at the entrance to the palace, since they did not
want anything to be lacking at the home of the king. But those
who were not so wise went on with their work, since they took
it for granted that it would take a long time for the banquet to
be prepared. Suddenly, the king asked his servants to come in.
Those who had been waiting outside were ready, but the others
had to go in in their dirty clothes. The king, happy at the sight
of the wise servants, and angry at the others, said, "Those who
are ready may come in and eat and drink; but those who are not
ready must stand around and watch them."

> Shabbat 153 (An analagous parable is
> attributed to R. Judah Hanasi, *Eccles.*
> *Rabbah,* ix, 8)

The following maxims presume a particular judgment
before God:

When R. Johanan ben Zakkai took sick, his disciples came to
visit him. When he saw them, he began to cry. They said to
him, "Light of Israel, right hand column of the Temple, mighty
hammer, why are you crying?"

He answered, "If I was about to be led to an earthly king,
who today is here and tomorrow is in the grave, whose anger
does not last forever and whose chains do not bind forever, who
cannot condemn me to an everlasting death, and can be bribed
by words or money—even then I would cry. But now I am being
taken to the King of kings, to the Holy One, blessed be He, who
always existed and will live forever, whose anger lasts forever

and whose chains bind forever, whose death sentence includes
all future ages, and who cannot be bribed by words or money.
I see before me two paths, one leading to the Garden of Eden,
and one to Gehenna, and I do not know which path I will have
to take; should I not be crying?"

Berakot 28b

The idea of a real judgment, pronounced immediately
after death, becomes more and more prominent in rabbinical literature (R. Eliezer ben Yose, *Sifre on Num.*, 13:8).
Some concrete details are suggested in a conversation attributed to R. Judah Hanasi:

Antoninus questioned our rabbi, the saintly one: "At the
moment when man dies and the body dissolves, does the Holy
One, blessed be He, make it appear for judgment?"
"Why do you ask me about the body, which is unclean? Ask
me rather about the soul, which is pure. Their relationship can
be understood by the story of an earthly king who owned a
beautiful garden. The king assigned two men to watch over it,
one of them blind, the other lame. The one whose legs were
paralyzed said to the blind man, 'I see some early fruit; let me
sit on your back.' The paralytic sat on the blind man's back, and
in this way they took all the fruit. Sometime later, the king
came and said to the blind man, 'Where is all my fine early
fruit?'
" 'How could I have seen them?' said the blind man.
"Then the king said to the paralytic, 'Where is my early
fruit?'
" 'I couldn't have taken it; don't you realize that I am lame?'
"Thereupon the king placed the paralytic on the back of the
blind man and pronounced judgment as if they constituted a
single man. It is in this way that the Holy One, blessed be He,
puts the soul back into the body and judges them both as a
single being. He calls on the heavens to bring forth the soul,
and he calls on the earth below so that he can judge the body
along with it."

Mekilta on Exod., 15:1; cf. also Sanhedrin 91a

The World to Come

What we have learned about man's fate after death helps us to see more clearly into the question of time and eternity. The ancient Semites had great difficulty in understanding this latter notion; to designate it, they had only the very imprecise term, *olam*. This word meant "time," considered as the mysterious mass of the past or future. By extending the meaning of the word, it was possible to come to a wider conception of time. At the eve of the Christian era and under the influence of Greek thought, *olam* had come to be understood not only in a temporal sense but also in spatial terms, corresponding to the Greek term, *kosmos*. The possibility of distinguishing between two periods, two kinds of time, was then considered. There would be the time of unhappiness and corruption in which humanity was living, and the "new age," a time in which unhappiness and corruption had been eliminated. This distinction appears first and above all in the Apocrypha; we find it mentioned by the rabbis from the first century on. The two ages succeed one another and prepare for one another; one is the vestibule, the other the main hall.

When will "the world to come" take place? If the time of reward is placed after the resurrection, in a renewed world, it means that happiness and the absence of corruption will only then make their appearance. But as belief in retribution and judgment after death becomes more accepted, the time of reward starts much earlier. The usual expression in referring to this time, *olam haba,* is commonly translated as "the world to come," the world that has not yet begun and will be inaugurated by the resurrection. But several second-century texts expect it to start immediately after death. We have, for instance, this commentary on Proverbs 6:22: "My law will guide you in your path in this world;

it will watch over you in your sleep, at the hour of death; and when thou awakest, it will converse with you, in the *olam haba"* (*Sifra on Lev.*, 18:4; see also 18:5 and *Mekilta on Exod.*, 16:25). That world can be called a future world only in relation to those who have not yet died, but it is already in existence. Therefore, to speak of the "future world" is not quite correct. As indicated by the present participle *haba,* one ought to say "the coming world." For it exists already and it is coming for those who wait for it. This was the way it was understood by a man who had a deeper knowledge of the language of rabbinical writings than we do, the compiler of *Tanhuma* (eighth or ninth century):

> The sages have taught us that we human beings cannot explain or appreciate the joys of the future age. Therefore, they called it "the coming world," not because it does not yet exist, but because for us, the living, it is still in the future. "The world to come" is the one awaiting man after this world. But there is no basis for the assumption that the world to come will only begin after the destruction of this world. What it does imply is that when the righteous leave this world, they ascend on high, as it is said (Ps. 31:20): "How great is the goodness, O Lord, which you have in store for those who fear you, and which, toward those who take refuge in you, you show in the sight of men."
>
> *Tanhuma Vayikra,* 8

Jewish and Christian thought and our vocabulary are here in agreement. In the Litany of the Saints we read: *"Quos praesens saeculum adhuc in carne retinet vel futurum iam exutos corpore suscepit. . . ."* For the Christian, too, the future is already present. It is impossible to give a better expression to the range and the intensity of our hopes.

The first recipients of the teaching of Jesus, and the apostles shared these beliefs, and we should not forget this in judging the eschatological doctrine of the New Testament. The Jews who lived at the time of the Gospel had neither uncertainty nor fear regarding the time after their deaths, and the traditional faith of the synagogue reassured the Christians concerning this momentous passage. Their hopes were enlightened and deepened by the assurance that "to leave the body means to make one's dwelling close to Christ." They understood very well the words of Paul: "For we know that if the earthly house in which we dwell be destroyed, we have a building from God, a house not made by human hands, in the eternal heavens. And indeed, in this present state we groan, yearning to be clothed over with that dwelling of ours which is from heaven" (2 Cor. 5:1 ff.). It is evident that except for those terms which refer to Christ, this Pauline declaration, together with the sentences preceding it, could very well have been repeated by a contemporary rabbi who believed in retribution for the righteous after death. It may have been difficult to define their state, but there was no doubt that it was quite different from resurrection. That is why St. Paul is very careful not to speak of body, but only of "that dwelling of ours."

Chapter Nine
Messianism

To what extent do the messianic concepts of Judaism at the time of Jesus prepare and explain the Christian message? Here we must first point out two specific differences between Jewish and Christian thinking.

Since Christian dogma is entirely centered on Christ, Christology is essential in its plan and arrangement. The messianic views in Jewish doctrine, on the other hand, do not emphasize the person of the Messiah but the restoration of the Jewish nation. Moreover, in Jewish thought messianism is less important than the Torah and the idea of the chosen nation. It is true that, according to an old saying, "All prophecies refer to the days of the Messiah." But in their actual exegesis the rabbis were to discover more references to the Torah and to Israel than to the Messiah. We can even read through certain ancient legal texts like the Mishnah without discovering any allusion to the Messiah.

Another question is whether messianic hopes were still flourishing in Israel at the time of Jesus Christ. Some historians tell us that the rabbis had eliminated messianism from their teaching and preaching, since they were only interested in the study of the Torah and the welfare of the individual, and were also afraid of arousing the suspicion of the Roman government.

As a matter of fact, we possess few statements from rabbis who lived at the time of Jesus. But what does such silence concerning the Messiah mean? The first certain rabbinic statement comes from R. Johanan ben Zakkai who, before his death, gave orders to prepare a throne for Ezechias, the Messiah (Ber. 28b). Let us also call attention to a disillusioned statement by the same rabbi: "If you should be busy planting when you hear that the Messiah has come, go on with your work and then go out to meet him" (Ab. R. N., 31). On the whole, the rabbis of the end of the first century undoubtedly believed in the Messiah. This is not simply a reaction against the reverses of the year 70; they shared one of the essential beliefs of the Jewish religion of their times, as it appears in official prayers, the Aprocrypha, and as we can discover it even in the books of Philo and Josephus, although—for different reasons—they were rather quiet on this point, which was so closely connected with national aspirations. We see also from the New Testament and from Josephus that the people at that time were excited about an imminent event of messianic character.

Those expectations showed different forms and various degrees of intensity, depending on the background in which they arose. Pietist and apocalyptic circles were naturally more ardent and more hotheaded than the rabbinic schools. Besides, the first century was a period of transition and gestation. The messianic doctrines adopted a classical and definitive form only at the end of the century; previously, as is evident from a study of the Apocrypha, the ideas were

varied and changeable. We shall try to explain these variations and the shifting state of messianic speculation.

Its central point is the restoration of the nation, at that
time destitute and subjected to the Romans. People hoped
for its deliverance and re-establishment, the return from
exile, and, finally, for God's universal rule by means of
Israel. This redemption of the nation could be thought of in
various ways. From an earthly point of view, ordinary historical rhythms would have been brought to completion;
but if we allow for a supernatural dimension, the reconstitution of Israel is conceived of as occurring in a new land,
miraculously fertile and transfigured. There is even a transcendental understanding of Israel's restoration, accompanied by the resurrection of the dead, and culminating in
eternal happiness or misfortune, heaven or hell. Finally, the
messianic times may be fulfilled on a more or less transformed earth, followed at the end of days by the resurrection and the last judgment.

This last plan, although it is the most rational, appears
only in *4 Ezra*. In the other apocryphal books we find
the most divergent presentations. We understand as messianism any description of a national consummation—the
presence of the Messiah, the restoration of the chosen
nation—that would occur in the land of Israel, which would
be more or less miraculously transformed. The presence of
any one of those elements calls for the term "messianic,"
even if the Messiah himself does not appear. By eschatology
we mean the whole complex of resurrection, last judgment,
and eternal life in heaven or hell.

The elements of both messianism and eschatology have
been combined in various ways. There is the single messianic
act: In a renewed world, around an Edenlike Palestine,
the Israelites (or the righteous) will enjoy endless bliss
(*The Book of Enoch*, first part; *The Apocalypse of the*

Weeks; The Book of Jubilees, The Jewish Sibyls; The Testaments of the Twelve Patriarchs, The Life of Adam and Eve). Sometimes the Messiah plays a more or less definite role (*The Book of Enoch, The Book of the Secrets of Enoch,* and *4 Ezra,* xi-xiii, *2 Baruch,* xxv-xxx, lxx-lxxiv); sometimes the resurrection is also the beginning of messianic times (*The Book of Enoch, The Book of the Secrets of Enoch, The Apocalypse of the Weeks, The Testaments of the Twelve Patriarchs, 2 Baruch,* xxv-xxx, lxx-lxxiv). This is a more or less eschatological messianism. There may also be emphasis on a single eschatological and transcendental act: all the righteous will taste eternal delights, either in heaven (*The Book of Enoch,* xcvi-civ), or in paradise, which is prepared in the third heaven (*The Book of the Secrets of Enoch).* Israel, raised to the highest heaven, will enjoy seeing the punishment of their enemies (*The Assumption of Moses,* x, 1-9). We find the idea of two successive acts—the eschatological era is preceded by the times of the Messiah. This is the case in most of rabbinical writings, in one of the descriptions in *4 Ezra* (vii, 26-43), and in the general conceptions in both that book and in *2 Baruch.* The same concept of the two different times is also found in *The Psalms of Solomon;* the two times are described in successive psalms, probably not the work of the same author (messianism, xvii, 36 ff.; eschatology, iii and xv). This view must have been that of the editor of the collection.

These indications show how easy it was to confuse messianism and eschatology, and then to conceive of messianic happiness in a transcendent and eschatological form. In many a description it is hard to state whether a certain feature refers to the messianic or the eschatological era.

The consummation will restore Israel to its former splendor, and it will give the righteous the happiness which is in store for them. Since the preaching of Jesus centered on the Kingdom of God, we are accustomed to recognize the establishment of the Kingdom of God as the end term of the Messiah's activity and of the great eschatological drama. Is this also the case in Jewish teaching?

In the Gospels, the phrase "Kingdom of God" has a basically ethical connotation, closely linked to messianism: Christ announces that the Kingdom is at hand. He calls it the Kingdom of the Son of Man. In Jewish literature, the rabbis speak constantly of the kingdom of God, but it is understood only in an ethical sense; it is a matter of recognizing the sovereign rule of God and submitting to his will by fulfilling his commandments. Thus we are told that by the recital of the *Shema* we "accept the yoke of the kingdom of Heaven" (R. Gamaliel, Ber. ii, 5, 16a); in the Temple the people exclaimed: "Blessed be the Name of the glory of his kingdom now and forever" (T. P. Yoma iii, 7, 40d; R. Tarfon claims to have heard it). R. Johanan ben Zakkai stated that any benediction which has no reference to the Kingdom is not a benediction (Ber. 40b). He also finds fault with an Israelite who sells himself into perpetual slavery, because "He rejects the yoke of Heaven and accepts instead the yoke of flesh and blood" (*Tos. B. K.*, vii, 5). R. Eleazar ben Azariah said: "He who avoids sin has accepted the Rule of Heaven" (*Sifra on Lev.*, 20:26). To live by the law in regard to usury is to accept the yoke of Heaven (*Sifra on Lev.*, 25:28).

Taken by itself, therefore, the kingdom of Heaven does not imply a messianic consummation. People believed, however, that it would usher in a splendid and universal rule of God. In ancient prayers we read: "Bring back our judges . . . and rule over us, Thou alone" (*Shemoneh Esreh*); "May his great Name be magnified, may he establish his kingdom and may the Messiah come" (*Kaddish*). *The Sibylline Books,* which bear a Hellenistic imprint, extol the future Kingdom, whether under a messianic or under an eschatological aspect. According to *The Testaments of the Twelve Patriarchs,* the consequence of the messianic Kingdom is that "The Holy One of Israel will rule over them"; "We shall worship the King of Heaven" (*The Testaments of the Twelve Patriarchs,* Dan. v, 13; Benj. x, 7), when Israel will be raised to the heaven, *"tunc parebit regnum illius"* (*The Assumption of Moses,* x, 1). Here is one excerpt from the *Sibyls* (iii, 49, 55): "Then the great rule of the immortal King will appear before men; a pure prince will arrive, holding the sceptre of the whole world, and for all times. . . . Alas, unfortunate one, when the judgment of the immortal God, the great King will come!"

In other words, in keeping with certain Jewish concepts, the messianic consummation will lead to the Kingdom of God, understood in a religious and moral sense.

But the essential and longed-for result, the object of all desires, is the restoration of the nation. The expression of this feeling is seen in the term reserved for this event, a term which is taken from the prophetic vocabulary, especially that of the great Isaias, *geullah,* redemption or liberation, the prelude for an intense life and prosperity for the nation. It is modeled after the redemption from Egyptian bondage and, like it, is the work of God. The national point of view is also present in expressions like "salvation" and "consolation." The decisive role of divine intervention is clear in the phrase, "God's mercy."

We shall present the various messianic acts in a chronological and logical order. The different concepts remind us of the prophetical oracles from which they flow. The messianic speculations vary according to the schools of their origin, but we do find a common kernel, proving that they are all based on the same tradition.

Preliminaries for Redemption

Shortly before the Christian era there were people who, by calculation or by observation of certain signs, tried to discover the moment when the Messiah would come and bring the present order of things to an end, changing this corrupt world into an incorruptible one. Such people still existed at the time of Origen: *"Forte quaniam apud Judaeos erant quidam sive per scripturas profitentes de temporibus comsummationis, sive de secretis."*[1] Such "calculators" could not be restrained by the threats of R. Joshua ben Halafta and others who declared that they would not have a share in the world to come (*Derekh Eretz Rabbah,* xi). Josephus denounces the regrettable consequences of such attempts:

Those people were incited to war by an ambiguous prophecy, also found in Scripture, that in this period someone from their land was to become the master of the universe. The Jews applied that prediction to themselves and many sages were mistaken in the interpretation. In fact, the oracle was announcing the kingdom of Vespasian, which had been proclaimed during his stay in Judea. Anyhow, man cannot escape his destiny, even were he to foresee it. But the Jews either scorned the omens or interpreted them in terms of their own fantasies, until their own ruin and that of their country convinced them of their folly.

Wars of the Jews, IV, v, 4, par. 312

We may conclude from this text that the historian believed in signs, and that the people saw in certain phenomena the signs of an end soon to come. All the documents suggest that the end is at hand, revealing again the intensity of the messianic expectations.

We find one of the many computations in the first-century

---

[1] *Commentar. ser. in Matth.* 55, P.G., XIII, col. 1686.

text, *The Assumption of Moses* (x, 12), announcing that two hundred and fifty years after Moses' death, God's reign would be established and idol worship would be destroyed. The messianic tribulations, to which we shall return, would be among the signs to be interpreted. Christian apologetics placed great emphasis on the prediction of Jacob: "The sceptre shall not depart from Juda, nor the staff from between his feet until he comes to whom it belongs" (Gen. 49:10). Here is how the Aramaic Targum translates that text: "There will be no lack of kings and governors from the house of Juda, nor of scribes teaching the Law, from among their children and grandchildren, until King Messiah comes, whose rule it is, and all kingdoms of the world will serve him" (*Targ. Jer.*, I; the other two give a similar interpretation).

Aside from the circle of R. Sela (beginning of the third century) who gives the Messiah the name of Shilo (Sanh. 98b), the messianic exegesis of that text appears only in late commentaries. Toward the end of the second century, R. Judah Hanasi—and afterward, others—apply that prediction to the two leaders of the captivity, in Babylonia and Palestine (*Sifre on Deut.*, 33:12). This may well have been a reaction against Christian apologetics.

Wise men felt how dangerous and demoralizing such calculations were, and they preferred to emphasize moral considerations. In the main text referring to this problem, we have first what the leaders of the Babylonian schools of the early third century have to say, and then a discussion between two rabbis of the end of the first century:

Rab said, "All terms have passed, and everything now depends on repentance and good deeds." R. Samuel said, "It is enough for the man in mourning (Israel) to remain in mourning. As R. Eliezer is reported to have said, 'If they do not do penance, they will not be redeemed.'"

R. Yose ben Hananiah: "It is true that if they do not do penance, they will not be redeemed. But the Holy One, blessed be He, will send them a king like Hanan, who will make severe decrees, and then the Israelites will repent and find happiness. R. Eliezer's opinion is based on the text of Jeremias: 'Return, rebellious children, and I will cure you of your rebelling.' "

R. Joshua: Is it not also said, "You were sold for nothing, and without money you shall be redeemed"? (Isa. 52:3)

R. Eliezer: Is it not also said, "If you wish to return, O Israel, says the Lord, return to Me"? (Jer. 4:1)

R. Joshua: But it is also said, "The man clothed in linen, who was upstream, lifted his right and left hands to heaven; and I heard him swear by Him who lives forever that it would be for a year, two years, a half-year; and that, when the power of the destroyer of the holy people was brought to an end, all these things should end" (Dan. 12:7).

Then R. Eliezer fell silent.

Sanhedrin 97b, 98a

R. Joshua is generally very close to the common opinion, and may well be expressing the sense of the tradition. Other rabbinical statements make the quick coming of redemption depend on various moral conditions; prayer and the merits of the Patriarchs may hasten it, but the most important things are penance (this is a frequent theme of the rabbis; see *The Assumption of Moses*, i, 18), good deeds, loyalty to the commandments, and the study of the Torah.

The rabbis use the expression "messianic tribulations" for the material and spiritual distress preceding the advent of the Messiah. Both the expression and the idea are derived from the vocabulary of the Prophets. Jesus, too, had this in mind when he spoke of the "beginning of sorrow," as heart-rending as the cries of a woman in labor (Mark 13:8).

The frequent allusions in the texts to these tribulations do not refer, as one might suppose, to what the Messiah will undergo, but to the sorrows that will mark the time of his arrival. We shall quote three of those descriptions. Here is one from *4 Ezra,* which represents a particular conception:

Then I asked, "Lord, what are the signs of those days? Will I live to see them?"

He answered, "I can tell you what I know about the signs you asked about. But I have not been informed concerning the span of your life. Now listen to the signs.

"In those days the inhabitants of the earth will be seized by a great fright. Truth will be hidden and faith will be uprooted. Some people will curse God and tell lies. Treacherous people will pose as saints. There will be more sins and more impudence than now or in the past. The land will be desolate and deserted. If you will live that long, you will witness that all of creation will be in chaos. The sun will suddenly rise at night, and then change to darkness. The moon will suddenly rise during the day and change into blood. The Pleiades will give tongue and Aldebaran will snarl. Orion and the stars will raise their voices, and Astra will respond. The screech owls and the wood owls will sing a dismal chant. The birds of the heaven will leave their places of habitation. The Dead Sea will bring forth fish. The demons will lift their voices, and they will be heard everywhere. At some places pits will open up, and fires will come out. The beasts of the steppe will leave their country. Women will give birth to monsters and will be enraged by imperfect embryos. Brothers will kill one another and friends will turn to enemies. Wisdom will escape to her chambers, and Intelligence will flee to her room. One will search for them in vain. Iniquities and lies will increase greatly. Arrogance will grow and impudence will be treasured. One country will ask its neighbor: Is there any piety to be found in you? Is there no justice left on your shores? But the answer will be in the negative. In that time a man will not receive his due, nor enjoy his work, and all roads will lead nowhere, . . . for they have not only changed the laws, but the Almighty himself. Therefore, evil will overcome them, and at the end of time they will be in distress and pain. The glory of the Most High will reveal itself to them, and he will reign in judgment. He will come and change them. He will pay them back with torments; their pride will turn into humiliation.

"This is what I have to tell you. But if you weep and pray, while fasting for seven days, you will hear of greater wonders than these."

4 Ezra, iv, 52-v,13

When Baruch, who was almost a contemporary, was asked how long the tribulation would last, he answered more systematically:

That time has been divided into twelve parts, and each of them has special features. The first is that of severe disturbances. In the second, the mighty and powerful will die. In the third, many more will die. In the fourth, the sword will hold sway. In the fifth, earthquakes. In the eighth, many ghosts and demons. In the ninth, fire. In the tenth, theft and great oppression. In the eleventh, iniquity and shamelessness. In the twelfth, confusion arising from a mixture of the above calamities. They will intermingle and help one another. Some of these parts will be incomplete, others complete, so that those alive at that time will not know that this is the consummation of the world.

2 Baruch, 26 ff.

The other description, which in its essential parts goes back to Gamaliel, seems to have a more primitive form:

(When the Messiah is about to come, pride will increase, and prices will be extremely high. The vine will bear its fruit but wine will be expensive. There will be no standards of correction, and the whole kingdom will go over to heresy.) The synagogue will be in the service of prostitution, Galilee will be devastated, and the inhabitants of the land will wander from city to city without finding pity. The wisdom of the scribes will be corrupted, and those who fear sin will be despised. (Young

people will insult the old, and the latter will stand out of respect before the children. The son will humiliate his father, the
daughter will rise up against her mother and the daughter-in-
law against her mother-in-law. Members of one family will hate
one another.) The face of that generation will resemble that of
a dog. Truth will be abandoned. The son will have no shame
before his father. (On whom can we rely? Only on our Father
who is in heaven.)[2]

These excerpts, however, do not furnish us with a clear
picture of the messianic tribulations. We are still unclear
as to how long they are supposed to last—perhaps this was
deliberately left undetermined. We hear of cosmic dis-
order, of various catastrophes, of religious persecutions,
apostasy, and of a wave of immorality and irreligion. The
times will be so terrible that many people will completely
despair; a man would have to store up many merits to be
preserved during such days (R. Eliezer, *Mekilta on Exod.*,
16:29).

The precursor of the Messiah is mentioned in the Book
of Malachias (3:23-24): "Lo, I will send you Elias, the
prophet, before the day of the Lord comes, the great and
terrible day, to turn the hearts of the fathers to their children, and the hearts of the children to their fathers, lest I
come and strike the land with doom."

This is the origin of the tradition recorded in Ecclesiasticus (48:10-11). When Jesus, the son of Sirach, addresses
Elias: "You are destined, it is written, in time to come to
put an end to wrath before the day of the Lord, to turn back
the hearts of fathers toward their sons, and to re-establish
the tribes of Jacob. Blessed is he who shall have seen you
before he dies, O Elias, enveloped in the whirlwind."

[2] *Derekh Eretz Zutta* 10, text of Gamaliel. The lines in parentheses come
from Sotah 9, 15, which gives an expanded text, with additions attributed to
third-century scholars.

From these and the preceding verses we see that the prophet Elias held a considerable place in Jewish thinking. He appears often in rabbinical statements; in his role of a heavenly scholar, he intervenes in order to ask questions, to offer solutions, and give reprimands. Above all, he was expected as the forerunner of the Messiah. Several New Testament texts show that that belief was widespread in the time of Jesus (Matt. 11:14; 14:10; 27:47, 49; Luke 1:17; John 1:21,25).

His task as a forerunner consisted primarily in calling Israel to repent (a contemporary of Hillel, Pes. 70b). He was also to resolve difficult questions which had remained without an answer (a common notion, B. M. i, 8; ii, 8), and finally to re-establish the true Israel, eliminating families that had been forcibly introduced into the holy nation, and bringing back those who had become unlawfully removed (*Tos. Eduyyot,* 3). According to a tradition found in St. Justin (*Dialogue with Trypho,* viii, 4), he will also announce the advent of the Messiah by bestowing royal consecration on him. The prophet would also have a priestly mission: he would restore to the Temple the jar of manna, the vial containing the water of purification, the staff of Aaron, and the bottle with the anointing oil (*Mekilta on Exod.,* 16:33). Because of all these characteristics, he was later to be regarded as the high priest of messianic times. Later traditions combine Moses with Elias in this mission of forerunner.

The Person of the Messiah

Jewish messianic speculations generally present a very vague picture of the Messiah. Sometimes we even have a messianism without a Messiah.

The word Messiah means "anointed"; the Messiah is the one who has received royal consecration. This term is more frequent in the literature we are studying than in the Bible (Dan. 11:25; perhaps Ps. 2:2). There he is more often called "the son of David" (several times in the New Testament, see Matt. 9:27; 12:23; 15:22; 20:30-31), or simply "David." These two terms remind us of his lineage as well as of his royal dignity. For the same reason, he is sometimes called "the king, the king of Israel, King Messiah."

The first question a Christian would ask is whether the Jews believed the Messiah to be a divine being. Several Old Testament texts show clearly that the Messiah would belong to the divine sphere. Isaias (7:14) calls him "God-Hero, Father-Forever" (9:5). No king in Israel could have said of himself: "The Lord said to me, 'You are my son; this day I have begotten you'" (Ps. 2:7). A supreme dignity also underlies the great royal Psalm 110: "The Lord said to my Lord: 'Sit down at my right hand . . . before the daystar, like the dew, I have begotten you.'" Jesus made an obvious reference to this psalm (Mark 12:53 ff); since the Jews interpreted it in a messianic sense, they were forced to ponder the meaning of its opening words. Similarly, Psalm 72 and Daniel's vision of the Son of Man sitting next to the eternal God (7:13,14,27) suggest the feeling that the Messiah was more than a man, more than a son of man.

This path is paved in revelation, but is continued only in the apocryphal books; the rabbis, on the other hand, try to deprive the Messiah of any divine halo. Here are some texts which give the Messiah a real transcendence. Half a century before the birth of Christ, a pious Jew wrote:

He is a righteous king, instructed by God, and appointed over the sons of Jerusalem. There is no iniquity as long as he lives with them. All are saints, and their king is Christ the Lord.

. . . The Lord himself is his king and his hope; he is mighty through his hope in God. He will have mercy on all those nations who fear him. He will subdue the earth forever with the words of his mouth. He will bless the people of the Lord with wisdom and joy. He will be free of sin, in order to command numerous peoples, reproaching their leaders and destroying sinners by the force of his word. Relying on his God, he will not weaken, for God has made him mighty through the Holy Ghost, and wise through counsel and intelligence, combined with strength and justice. He is powerful in his deeds and strong through the fear of God. He feeds the flocks of the Lord in faith and justice and he will not allow them to grow sick in their pasture. . . . This is the glory of the king of Israel whom God has appointed over the house of Israel in order to correct them.

The Psalms of Solomon, xvii, 35-47

When we realize the close ties which unite this Messiah to his God, the spiritual gifts he has received from the Almighty, and his supernatural power, can we still think of him as of an ordinary creature?

Here is a detailed representation, which is derived from Daniel's revelations concerning the Son of Man and is found in *The Book of Enoch,* a work antedating the public life of Jesus, and in which there does not seem to be Christian influence. In it we meet a mysterious person, called either the Chosen One or the Son of Man:

There I saw someone who had the Head of Days, and his head was like white wool; and with him was another man, his face full of grace like a holy angel. I asked the angel who accompanied me and who revealed all the secrets to me about that Son of Man, "Who is he, and where does he come from? Why does he walk with the Head of the days?"

He answered, "This is the Son of Man. He possesses justice and justice lives with him. He will reveal the most precious secrets, because the Lord of spirits has chosen him, and his fate has vanquished spirits for all eternity. The Son of Man, whom you have seen will make kings and mighty ones rise from their couches, and drive the powerful from their seats. He will throw off the reins of the strong and break the teeth of sinners. He will remove kings from their thrones and their power because they failed to glorify him, and did not humbly confess from whom they received their kingship" (xlvi, 1 ff.).

And at that hour that Son of Man was named
In the presence of the Lord of Spirits,
And his name before the Head of Days.
Yea, before the sun and the signs were created,
Before the stars of the heaven were made,
His name was named before the Lord of Spirits.
He shall be a staff to the righteous whereon to stay themselves
    and not fall,
And he shall be the light of the Gentiles,
And the hope of those who are troubled of heart.
All who dwell on earth shall fall down and worship before him,
And will praise and bless and celebrate with song
The Lord of Spirits.
And for this reason hath he been chosen and hidden before him,
Before the creation of the world and for evermore (xlviii, 2-6).

Because the Elect One standeth before the Lord of Spirits,
And his glory is for ever and ever,
And his might unto all generations.
And in him dwells the spirit of wisdom,
And the spirit which gives insight,
And the spirit of understanding and of might,
And the spirit of those who have fallen asleep in righteousness.
And he shall judge the secret things,
And none shall be able to utter a lying word before him;
For he is the Elect One before the Lord of Spirits according to
    his good pleasure (xlix, 2-4).

And he (the Elect One) shall choose the righteous and holy
    from among them:

For the day he has drawn nigh that they should be saved.
And the Elect One shall in those days sit on My throne,
And his mouth shall pour forth all the secrets of wisdom and
    counsel:
For the Lord of Spirits hath given (them) to him and hath
    glorified him (li, 2-3).
And the Lord of Spirits placed the Elect One on the throne of
    glory.
And he shall judge all the works of the holy above in the heaven,
And in the balance shall their deeds be weighed.
And when he shall lift up his countenance
To judge their secret ways according to the word of the name
    of the Lord of Spirits,
And their path according to the way of the righteous judgment
    of the Lord of Spirits,
Then shall they all with one voice speak and bless,
And glorify and extol and sanctify the name of the Lord of
    Spirits (lxi, 8-9).

And thus the Lord commanded the kings and the mighty and
    the exalted, and those who dwell on the earth, and said:
"Open your eyes and lift up your horns if ye are
    able to recognize the Elect One."
And the Lord of Spirits seated him on the throne of his glory,
And the spirit of righteousness was poured out upon him,
And the word of his mouth slays all the sinners,
And all the unrighteous are destroyed from before his face. . . .
And pain shall seize them
When they see that Son of Man
Sitting on the throne of his glory (lxii, 1-2,5).

And from henceforth there shall be nothing corruptible,
For that Son of Man has appeared,
And has seated himself on the throne of his glory,
And all evil shall pass away before his face,
And the word of that Son of Man shall go forth
And be strong before the Lord of Spirits (lxix, 29).

These texts, which we have quoted at length, define the Chosen One, the Son of Man, as a transcendental being, pre-existent, close to God. He is invested with divine gifts, shares God's throne and exercises the divine function of judgment; the support of men, he is the object of their adoration and reigns with God for all eternity. If we cannot discover here a true Son of God in the theological sense, we must agree with F. Martin that "This is nevertheless the most ideal type conceived of by Jewish Messianism before Christianity."[3]

The person described in one of the visions in *4 Ezra* (probably before 70) also has a transcendental character. The lion of Judah destroys the eagle of Rome with his breath: this is the Messiah whom God has reserved for the end of the days (xi, 37; xii, 2,32). In another vision he sees Christ, the Son of God, who rules in glory during the four hundred years of the messianic kingdom, or who is in heaven with the righteous (vii, 28).[4]

In another vision he sees a human form rising from the sea and flying upwards to heavenly clouds. The sight of him makes everything tremble, and his voice melts objects, like wax melts in the presence of fire. He disperses his enemies with the burning breath of his mouth, which changes into a river of fire and storm. God explains that this is his son[5] whom he has kept in reserve for a long time (xiii, 3,10,26,32, 37). Here is another transcendent being, pre-existent, endowed with divine powers, if not a "Son of God."

Thus it seems that certain Jewish schools thought of the Messiah as a divine being. But in their commentaries on the

---

[3] F. Martin, *Le livre d'Henoch, tranduit sur le texte ethiopien* (Paris, 1906), p. xxxviii.

[4] Scholars disagree concerning the authenticity of *filius meus*. Cf. Vaganay, *Le probleme eschatologique dans le IVe Esdras*, pp. 87 ff.; L. Gry, *Les dires prophètiques d'Esdras* (Paris, 1938), pp. 45-47, 397.

[5] Gry again reads "my servant."

biblical texts the rabbis tried to minimize the transcendence of the Messiah. In several passages, they see instead Ezechias;[6] others are interpreted in a human and earthly way. Here is a commentary on the second Psalm, which at that time was generally believed to have messianic connotations:

The Holy One, blessed be He, said to the Messiah, the son of David, who will soon be revealed in our days, "Ask one thing of me, and I will give it to you, as it is written: I shall announce the law . . . today, I have given birth to you. Ask me, and I will give you the nations as your portion."

When he saw that the Messiah, the son of Joseph, had been killed, he said, "Master of the universe, all I want is life."

"Your father, David, had already prophesied life before you spoke up (Ps. 21:5)—'He asked life of you: you gave him length of days forever and ever.'"

Sukkah 52a

If the rabbis call the Messiah "God" or "son of God," they see this only as a human title which God also bestowed on Israel. We feel that they definitely tried to eliminate any exegesis which would elevate the Messiah to the level of God. An interesting example is found in connection with Daniel 7:9: "Thrones were set up." R. Akiba commented, "One is for the Ancient of Days, one for David the Messiah." But R. Yose rebuked him, "Akiba, how long will you profane the Shekinah? One is for justice, and one for mercy" (Sanh. 38b).

The general sentiments of the rabbis are expressed in this affirmation of Trypho (*Dialogue with Trypho*, xlix, 1; l, 1): "It seems to me that those who maintain that Jesus has been chosen to be anointed, that he has been Christ-Anointed, say something which is more believable than

[6] See *Dialogue with Trypho*, xliii, 8; lxvii; lxviii; lxxi, 3; lxxvii, 1-2.

those who share your opinion. All of us wait for a Christ who is a human being, and for Elias who will anoint him when he comes. . . . But first answer this: How can you prove that there is another God in addition to the One who created the universe?"

In addition, the rabbis attribute a very restricted role to the Messiah, placing him below the great personalities of the Bible. They admit only that his name is one of the things created before the world (Pes. 54a), a characteristic shared with Manna, the rainbow, and the Tablets of the Law. It does not imply a real pre-existence: "Since you say that there was a pre-existent God who became flesh by the will of God in order to be born by a virgin, how then can one prove that he was pre-existent, since he was filled by the powers of the Holy Spirit—as enumerated by the mouth of Isaias—indicating he was previously devoid of them?" (*Dialogue with Trypho,* lxxxvii, 3)

The Apocrypha and the rabbis also differ greatly in regard to the Messiah's life and activities. The Apocrypha show a Messiah pre-existing with God, and his manifestation is presented as a heavenly revelation. This seems to exclude the possibility of a human origin. Nevertheless, even the Apocrypha often mention his descent from David; it is a generally accepted doctrine that the Messiah is the son of David. This belief was not absolute, since R. Akiba declared Bar Kochba, who was not of the house of David, to be the Messiah. Also, at the time of the triumph of the Asmoneans, who came from the tribe of Levi, the writers whose opinions are preserved in *The Book of Jubilees* and in *The Testaments of the Twelve Patriarchs* give the future supremacy to a descendant of Levi, neglecting the tribe of Judah altogether. All agree that the Messiah must be born at Bethlehem, according to the prophecy of Micheas, a

prophecy well known to Jesus' contemporaries and interpreted in this sense (John 7:42; Matt. 2:5-6).

We shall soon see that part played by the Messiah in the
national restoration. He is not very active in this, playing
a rather secondary role, especially according to the rabbis.

Will he have to die? Only in *4 Ezra* (vii, 29) do we find
the statement that at the end of his reign he will die like all
men. The Apocrypha, which attributed to the Messiah a
glorious and quasi-eternal rule, apparently do not concede
that he might die. The rabbinical texts are vague on this
point, since in them the Messiah often appears as a being
without concrete reality.

The suffering and death of the Messiah, a central doctrine
for Christians, is a difficult conception for Jewish minds. It
is useful to recall how obstinately the apostles rejected the
predictions by Jesus of his own passion. They did not wish
to understand (Luke 9:45), and they could be convinced
only after the Resurrection (Luke 24:26,46). We also
know how hard Paul tried to prove to his co-religionists
that Christ had been subject to suffering (Acts 26:23). From
its first beginnings Christian apologetics had no difficulty in
finding several biblical prophecies regarding Christ's sufferings and death. But how did Judaism interpret those
passages? In accordance with Scripture, Judaism at first admitted that the Messiah would be subject to some suffering,
but later, as a reaction against Christianity, it either gave
these texts another meaning or applied them to a Messiah
other than the son of David.

The first attitude is present in the way Trypho answers
Justin's demonstrations: "The passages from Scriptures
which you have quoted prove abundantly that a suffering
Christ has been foretold, who will return in glory to receive
the eternal kingdom from all nations. But now prove that
this man is that Christ. ... We know that he must suffer and

that he will be led away like a lamb. But we cannot believe that he will fail and be crucified, that he will die in such shame and dishonor" (*Dialogue with Trypho,* xxxix, 7; xc,1).

Such declarations, with their mixed emphasis, are confirmed in certain rabbinical writings. The clearest statements concerning Christ's suffering and death are taken from Isaias' prophecies about the suffering servant, especially chapter 53. But toward the end of the second century it was said in the school of R. Judah Hanasi: "Because of his suffering, the Messiah will be called the leper of the house of Juda, as it is said (Isa. 53:4): 'Yet it was our infirmities that he bore, that he endured, while we thought of him as striken, as one smitten by God and afflicted' " (Sanh. 98b, *baraita*).

About fifty years later, R. Johanan interpreted Ruth 2:14 —"dip your bread in the sauce"—as an allusion to sufferings of the King Messiah: "He was crushed because of our sins" (*Ruth Rabbah,* 2:14). These texts usually received a non-messianic interpretation, or, like *Targum Jonathan* on the Prophets, celebrated the triumph of the Servant of God, victor over the nations.

The same holds true of Psalm 22, which Jesus recited on the cross. St. Justin uses it as one of his main pieces of apologetics, but his extended speeches do not convince his adversary (*Dialogue with Trypho,* xcvii, iii-cvi). Rabbinical exegesis was well aware of the messianism in that psalm, since one rabbi of the end of the third century, R. Simeon ben Pazzi, applies it to the Messiah of Ephraim (*Pesikta Rabbati,* 163a). A century earlier, R. Hiyya bar Abba and R. Simeon ben Talafta thought the psalm dealt with redemption and gave an exegesis based on the title: "Passing through a valley, they saw 'the hind of the dawn' starting to penetrate the dark. R. Hiyya said: "The redemption of Israel will be

like this.' R. Simeon: 'This is what is meant by Micheas 7:8
—Though I sit in darkness, the Lord is my light. In the beginning, the light is small; then it breaks forth and increases, until it becomes more and more glorious. Likewise,
at the beginning, Mardochai was sitting at the king's
gate . . .' " (*Midrash on Ps.*, 22:13).

Those last lines indicate the accepted interpretation, ap-
plying the Psalm to Esther and Mardochai. Whatever could
humiliate the Jewish spirit is turned to its advantage and
glory. Here is another instance. We read in Zacharias (12:
11): "And the land shall mourn, each family apart." St. John
(19:37) applied this to the crucified Christ. But at the end
of the second century, R. Dosa understood it as referring to
the Messiah the son of Joseph, who will be put to death,
supporting his reading with the text, "They shall look upon
him whom they have thrust through, and they shall mourn
for him as one mourns for an only son" (Zach. 12:10). The
rabbis, however, apply this passage to the evil nature which
will be destroyed. But it is pointed out that in that case one
ought to rejoice rather than mourn (Suk. 52a).

These last interpretations reveal what is at the bottom
of Jewish thinking. On the one hand, Jews cannot admit a
suffering Messiah, and this gives us an idea of the importance
of late or isolated statements which do mention the sufferings of the Messiah. On the other hand, they must recognize
the true meaning of certain biblical passages, but they apply
them to other Messiahs, either the one of Ephraim or of Joseph.

The latter figure made its appearance toward the end
of the Tannaitic age (end of second century); we do not
know whether it existed earlier. The Messiah of Ephraim,
whose exploits constantly seemed to grow, became the subject of all warlike actions. He will defeat the Roman Empire
and all nations that are in league against Israel—above all,

Gog and Magog. In order to achieve victory, he will accept
death. His people will mourn for him, and God will reward
him by giving him a share in heavenly glory. In his classical
work on the suffering Messiah, Dalman points out that his
death is not presented as having an expiatory value.[7]

The Establishment of the Messianic Kingdom

God's role is primary; he takes the initiative and directs
everything, and the persons whom he uses in the execution
of his plans are only instruments. Therefore the title of
Savior ought to be reserved to him: " 'Give thanks to the
Lord, for he is good, for his kindness endures forever! Thus
let the redeemed of the Lord say' (Ps. 107: 1-2). R. Berechiah
[ca. 340] reported in the name of R. Helbo [ca. 300], who
said it in the name of R. Samuel [d. 254 or 257]: 'Who are
redeemed of the Lord? They are the Israelites, as Isaias (35:
10) said, Those whom the Lord has ransomed will return.
Not redeemed by Elias or the Messiah, but by God' " (Midrash on Ps., 7:1).

The restoration of the nation will be accomplished by
the return of the exiles to their fatherland. As a prelude to
this, there will be the liberation of Israel; those nations
which have enslaved the Jews will be forcibly dispossessed,
either by wars or divine punishments. What part does the
Messiah have in these developments?

Jewish tradition is divided and hesitant in dealing with
the way the Messiah would make his appearance. This is
evident once again in the secondary role it assigns to him.

According to *The Book of the Secrets of Enoch,* the Chosen One is revealed only at the Last Judgment. The presen-

---

[7] Dalman, *Der leidende und der sterbende Messias der Synagogue in ersten
nachchristlichen Jahrtausend* (Berlin, 1888).

tation in *The Book of Enoch* is no less disturbing; after the triumph of the Asmoneans and the punishment of treacherous and disloyal Israelites, God establishes the New Jerusalem:

And I stood up to see till they folded up that old house; and carried off all the pillars, and all the beams and ornaments of the house were at the same time folded up with it, and they carried it off and laid it in a place in the south of the land. And I saw till the Lord of the sheep brought a new house greater and loftier than the first, and set it up in the place of the first which had been folded up. . . .
(Conversion of the surviving gentiles and their spontaneous submission to Israel.) And I saw till they [the Israelites] laid down that sword, which had been given to the sheep, and they brought it back into the house, and it was sealed before the presence of the Lord, and all the sheep were invited into that house, but it held them not. . . .
And I saw that a white bull was born, with large horns, and all the beasts of the air feared him and made petition to him all the time. And I saw till all their generations were transformed, and they all became white bulls; and the first among them became a lamb, and that lamb became a great animal and had great black horns on its head; and the Lord of the sheep rejoiced over it and over all the oxen (xc,28-38).

In this picture the Messiah (the bull) appears only after the acts of consummation are fulfilled, in order to enjoy the supreme bliss with those who belong to him, after they have been transformed in his own image.

There is a similar description in *4 Ezra*:

For behold the days come, and it shall be when the signs which I have foretold unto thee shall come to pass,
Then shall the city that now is invisible appear, and the land which is now concealed be seen;

And whosoever is delivered from the predicted evils, they shall see my wonders. For my Son the Messiah shall be revealed, together with those who are with him, and shall rejoice the survivors four hundred years. And it shall be, after these years, that my Son the Messiah shall die, and all in whom there is human breath. Then shall the world be turned into the primeval silence seven days, like as at the first beginnings (vii, 26-30).

Logically, the Messiah ought to appear at the first hour of redemption, in order to direct all of its acts. This is suggested in *The Psalms of Solomon*:

Behold, O Lord, and raise up unto them their king, the son of
       David
At the time in which thou seest, O God, that he may reign over
       Israel Thy servant.
And gird him with strength, that he may shatter unrighteous
       rulers,
   And that he may purge Jerusalem from nations that trample
       [her] down to destruction (xvii, 23-24).

The rabbis who give a preponderant role to the Messiah place his appearance at the beginning of the messianic era. Some insist that it will occur in an extraordinary manner, as suggested by frequent expressions in the Apocrypha and rabbinic literature: God "raises up" the Messiah; the Messiah is "revealed" or "reveals himself." In what way? There are two traditions. The first occurs quite often (*Gen. Rabbah*, 75 and 98, on Gen. 32:6 and 49:11; Ber. 57a, etc.) and is based on the prophecies of Zacharias 9:9, "See, your king shall come to you; a just savior is he, meek, and riding on an ass," and of Jacob, "He [Juda] tethers his ass to the vine" (Gen. 49:11). According to this tradition, the Messiah will come riding on an ass if Israel is not pure (Sanh. 98a). The second tradition takes into account the vision of Daniel, in which the Messiah is seen in the clouds of heaven; "If the Israelites are just, the Messiah will come on the clouds of heaven." Then one quotes the words of Sapor, who offered a white horse to R. Samuel to replace the ass "on which you say the Messiah will come" (Sanh. 98a).

We already know that Elias will anoint the Messiah when he comes, but we do not know under what conditions.

We will not report other later statements, giving details on the manifestation of the Messiah. We retain only one, which appears several times, beginning in the third century, and is repeated in the statement of Trypho (*Dialogue with Trypho*, viii, 4; cx, 1), that after the Messiah appears, he will remain hidden for forty-five days, or, at least he will disappear and remain unknown (*Pesikta Rabbati*, 72; T. P. Ber. ii, 4, 5a).

The return of the Israelites to their land and their dominion over the rest of the world imply that the nations who had enslaved them will grant them freedom. In some descriptions the return from exile and the triumph of the chosen nation is accomplished peacefully. The more frequent conception is that the nations will either be defeated in a decisive war or completely destroyed by God. In *The Book of Enoch*, before the great day which inaugurates the messianic era, and even before the appearance of the Messiah, the Jews receive a big sword with which to fight the persecuting nations. These nations are put to flight and the earth swallows them up (xc, 18-19). In *The Psalms of Solomon*, the Messiah defeats the enemy, but the text seems to attribute the victory to God as well, and elsewhere the vengeful activity of the Messiah is much less warlike:

Behold, O Lord, and raise up unto them their king, the son of David. . . .

And gird him with strength, that he may shatter unrighteous
   rulers,
   And that he may purge Jerusalem from nations that trample
      [her] down to destruction.
Wisely, righteously he shall thrust out sinners from [the] in-
      heritance,
   He shall destroy the pride of the sinner as a potter's vessel.
With a rod of iron he shall break in pieces all their substance,
   He shall destroy the godless nations with the word of his
      mouth;
At his rebuke nations shall flee before him,
   And he shall reprove sinners for the thoughts of their
      heart. . .

May God cleanse Israel against the day of mercy and blessing.
   Against the day of choice when He bringeth back His
      anointed (xvii, 23-25; xviii,6).

The Messiah of *4 Ezra* and *2 Baruch* is more awe-inspiring, but not usually more warlike. Either he is the Lion of
Juda who condemns the nations for their injustice and then
mercifully delivers his people and showers them with blessings (*4 Ezra*, i, 31-34), or he has the form of a man who rises
from the sea and sees that all nations are united against him;
whereupon he reproves them from the heights of Mount
Zion and destroys them "without lifting his head or taking
up a sword or any other instrument of war," but simply with
the fiery breath of his mouth (xiii, 8-11, 33-38). The Messiah
of *2 Baruch* also destroys enemies and pagan Rome without
any effort (xxxvi, 2-11; xl; lxxii); it is nevertheless added
that they will be handed over to the sword (lxxii, 6). The
rabbis leave warlike activity almost entirely to the Messiah
of Ephraim. R. Eliezer says that Israel will be avenged on
Rome in accordance with Ezechiel 25:14 (*Lev. Rabbah*, 34:
11). Other rabbis state that at the time of the Messiah, as in

time past, the angels who protect Israel (Dan. 12:1) will destroy its enemies (*Exod. Rabbah,* 18:5).

Thus we see that punitive measures have an extremely important role; they are exercised either by God or his angels, by the Messiah or Israel. This conception is well received for two reasons. These punishments seem to be identical with the Day of the Lord, so often invoked by the prophets in order to threaten their listeners. Instinctively Jewish thought tends to blend messianism and eschatology. The nations are usually threatened with the punishment of fire, the Gehenna:

In these days downcast in countenance shall the kings of the
    earth have become,
And the strong who possess the land because of the works of
    their hands.
For on the day of their anguish and affliction they shall not [be
    able to] save themselves.
And I will give them over into the hands of Mine elect:
As straw in the fire so shall they burn before the face of the holy:
As lead in the water shall they sink before the face of the right-
    eous,
And no trace of them shall any more be found. . . . (xlviii, 8-9)

And I looked and turned to another part of the earth. And saw there a deep valley with burning fire. And they brought the kings and the mighty, and began to cast them into this deep valley.

The Book of Enoch, liv, 1-2

This is an eschatological view, but even in a this-worldly messianism—as in *The Sibylline Books*—God dispatches fiery swords against his enemies, and judges men by war, fire, and sword, and by sulphur sent down from the heavens (iii, 673 ff., 690 ff., 761). We also read that if God no longer sends

a deluge of water, he will send fire and plague against the
nations (*Mekilta on Exod.,* 18:1; *Tos. Taan.,* iii, 1). The
rabbis also imagined other tortures for pagans.

The eschatological form of the punishment of the nations
is further indicated by the frequently recurring idea that
the nations will be so annihilated that no trace will be left
of them: " 'Your anger consumes them like stubble.' It does
not say, 'It has consumed them' but 'It *will* consume them,'
as it is written (Abdias 18), 'The house of Jacob shall be a
fire, and the house of Joseph a flame,' and it is written (Zach.
12:6), 'I will make the princes of Juda like a brazier of fire
in the woodland, and like a burning torch among sheaves' "
(*Mekilta on Exod.,* 15:7).

God brought about this suppression of the nations: "The
Lord alone was their leader" (Deut. 32:12). God said to the
Israelites, "Since you lived alone in this world and did not
benefit from the goods of idolators, I shall let you dwell
alone in the world to come and none of the idolators will
benefit from you" (*Sifre on Deut.,* 33:12).

However, we also find that the nations will exist in the
messianic age, paying tribute to Israel and adoring the true
God. This apparent contradiction can be explained in two
ways: the messianic consummation is thought of as a definitive consummation; and Israel is pleased to see the destruction of the enemy nations while the chosen people will be
in bliss.

In the reconstitution of the nation, three moments may be
distinguished: the deliverance, the return from exile, and
the inauguration of the new order. Liberation is the chief
and indispensable element of messianic times. Although
there are different opinions regarding the concrete realization, the statement of R. Samuel (d. 257) may well represent
the common opinion: "The only difference between this
world and days of the Messiah is that submission to foreign

nations will cease; as it is said in Deuteronomy 15:11, 'The needy will never be lacking in the land' " (Ber. 24b). This liberation is called for in several official prayers. It is demanded by Zachary, the representative type for those Jews who await the redemption of Israel: "Salvation from our enemies, and from the hand of all who hate us. . . . That, delivered from the hand of our enemies, we should serve him without fear, in holiness and justice before him all our days" (Luke 1:71, 74-75).

It is God himself who will liberate his people, just as he delivered them from Egyptian bondage; this time, liberation will be definitive. This is demonstrated by the following rabbinic exegesis:

In the time to come they will sing a tenth song, as it is said, "Sing to the Lord a new song, his praise from the end of the earth" (Isa. 42:10). And again, "Sing to the Lord a new song of praise in the assembly of the faithful" (Ps. 149:1). The songs that were sung in the past are designated by a feminine noun. For just as a woman who gives birth, the liberations of past times were followed by a servitude. But future salvation will not be followed by servitude; therefore, it is designated by a masculine noun, in accordance with the text (Jer. 30: 6), "Inquire, and see: since when do men bear children? Why, then, do I see all these men, with their hands on their loins like women in childbirth?" Just as a man does not give birth to a child, the salvation that is to come will not be followed by servitude, as it is said (Isa. 45:17), "Israel, you are saved by the Lord, saved forever! You shall never be put to shame or disgrace in future ages.

Mekilta on Exod., 15:1

The return from exile is a major aspect of the restoration, for the holy nation can only be reconstituted in the Holy Land, around the Temple. Therefore, the hope of the return holds a considerable place in the Psalms, the Prophets, and later in the post-biblical literature, especially that of the rabbis. Listen to the tenth blessing of the *Shemoneh Esreh,* recited in the Temple and later in the synagogue: "Sound the great trumpet for our liberation, and raise the standard for the gathering in of our exiles. Blessed be Thou, Yahweh, who gathers together the exiles of his people Israel!" A half century before Christ, a pious Jew wrote in the same spirit:

Blow ye in Zion on the trumpet to summon [the] saints,
    Cause ye to be heard in Jerusalem the voice of him that bring-
        eth good tidings;
    For God hath had pity on Israel in visiting them.
Stand on the height, O Jerusalem, and behold thy children,
    From the East and the West, gathered together by the Lord;
From the North they come in the gladness of their God,
    From the isles afar off God hath gathered them.
High mountains hath he abased into a plain for them;
    The hills fled at their entrance.
The woods gave them shelter as they passed by;
    Every sweet-smelling tree God caused to spring up for them,
    That Israel might pass by in the visitation of the glory of their
        God.
Put on, O Jerusalem, thy glorious garments;
    Make ready thy holy robe;
    For God hath spoken good concerning Israel, for ever and
        ever.
Let the Lord do what He hath spoken concerning Israel and
        Jerusalem;
    Let the Lord raise up Israel by His glorious name.

                          The Psalms of Solomon, xi

    In this description the return is attributed to God him-self. Less frequently it is presented as accomplished by the Messiah: "And he shall gather together a holy people, whom he shall lead in righteousness" (*The Psalms of Solomon*, xvii).

All of Israel must be included in this return. The question is raised as to whether the ten lost tribes will come back. It is stated in *4 Ezra* that the Messiah will also gather in those who had fled beyond the river Euphrates in order to be able to observe the laws; God will halt the river, so that they may cross it and return (xiii, 39-47).

Here we see again that wonders will accompany the return from exile; it is indeed a classical theme. Clouds will protect those who return, according to the symbolic exegesis of R. Akiba on "Setting out from Sukkot" (Exod. 13:20). Other rabbis interpreted these words literally, as referring to a place name, but he understands Sukkot as referring to clouds of glory, and invokes Isaias 4:5, "Then will the Lord create, over the whole site of Mount Sion and over her place of assembly . . . over all, his glory will be shelter and protection." This refers to the past; as to the future, it says (Isa. 4:6 and 35:10), "Shade from the parching heat of day, refuge and cover from storm and rain. . . . Those whom the Lord has ransomed will return and enter Sion singing, crowned with everlasting joy" (*Mekilta on Exod.*, 12:37; 13:20).

One of the miracles deduced from Scripture is the return on the clouds: "God heals by the same methods that he wounds. When the Holy One, blessed be He, sent Israel into exile, it was by means of clouds, as it is said (Lam. 2:1), 'How is it that the Lord in his anger covered the daughter of Sion with a cloud?' In the same way, he will also reassemble them by means of clouds, as it is said (Isa. 60:8), 'What are these that fly along like clouds, like doves to their cotes?' " (*Mekilta on Exod.*, 14:24)

This is an ancient tradition. For example, in *The Book of Enoch* the following fragment is suddenly inserted: "And it came to pass after this that I saw another host of wagons, and men riding thereon, and coming in the winds from the east, and from the west to the south. And the noise of their wagons was heard, and when this turmoil took place the holy ones from heaven remarked it, and the pillars of earth were removed from their place, and the sound thereof was heard from one end of heaven to the other, in one day" (lvii, 1-2).

However, this traditional statement concerning the return from exile is absent from some descriptions, especially those in the Apocrypha. In several it is said that messianic bliss will be the portion of all those who will be alive in Palestine at the time of his arrival; thus we read in *4 Ezra,* xii, 34: "But my people who survive, he shall deliver with mercy, even those who have been saved throughout my borders, and he shall make them joyful until the End come, even the Day of Judgment, of which I have spoken unto thee from the beginning."

The Days of the Messiah

This classical expression designates the state of happiness which the messianic era will bring about. The Jewish soul wavers between two conceptions of these times. We have quoted the statement of R. Samuel, according to which the only difference between our times and the messianic age is the ending of servitude, but this principle always produces objections. It seems that the eschatological mirage led many astray; it was hard to imagine that these times, so long awaited, should not be full of wonders. This popular expectation of the marvelous won the day, and the messianic times are often painted in colors appropriate to the age which inaugurates the resurrection. This confusion is also seen in the use of terms; the messianic times are sometimes called "the world to come," or "the future to come," an expression which includes the whole eschatological period.

How, then, can we distinguish the joys of messianic times from those of the eschatological period? Sometimes this is impossible, since certain traits are present in descriptions of both. In other cases it would seem that a more national note characterizes a messianic representation.

Before clarifying the details of the messianic reign, we shall present three texts showing the different possible types of messianism. The first, an extract from the great messianic Psalm of Solomon, is quite in the tradition of the prophets. It describes an earthly and human messianism, in which the nations are welcomed:

And he shall gather together a holy people, whom he shall lead
    in righteousness,
    And he shall judge the tribes of the people that has been
        sanctified by the Lord his God.
And he shall not suffer unrighteousness to lodge any more in
    their midst,
    Nor shall there dwell with them any man that knoweth wick-
        edness,
    For he shall know them, that they are all sons of their God.
And he shall divide them according to their tribes upon the
    land,
    And neither sojourner nor alien shall sojourn with them any
        more.
He shall judge peoples and nations in the wisdom of his right-
    eousness. *Selah.*
And he shall have the heathen nations to serve him under his
    yoke;
    And he shall glorify the Lord in a place to be seen of all the
        earth;
    And he shall purge Jerusalem, making it holy as of old:
So that nations shall come from the ends of the earth to see his
    glory,

Bringing as gifts her sons who had fainted,
And to see the glory of the Lord, wherewith God hath glorified
her,
And he [shall be] righteous king, taught of God, over them,
And there shall be no unrighteousness in his days in their midst,
For all shall be holy and their king the anointed of the Lord.

For he shall not put his trust in horse and rider and bow,
Nor shall be multiply for himself gold and silver for war,
Nor shall he gather confidence from a multitude for the day
of battle.
The Lord Himself is his king, the hope of him that is mighty
through [his] hope in God.

All nations [shall be] in fear before him,
For he will smite the earth with the word of his mouth for
ever.
He will bless the people of the Lord with wisdom and gladness,
And he himself [will be] pure from sin, so that he may rule a
great people.
He will rebuke rulers, and remove sinners by the might of his
word,
And [relying] upon his God, throughout his days he will not
stumble;
For God will make him mighty by means of [His] holy spirit,
And wise by means of the spirit of understanding, with
strength and righteousness.
And the blessing of the Lord [will be] with him; he will be
strong and stumble not.
His hope [will be] in the Lord; who then can prevail against
him?
[He will be] mighty in his works, and strong in the fear of God,
[He will be] shepherding the flock of the Lord faithfully and
righteously,
And will suffer none among them to stumble in their pas-
ture.

He will lead them all aright
   And there will be no pride among them that any among
      them should be oppressed.
This [will be] the majesty of the king of Israel whom God know-
      eth;
He will raise him up over the house of Israel to correct him.
His words [shall be] more refined than costly gold, the choicest;
Blessed be they that shall be in those days,
   In that they shall see the good fortune of Israel which God
      shall bring to pass in the gathering together of the tribes.
May the Lord hasten His mercy upon Israel!
   May He deliver us from the uncleanness of unholy enemies!
   The Lord Himself is our king for ever and ever.
                                 The Psalms of Solomon, xvii, 26-51

The second example is taken from 2 *Baruch.* Here are
themes dear to Jewish imagination; the earth has been miraculously transformed into a paradise, and life is an endless
delight. The role of the Messiah is clearly asserted, but is
already somewhat reduced. A frank nationalism is coupled
with a limited universalism:

And it shall come to pass when all is accomplished that was
to come to pass in those parts, that the Messiah shall then begin to be revealed. And Behemoth shall be revealed from his
place and Leviathan shall ascend from the sea, those two great
monsters which I created on the fifth day of creation, and
shall have kept until that time; and then they shall be for food
for all that are left. The earth also shall yield its fruit ten
thousandfold . . . (xxix, 3-5).

After the signs have come, of which thou was told before,
when the nations become turbulent, and the time of the Messiah is come, he shall both summon all the nations, and some
of them he shall spare, and some of them he shall slay. These
things therefore shall come upon the nations which are to be
spared by Him. Every nation, which knows not Israel and has

not trodden down the seed of Jacob, shall indeed be spared. And this because some out of every nation shall be subjected to thy people. But all those who have ruled over you, or have known you, shall be given up to the sword ... (lxxii, 2-6).

And it shall come to pass, when He has brought low everything that is in the world,

And has sat down in peace for the age on the throne of His
kingdom
That joy shall then be revealed
And rest shall appear.
And then healing shall descend in dew,
And disease shall withdraw,
And anxiety and anguish and lamentation pass from amongst
men,
And gladness proceed through the whole earth.
And no one shall again die untimely,
Nor shall any adversity suddenly befall.
And judgments, and revilings, and contentions, and revenges,
And blood, and passions, and envy, and hatred,
And whatsoever things are like these shall go into condem-
nation when they are removed.
For it is these very things which have filled this world with
evils,
And on account of these the life of man has been greatly
troubled.
And wild beasts shall come from the forest and minister unto
men,
And asps and dragons shall come forth from their holes to
submit themselves to a little child.
And women shall no longer then have pain when they bear,
Nor shall they suffer torment when they yield the fruit of the
womb (lxxiii).

And it shall come to pass in those days that the reaper shall
not grow weary,

Nor those that build be toilworn;
For the works shall of themselves speedily advance
Together with those who do them in much tranquility.
For that time is the consummation of that which is corrupt-
ible,
And the beginning of that which is not corruptible.
Therefore those things which were predicted shall belong to
it:
Therefore it is far away from evils, and near to those things
which die not (lxxiv, 1-3).

We take our third example from *The Book of Enoch*.
Here is a completely transcendent perspective. It was not
very popular, since people believed that in a good economy
of retribution, material rewards should be included. After
judgment has been given, the Chosen One has only to live
quietly with his elect in the calm of beatitude:

Then I will cause My Elect One to dwell among them.
And I will transform the earth and make it a blessing:
And I will cause Mine elect ones to dwell upon it:
But the sinners and evil-doers shall not foot thereon.
For I have provided and satisfied with peace My righteous
ones
And I have caused them to dwell before Me:
But for the sinners there is judgment impending with Me,
So that I shall destroy them from the face of the earth (xlv,
4-6).

And in those days shall the mountains leap like rams,
And the hills also shall skip like lambs satisfied with milk,
And the faces of all the angels in heaven shall be lighted up
with joy.
And the earth shall rejoice,
And the righteous shall dwell upon it,
And the elect shall walk thereon (li, 4-5).
And the righteous shall be in the light of the sun,

And the elect in the light of eternal life:
The days of their life shall be unending,
And the days of the holy without number (lviii, 3).

And the righteous and elect shall be saved on that day,
And they shall never thenceforward see the faces of the sinners and unrighteous.
And the Lord of Spirits will abide over them,
And with the Son of Man shall they eat
And lie down and rise up for ever and ever. . . .
And they shall be clothed with garments of glory,
And these shall be the garments of life from the Lord of Spirits:
And your garments shall not grow old,
Nor your glory pass away before the Lord of Spirits (lxii, 13-16).

There was a strong tendency to represent messianic happiness in terms of eternity. In *4 Ezra* the four hundred years granted to the righteous goes beyond ordinary limits. In the Apocrypha, messianic times seem to be without any limit, or at least to last for an extraordinary period. According to *The Book of Jubilees* (xxiii, 27), the Golden Age, a national messianism without a Messiah, lasts a thousand years, and *The Book of Enoch* speaks of an even longer period:

And then shall all the righteous escape,
And shall live till they beget thousands of children,
And all the days of their youth and their old age
Shall they complete in peace.

And then shall the whole earth be tilled in righteousness, and shall be planted with trees and be full of blessing. And all desirable trees shall be planted on it, and they shall plant vines on it, and the vine which they plant thereon shall yield wine in abundance, and as for all the seed which is sown thereon each measure [of it] shall bear a thousand, and each measure of olives shall yield ten presses of oil. . . . And the earth shall be cleansed from all defilement, and from all sin, and from all punishment, and from all torment (x, 17-22).

Some rabbis give exact numbers, often rather low ones, for the duration of messianic times. It seems we are dealing with classroom exercises, since the same rabbi, Eliezer, comes to four different results:

"Yahweh is at war with Amalek from generation to generation"; the rabbis wondered what these words meant. Eliezer sees in them the generation of the Messiah, lasting for three generations, according to Psalm 72:5, "May he endure as long as the sun, and like the moon through all generations." (The first word, in the singular, counts for one generation; the second, in the plural, for two.)

Melita on Exod., 17:16

There is also a tradition that Eliezer said, "The days of the Messiah last forty years." He proves it the first time by Psalm 95:10, "Forty years I loathed that generation." He proves it again by using two related texts: "He therefore let you be afflicted with hunger, and then fed you with manna" (Deut. 8:3), and "Make us glad, for the days when you afflicted us" (Ps. 90:15).

Sanhedrin 99a (where there are more computations to be found, similarly derived from biblical texts)

R. Eliezer said, "The days of the Messiah last four hundred years." For it is written, "[Your posterity] shall be subject to slavery and shall be oppressed four hundred years" (Gen. 15:13), and "Make us glad, for the days when you afflicted us" (Ps. 90:15).

Pesikta Rabbati, 4a

R. Eliezer said, "The days of the Messiah will last a thousand years." For it is written, "A thousand years in your sight are as yesterday" (Ps. 90:4). R. Joshua [his usual opponent in debate] replied, "They will last two thousand years, since it says (Ps. 90:15), 'Make us glad, for the days when you have afflicted us.' This implies at least two days, and one day for the Holy One, blessed be He, is like a thousand years, since 'A thousand years in your sight are as yesterday.' "

Midrash on Psalms, 90:17

All this should be considered merely scholastic and exegetical pastime. It leads to the statement by R. Judah Hanasi, who knew how to evaluate such calculations: "We cannot determine the days of the Messiah, for 'The day of vengeance was in my heart, my year for redeeming was at hand' (Isa. 63:4). And the days of the Messiah will last 265,000 years" (*Pesikta Rabbati,* 4b). One might as well say that they are of infinite duration. It is this conviction that may have been behind the objection of those Jews who said to Jesus, "We have heard from the Law that the Christ abides forever" (John 12:34).

Transcendent messianism—as in *The Assumption of Moses* or *The Book of Enoch*—sends Israel or the chosen ones to heaven. Other works situate the national restoration in Palestine, naturally, but a Palestine that has been totally transformed, along with the whole earth. The center of the renewed kingdom, of course, is the holy city of Jerusalem, which seems to attract and absorb the rest of the universe. This hope is expressed in prayers calling on God as "he who builds Jerusalem." We find this in The Book of Tobias, in a sort of vision with many marvelous features also reported in later documents:

Jerusalem, city of God, the Lord hath chastised thee for the works of thy hands. Give glory to the Lord for thy good things, and bless the God eternal, that he may rebuild his tabernacle in thee. . . . Nations from afar shall come to thee, and shall bring gifts, and shall adore the Lord in thee, and shall esteem thy land as holy. For they shall call upon the great name in thee. They shall be cursed that shall despise thee; and they shall be condemned that shall blaspheme thee; and blessed shall they be that shall build thee up. But thou shalt rejoice in thy children, because they shall all be blessed, and shall be gathered together to the Lord. Blessed are all they that love thee, and that rejoice in thy peace. . . . The gates of Jerusalem shall be built of sapphire, and of emerald, and all the walls thereof round about of precious stones. All its streets shall be paved with white and clean stones, and Alleluia shall be sung in its streets. Blessed be the Lord who hath exalted it, and may he reign over it forever and ever, Amen.

The Book of Tobias, 13:11-23

This is a copious prelude to the variations which Jewish literature develops in its presentation of the splendors of the new Jerusalem. The following text, for example, depicts the Holy City as covering the whole world:

"The word of the Lord is upon the land of Hadrach, and Damascus is its resting place, for the cities of Aram are the Lord's, as are all the tribes of Israel" (Zach. 9:1). R. Judah interpreted this verse to mean that the Messiah will be harsh with the nations but kind to Israel.

R. Joshua (whose mother was from Damascus) replied, "Why do you misinterpret Scriptures for us? I am from Damascus, and I call upon heaven and earth to witness that there is a place called Hadrach."

"How do you explain the phrase, 'Damascus is its resting place'? How will it be realized?"

"In the future Jerusalem will extend as far as Damascus. 'Damascus is its resting place'—but the word of the Lord has no other resting place than Jerusalem, as it says (Ps. 132:14), 'Sion is my resting place forever.' "

"And how will there come to pass that '[Jacob's] city shall be rebuilt upon its hill'?" (Jer. 30:18)

"It will not be shaken from its place."

"And how do you explain that description of the temple: 'The temple had a broad way running upward so that one could pass from the lowest to the middle and the highest story'?" (Ezech. 41:7)

"The land of Israel will go larger and rise higher on all sides, like a figure that is narrow at its base, and the gates of Jerusalem will reach as far as Damascus. This is in keeping with the verse, 'Your nose is like the tower on Lebanon, that looks toward Damascus' (Cant. 7:5). Then the exiles will come and camp in its midst, as it is said, 'Damascus is its resting place.' And it is also written, 'In days to come, the mountain of the Lord's house shall be established as the highest mountain and raised above the hills. All nations shall stream toward it; many peoples shall come and say: Come, let us climb the Lord's mountain, to the house of the God of Jacob, that he may instruct us in his ways, and we may walk in his paths. For from Sion shall go forth instruction, and the word of the Lord from Jerusalem' " (Isa. 2:2-3).

Sifre on Deuteronomy, 1:1

Let us add this statement of R. Eliezer ben Jacob: "In the future Jerusalem will extend as far as the throne of glory, and it will say to the Holy One, blessed be He, 'This place is too narrow for me; give me more room in which to live' " (*Pesikta de Rav Kahana,* 143b).

The Temple, of course, will be rebuilt; it will be more splendid than the old one, and will occupy three holy mountains. According to R. Yose ben Halafta:

Mount Sinai has been separated from Mount Moriah, just as one would separate the challah from the dough, from the place where Isaac, our father, was bound. The Holy One, blessed be He, said that since their father, Isaac, was tied on its summit, it is only fitting that his sons receive the Torah at the same place. But how do we know that it will eventually return to its former place? Because it is written, "The mountain of the Lord's house shall be established as the highest mountain" (Isa. 2:2). The mountains are Tabor, Carmel, Sinai and Zion. This makes five mountains [by dissociating the article *ha,* which has the value of five, from the substantive *harim,* mountains], in analogy with the five parts of the Torah (Pentateuch).

Midrash on Psalms, 68:9

The new Palestine will be equally divided among the thirteen tribes: "In the present world, those who sow wheat have no garden, and those who have a garden do not sow wheat; but in the future everybody will have land on the mountains, in the plains and in the valley, as it is said, " 'There shall be three gates: the gate of Ruben, the gate of Juda, and the gate of Levi (Ezech. 48:31), for God Himself will give every one his share" (B. B. 122a).

This new soil, inevitably, will be miraculously fertile. Here are two testimonies, one from the Apocrypha and one from rabbinic literature:

The earth also shall yield its fruit ten thousandfold and on each vine there shall be a thousand branches, and each branch shall produce a thousand clusters, and each cluster produce a thousand grapes and each grape produce a cor [about 120 gallons] of wine. And those who have hungered shall rejoice: moreover, also, they shall behold marvels every day. For winds shall go forth from before Me to bring every morning the fragrance of aromatic fruits, and at the close of the day clouds distilling the dew of health. And it shall come to pass at that self-same time that the treasury of manna shall again descend from on high, and they will eat of it in those years, because these are they who have come to the consummation of time.

2 Baruch, xxix, 5-8

R. Gamaliel said, "Women will have children every day, as it is written (Jer. 31:8), 'the mothers and those with child.' "

One of his students made fun of him, saying, "There is nothing new under the sun." Thereupon his teacher went out and showed him a hen. Then he went on, "The trees will bear fruit every day, as it says (Ezech. 17:23), 'It shall put forth branches and bear fruit.' This means that as it brings forth branches every day, so it will yield fruit every day."

The student made fun of him again by quoting, "There is nothing new under the sun." Thereupon R. Gamaliel showed him a caper-bush, and continued, "The land of Israel will produce cakes and precious cloth, as it is written, 'May there be plenty of wheat in the land.' "

Shabbat 30b

All the rabbinic schools enjoyed these elaborations, and we also find them in the Hellenistic circles of *The Sibylline Oracles* (see iii, 741, 750). We do not know to what extent such exaggerations were taken literally, or where the line was between reality and symbol. In any event, these details of a future life of plenty answered hopes of a quite earthly nature, and provided encouragement for many.

The deliverance from servitude will be accompanied by an unexpected and rare peace. This is the realization of the prophecies:

The Messiah, called Shalom [Peace], will begin by preaching peace, as it says (Isa. 52:7), "How beautiful up on the mountains are the feet of the one who brings glad tidings of peace."

R. Yose of Galilee, *ca.* 150, "Perek Ha-shalom"

"I will establish peace in the land, that you may lie down to rest without anxiety. I will rid the country of ravenous beasts, and keep the sword of war from sweeping across your land" (Lev. 26:6). This is what is meant by, "Then the wolf shall be a guest of the lamb" (Isa. 11:6). The Israelite will put his hand in the very eye of the serpent, and draw the poison out of its mouth. Not only will they no longer go to war against you, but neither conquerors nor captives will march through the provinces, as they did in the days of King Josia.

Sifra on Leviticus, 26:6

Nevertheless, R. Eliezer felt sure that even in messianic times people will still wear swords, but only as ornaments. This is in keeping with the opinion that the only difference between this world and messianic times will be the cessation of servitude (Shab. 63a).

What will be the political condition of the new Israel? There are prayers for the restoration of judges and princes, as well as for the coming of King Messiah. But what will be the function of this king? *The Psalms of Solomon* shows him establishing perfect justice; the rabbis repeat the prophecy that "The Spirit of the Lord shall rest upon him" (Isa. 11:2), and that he will decide cases simply by his sense of smell. When the rabbis found out that Bar Kochba did not possess that faculty, they killed him (Sanh. 93b). In all other representations the Messiah is like the peaceful and passive president of a people dwelling in bliss.

Our sources have much to say about a spiritual renewal, indicating again that the Jewish mind is as much concerned with the life of the spirit as with that of the body.

The foremost characteristic of the future world is that it will contain nothing but saints; in order to purify the earth and the house of Israel, God will suppress all sinners and strangers. On the basis of Ecclesiastes 12:1, "the year . . . of which you will say, I have no pleasure in them," R. Simeon ben Eleazar deduced that one would be unable to sin or to store up merits. But he was told that the messianic times would not differ from ours (Shab. 151b).

God himself will bring about that holiness, for he will

dwell in the midst of his people and again place his Shekinah in Jerusalem and the Temple. This opinion is emphasized in all the literature of the period, including the Messiahless messianism of *The Book of Jubilees*:

And I will build My sanctuary in their midst and I will dwell with them, and I will be their God and they shall be My people in truth and righteousness. And I will not forsake them nor fail them; for I am the Lord their God. . . . And after this they will turn to Me in all uprightness and with [their] heart and with all [their] soul, and I will circumcise the foreskin of their heart, and the foreskin of the heart of their seed, and I will create in them a holy spirit, and I will cleanse them so that they shall not turn away from Me from that day unto eternity. And their souls will cleave to Me and to all My commandments, and they will fulfil My commandments, and I will be their Father and they shall be My children. And they all shall be called the children of the living God. . . . And the Lord shall appear to the eyes of all, and all shall know that I am the God of Israel and the Father of the children of Jacob, and King on Mount Zion for all eternity. And Zion and Jerusalem shall be holy (i, 19-28).

Future holiness will be assured by fidelity to the Law. The latter will not be altered in messianic times, the commandments will remain the same (*Sifre on Deut.*, 11:17). In accordance with Jeremias 31:33, this law will be engraved in the very hearts of the Israelites (R. Judah, *Cant. Rabbah*, 1:2). They will know it well, because they will be able to devote themselves completely to its study. R. Eleazar Hakkappar is said to have stated that the synagogues and academies in Babylonia would be transferred to the land of Israel. This was in accordance with Jeremias 46:18, "Like Tabor among the mountains he shall come, like Carmel above the sea." His interpretation: "If Mount Tabor and

Carmel, which came for only one hour to receive the Torah, will be established in Israel, this is all the more true of Babylonian synagogues and schools, where the Torah was read and taught" (Meg. 29b).

Since the Temple cult is indispensable to religion, there was hope that it, too, would be re-established. We have already quoted the sixteenth prayer of the *Shemoneh Esreh*, calling for the restoration of sacrifices. People believed that the entire liturgy would be revived (*Tos. Shab.*, i,13):

A heathen once asked R. Akiba, "Why do you observe your festivals? Has not God said to you, 'Your new moons and festivals I detest'?" (Isa. 1:14)

"If he had said, 'My new moons and festivals I detest,' you might be right. He only spoke of 'your new moons and fes-tivals'—referring to those instituted by Jeroboam (3 Kings 12:32). The other festivals will never cease, because they be-long to the Holy One, blessed be He, for it is written, 'The following are the festivals of the Lord' (Lev. 23:2). Of them it is said (Ps. 111:8) that they are 'reliable forever and ever, wrought in truth and equity.' "

Numbers Rabbah, 21:23

Nevertheless, a rabbi at the end of the second century, aware that future conditions would be quite different, said that "In the future all prayers will cease, except that of thanksgiving, which will never be halted. All sacrifices will cease, but not the sacrifice of thanksgiving. This is written in Nehemias 12:39, 'And the two choirs of them that gave praise stood still at the house of God'—the two choirs being the thanksgiving of prayer and the thanksgiving of sacrifice" (*Midrash on Psalms,* 56:4).

Two possibilities were seen for other nations: they could be allies of the Israelites by becoming proselytes, or they could remain their enemies and eventually be defeated. The first approach has a universalist tendency, and is in accordance with the teachings of the prophets. The relevant text from 2 *Baruch* (lxxii, 2-6) has already been quoted. Some rabbis also believe in the future conversion of the nations: "Just as in the past the nations gave up idol worship when they witnessed the destruction of Pharaoh and the Egyptians, in our day they will reject idol worship, as it is said (Jer. 16:19), 'To you will the nations come from the ends of the earth, and say, Mere frauds are the heritage of our fathers, empty idols of no use.' And it is also said (Isa. 2:20, 18), 'On that day men will throw to the moles and the bats the idols of silver and gold,' and 'The idols will perish forever' " (*Mekilta on Exod.*, 15:11).

R. Ishmael ben Yose was fond of remembering his father's interpretations of Psalms 118:1 and 68:32, "The nations will praise God, Egypt and Ethiopia will bring gifts to the Messiah, and since he hesitates to accept them, God commands him to do so" (Pes. 118b).

But is this not contrary to the proposition that in times of prosperity no proselytes ought to be accepted, so that they will not be attracted by motives of self-interest? The question is debated in an interesting text:

R. Isaac had said that the only time when God would laugh would be at the judgment of the nations. R. Yose added that in the future idolators would come to be made proselytes. But can they be accepted, since tradition says they should no more be received at the time of the Messiah than at the time of David and Solomon? They will be insincere converts, even if they wear phylacteries and fringes, and put a mezuzah on their door posts. But when they see the war of Gog and Magog, the former will ask, "Against whom are you fighting?" And they will answer, "Against Yahweh and his Messiah." For it is written (Ps 2:1,3), "Why do the nations rage?" They reject the commandments: "Let us break their fetters

and cast their bonds from us." Then the Holy One, blessed
be He, will be sitting in heaven and smiling, as it is written,
"He who is seated in heaven smiles."

Abodah Zarah 3b

These rabbis are hardly very receptive, but a little later
there were others, basing their opinions on Isaias 9:7 and
Sophonias 3:9, who seem to admit the validity of sacrifices
offered by the nations and the sincerity of their prayers.
According to a prophecy of Jeremias (3:17), all the nations
will assemble in Jerusalem in the name of Yahweh (Ab.
R. N. xxxv, 9). They will bring gifts for the King Messiah,
especially the exiles whom they will lead back, according
to the prophecy of Isaias 66:20. This tradition, also found
in *The Psalms of Solomon* (xvii, 34), reappears in the writing of a fourth-century rabbi, Juda ben Simeon *(Midrash
on Ps.,* 87:6). Another idea, formulated after the third century but suggested earlier, is that Israel will possess the
wealth of the nations. The latter will be the slaves of the
Israelites; they will take care of their sheep, wait on them,
and do all their hard work (Pes. 68a, based on Isa. 61:5).

On the whole, these rabbinical texts show little confidence
in the nations who wish to become attached to the Israelites,
and tend to keep them in a state of inferiority and depend-
ence.

Other documents—it is the second possiblity considered
—present the other nations as enemies at all times *(The
Sibylline Oracles,* iii, 661 ff.; *4 Ezra,* xiii, 33 ff.). They will
rise up against the Messiah and go to war against him. This
is a traditional theme, which the editor of *The Book of
Enoch* has inserted in the midst of the Parables, where it
hardly belongs:

And in those days the angels shall return
And hurl themselves to the east upon the Parthians and
   Medes:

They shall stir up the Kings, so that a spirit of unrest shall
  come upon them,
And they shall rouse them from their thrones,
That they may break forth as lions from their lairs,
And as hungry wolves among their flocks.
And they shall go up and tread under foot the land of His
  elect ones,
And the land of His elect ones shall be before them a thresh-
  ing floor and a highway:
But the city of my righteous shall be a hindrance to their
  horses.
And they shall begin to fight among themselves,
And their right hand shall be strong against themselves,
And a man shall not know his brother,
Nor a son his father or his mother,
Till there be no number of the corpses through their slaugh-
  ter,
And their punishment be not in vain
In those days Sheol shall open its jaws,
And they shall be swallowed up therein,
And their destruction shall be at an end;
Sheol shall devour the sinners in the presence of the elect
  (lvi, 5-8).

The special character of this fragment is the role attributed to the wicked angels, who will stir the nations to rebellion, forcing God's intervention in order to destroy them.

In rabbinic literature, which found an echo in St. John's
Apocalypse (20:8 ff.), the attack of the enemy nations becomes the war of Gog and Magog. That episode in Ezechiel
(38 ff.) has always intrigued Jewish thinking; those mysterious names seemed the incarnation of all evil forces which
will ultimately line up against God and the messianic kingdom. It is believed, therefore, that this war will break out
once the Messiah is in power. Such a war will be a plague
from which we pray to be delivered:

"Remember not the events of the past" (Isa. 43:18)—this refers to the yoke of the other kingdoms. "The things of long ago consider not"—this means the Egyptian yoke. "I am doing something new! Now it springs forth, do you not perceive it?"—this is the war of Gog and Magog. This may be compared to a man who was successful in freeing himself from a bear who had attacked him. While he was recounting the incident of the bear, he was assailed by a lion, and again he escaped. Now he forgot about the bear and remembered only the lion. Then a poisonous snake threw himself on him, and again he was saved. He forgot the first two incidents and talked only about the last one. In the same way Israel's final tribulations will make them forget the first ones.

Tosefta Berakot, i,13

In the Golden Age of the messianic era Israel will have to undergo the most terrible catastrophe of its history. God himself will destroy Gog and Magog as one of his main acts of intervention: "He shone forth from Mount Pharan (Deut. 33:2). There are four dazzling manifestations of the Holy One, blessed be He. The first was in Egypt, as it says (Ps. 80:20), 'O Shepherd of Israel, hearken. . . . From your throne over the cherubim, shine forth.' The second is at the giving of the Law: 'He shone forth from Mount Pharan.' The third is at the time of the Messiah, as it says (Ps. 50:2), 'From Sion, perfect in beauty, God shines forth' " *(Sifre on Deut., 33:2).*

The defeat of this typical enemy inaugurates the final salvation: " 'When in your own land you go to war against an enemy that is attacking you' (Num. 10:9). This refers to the war of Gog and Magog. Does this really only refer to that war to the exclusion of all others? The verse continues, 'The Lord will save you from your enemies.' The only war which will not lead to another servitude is that of Gog and Magog. Therefore, it says (Zach. 14:3), 'The Lord shall go forth and fight against those nations' " (*Sifre on Num.*, 10:9).

These speculations about Gog and Magog show that the Jews had two preoccupations: The nation will never be absolutely secure, it will always have powerful enemies to contend with, but each time God will lead them to a triumphant victory. Moreover, we find here a sketch of the doctrine of the Antichrist. Like the nations which rise against the Messiah in Psalm 2, this powerful adversary represents those powers which will never give up their fight against God and his kingdom.

Chapter Ten
General Eschatology

Under this term we understand mankind's last destiny—the
resurrection and the last judgment. Jewish thinking is beset
by several difficulties when it comes to these basic questions.
We recall the discussions between Sadducees and Pharisees,
with the former rejecting the belief in resurrection. There
is also the problem of how to reconcile a universal eschatology with messianism. Is the resurrection part of the messianic event? Can Israel expect a privileged situation in the
general consummation? Does the last judgment—which
basically affects whole nations—also concern individuals
and their moral actions, so that a broad universalism results
in a truly moral individualism? It is quite natural that these
views about man's final ends occupy an important place in
Jewish theology, and that debate on them was often vigor-
ous.

Resurrection

We have already pointed out that in the first Christian century, belief in resurrection was far from being commonly accepted among the Jews. Josephus, who employed terms borrowed from Greek philosophy, informs us that the Pharisees considered the soul imperishable, whereas the Sadducees are said to have believed that it disappeared together with the body. We read in the Gospels, which reflect the local Jewish feeling so well, that the Sadducees deny the resurrection (Mark 12:18-27). The stories found in the Acts of the Apostles (23:6-10) recall the passion with which the two parties expressed themselves on this point. When Paul simply declares himself a defender of the hope in resurrection, a storm erupted, and he is reconciled with his Pharisaic brethren. When we look through the Apocrypha, we can easily notice that their position is far from what was to become Maimonides' third article of faith. Neither in *The Book of Jubilees, The Assumption of Moses,* nor *The Book of Enoch* is resurrection even mentioned, whereas in *The Book of the Secrets of Enoch* it is affirmed only in the last section and is taken for granted in the Parables. Is the life promised to the righteous in *The Psalms of Solomon* the result of resurrection? In *2 Baruch* and *4 Ezra,* on the other hand, the resurrection is clearly announced. By the end of the first century it seems to have become dogma for the Pharisees. Among those who have no share in the world to come, the Mishnah mentions "the man who says that the revival of the dead cannot be deduced from Scriptures" (Sanh. xi, 1). We would call this nowadays an obligatory dogma of divine faith.

But this dogma was rejected by various heretics—by pagans, Samaritans, and, above all, the Sadducees. A whole system of apologetics is directed against the latter, with counterproofs based on the Bible as the sole authority recognized by both adversaries. We shall quote one of the most complete of these arguments, and one that goes back to the end of the first century:

Some heretics asked R. Gamaliel, "How can one prove that God will revive the dead?"

He answered, "From the Torah, the Prophets and Holy Scripture." Since they did not accept his argument, he continued, "From the Torah, for it says (Deut. 31:16), 'Soon you will be at rest with your fathers.' "

They said to him, "But it says, 'Then this people will take to rendering wanton worship to the strange gods.' "

"From the Prophets, for it is written (Isa. 26:19), 'But your dead shall live, their corpses shall rise; awake and sing, you who lie in the dust. For your dew is a dew of light and the land of shades gives birth.' "

But they countered, "Perhaps this refers to those whom Ezechiel brought back to life."

"From Scripture, as it says (Cant. 7:10), 'Your mouth [is] like an excellent wine—that flows smoothly for my lover, spreading over the lips of sleepers [the dead, in Hebrew edition].' "

But again they replied, "Perhaps this refers to the lips of the rabbis which start moving in their graves whenever someone quotes one of their sayings." They continued to argue with him, until he quoted Deuteronomy 11:9, "[Long life] which the Lord swore to your fathers he would give to them." "It does not say, 'to you' but 'to them,' and this proves that the revival of the dead can be deduced from the Torah." Others report that he cited another text (Deut. 4:4), "You, who clung to the Lord, your God, are all alive today." "It means that not only are you alive today—this is self-evident—but that you will be alive even at the time when all others will be dead. Or: just as you are here today, you will be here in the world to come."

Sanhedrin 90b

For the Sadducees, but more for the benefit of the pagans who could not be convinced by proof from the Bible, arguments from reason were attempted. Here is one, repeated several times by the Fathers of the Church, starting with St. Justin:

An emperor asked R. Gamaliel, "You say that the dead will come back to life. But how can dust become alive?"

The rabbi's daughter asked for permission to answer him and said, "There are two potters in our city. One of them makes his vessels out of water, and the other with clay. Which of the two is more praiseworthy?"

"The one who uses only water."

"Now if God can make a man by using only water, which is harder to accomplish, he can certainly make him out of clay."

Sanhedrin 90b[1]

The nature of the resurrection is clear from the words used to describe it in the Bible, the Apocrypha, and various Greek writings: *kum,* to arise, and *anastasis,* which contains the idea that the body will emerge from the grave in order to rejoin the soul. The expression most common in Hebrew documents, in prayers and sayings by the rabbis, is *tehiyyat hametim,* the revival of the dead. God is called "the One who revives the dead." This shows that the essential character of the resurrection is life as a reward for the righteous.

As a matter of fact, in many representations the resurrection is reserved exclusively for the righteous, and only they

---

[1] St. Justin, *I Apol.,* xviii ff. See J. Rivière, *S. Justin et les apologistes du deuxième siècle* (Paris, 1907), pp. 318 ff.

will enter eternal life. This is Josephus' feeling in the matter, and he attributes it to the Pharisees: "The Pharisees believe the soul to be immortal, and that rewards and punishments will be awarded to those who, while alive, had devoted themselves to vice or virtue. The soul will then be taken to eternal prison or it will receive the faculty to come back to life" (*Antiquities of the Jews*, XVIII, i, 3, par. 14).

The distinction between soul and body lends Jewish beliefs a Greek coloring. In the fifth part of *The Book of Enoch* they are expressed in their authentically Semitic form:

And all the idols of the heathen shall be abandoned,
And the temples burned with fire,
And they shall remove them from the whole earth,
And they [i.e., the heathen] shall be cast into the judgment of
fire,
And shall perish in wrath and in grievous judgment for ever.
And the righteous shall arise from their sleep,
And wisdom shall arise and be given unto them (xci, 9-10).

A disciple of R. Judah Hanasi, R. Hiyya, limits resurrection to the righteous. Commenting on a passage which deals with the benefit of rain (Gen. 2:5), he says that rain is a greater benefit than the resurrection: "The latter is for men, the former for men and animals alike; revival of the dead is for the Israelites, rain for all nations" (*Gen. Rabbah*, 13: 7).

Similarly, in the classical texts which deny certain people a share in the world to come (Sanh. xi, 3; *Tos. Sanh.*, xiii, 2, 6), this detail is added: "They do not live and they are not judged." This particularist conception may be derived from the connection made between messianism and eschatology, and it was thought that only Israel could be the subject of either of them. This led to the further conviction that burial in Israel was a guarantee of future resurrection, and that those interred there would be the first to be revived at the time of the Messiah (*Gen. Rabbah,* 74:1). A permanent and material witness to this belief is given by the numerous Jewish graves found on the slopes of the Mount of Olives and in the neighborhood of Jerusalem. This is a very ancient practice, and Josephus speaks of pious Jews and of proselytes who wish to lie in the holy soil. He also reports that King Monbaz sent the bodies of his mother and brother to Jerusalem in order to be buried (*Antiquities of the Jews,* XX, iv, 3, par. 95); their impressive mausoleum can still be seen there.

Nevertheless, the universalist concept was also maintained. It was the only logical position if resurrection was for the sake of judgment, as suggested by Daniel (12:2), "Many of those who sleep in the dust of the earth shall awake; some shall live forever, others shall be an everlasting horror and disgrace."

The Apocalypse of Baruch combines Jewish traditions with Greek conceptions:

And it shall come to pass after these things, when the time of the advent of the Messiah is fulfilled, that He shall return in glory.

Then all who have fallen asleep in hope of Him shall rise again. And it shall come to pass at that time that the treasuries will be opened in which is preserved the number of the souls of the righteous, and they shall come forth, and a multitude of souls shall be seen together in one assemblage of one thought, and the first shall rejoice and the last shall not be grieved. For they know that the time has come of which it is said that it is the consummation of the times. But the souls of the wicked, when they behold all these things, shall then waste away the more. For they know that their torment has come and their perdition has arrived.

2 Baruch, xxx

A rabbi of the end of the second century, R. Eleazar Hak-kappar, formulates the classical thesis: "Those who are born will have to die, and the dead will be revived. Those revived will be judged, in order to know and to make known that God is builder, creator, the one who understands; he is the judge, the witness, and the adversary, and that he will judge" (Ab. iv, 22).

This sentence bases the universality of the resurrection on the dogma of God the Creator. This idea is also expressed in a verse in Deuteronomy (32:39), "It is I who brings both death and life." This verse finds appropriate commentary: "Could this mean death for one person and life for another? No, for the text continues, 'I . . . inflict wounds and heal them'; just as wounding and curing refer to the same person, death and life apply to the same subject" (*Sifre on Deut.*, 33:39). There are also various rabbinical proofs which assume that resurrection is universal.

As only God can create, he alone can bring someone back to life. Therefore he is sometimes called "the One who revives the dead." How will this be achieved? Those authors influenced by Greek thinking believe that the soul will re-enter the same body it had inhabited before. But this view raises the problem as to how the body will be re-animated. For those trained in Semitic thinking, that question is even graver, since for them man's personal expression is found in his body. Some rabbinic statements seem to be answering real or assumed contradictions:

> Hadrian (the accursed one) asked R. Joshua ben Hananiah, "Out of what will the Holy One, blessed be He, have man spring up in the future?"
> "The spine."
> "How do you know this?"
> "Bring me a spine and I will show you."
> He threw it into the fire, and it was not consumed. He threw it into water, and it was not destroyed. He placed it under

a millstone, and it was not crushed. It was put on an anvil and pounded with a hammer, but whereas both anvil and hammer went to pieces, the spine was not damaged.

Genesis Rabbah, 28:3

The following reminds us of the answers which St. Paul gave to the Corinthians (1 Cor. 15:35):

Queen Cleopatra asked R. Meier, "I know that those who sleep will come back to life, for it says (Ps. 62:16), 'They will flourish in the city like grass in the field.' But when they do arise, will they be clothed or naked?"

I will use a grain of wheat as an example. If that grain is put into the soil naked but emerges clothed in many garments, does it not stand to reason that if the righteous are buried in their clothes, they will certainly come out fully dressed?

Sanhedrin 90b

"In what shape will those live who live in Thy day?
Or how will the splendour of those who [are] after that time continue?
Will they then resume this form of the present,
And put on these entrammeling members,
Which are now involved in evils,
And in which evils are consummated,
Or wilt Thou perchance change these things which have been in the world,
As also the world?"
And He answered . . . "The earth shall then assuredly restore the dead,
[Which it now receives, in order to preserve them].
It shall make no change in their form,
But as it has received, so shall it restore them. . . ."

"For then it will be necessary to show to the living that the dead have come to life again, and that those who had departed have returned [again]. And it shall come to pass, when they have severally recognized those whom they now know, then judgment shall grow strong, and those things which before were spoken of shall come.

"And it shall come to pass, when that appointed day has gone by that then shall the aspect of those who are condemned be afterwards changed, and the glory of those who are justified. For the aspect of those who now act wickedly shall become worse than it is, as they shall suffer torment. Also [as for] the glory of those who have now been justified in My law . . . then their spendor shall be glorified in . . . the light of their beauty. . . . They shall respectively be transformed, the latter into the splendour of angels, and the former shall yet more waste away in wonder at the visions and in the beholding of the forms."

2 Baruch, xlix, 2; li, 5

Judgment

As we have seen, many of these texts present resurrection as a prelude to judgment. *4 Ezra* (vii, 30-33) says clearly that after the seven days of sleep which follow the end of the corrupt world, the earth will give back those who sleep in its depths, and their souls will be returned to them. "The Exalted One will appear in the seat of judgment, there will be no more mercy, and patience will be removed."

In the Bible, judgment, the day of Yahweh, plays a considerable role; the prophets often refer to it as an object of hope and of fear. In post-biblical literature it continues to be the culminating point of the eschatological horizon. The introduction to *The Book of Enoch* is interesting in this regard, making clear that the judgment is the predominant preoccupation of all the apocalyptic writings:

The words of the blessing of Enoch, wherewith he blessed the elect and righteous, who will be living in the day of tribu-

lation, when all the wicked and godless are to be removed.
And he took up his parable and said ... from them the angels
I heard everything ... not for this generation, but for a remote
one which is for to come. Concerning the elect I said, and took
up my parable concerning them:

The Holy Great One will come forth from His dwelling,
And the eternal God will tread upon the earth, [even] on
 Mount Sinai,
[And appear from His camp]
And appear in the strength of His might from the heaven of
 heavens.
And all shall be smitten with fear,
And the Watchers shall quake,
And great fear and trembling shall seize them unto the ends
 of the earth.
And the high mountains shall be shaken,
And the high hills shall be made low,
And shall melt like wax before the flame.
And the earth shall be wholly rent in sunder,
And all that is upon the earth shall perish,
And there shall be a judgment upon all [men].
But with the righteous He will make peace,
And will protect the elect,
And mercy shall be upon them.
And they shall all belong to God,
And they shall be prospered,
And they shall all be blessed. . . .
And light shall appear unto them. . . .
And behold! He cometh with ten thousands of His holy ones
To execute judgment upon all,
And to destroy all the ungodly:
And to convict all flesh
Of all the works of their ungodliness which they have ungodly
 committed.

The Book of Enoch, i

In this development, judgment seems to affect only the wicked, and the righteous have nothing to fear. The prophets protested, however, against this popular attitude.

Let us also quote a statement from *4 Ezra* (vii, 70), in which judgment is presented as intended by God from the very first moment of creation: *Et quando Altissimus faciens faciebat saeculum et Adam et omnes ex eo venerunt, primum praeparavit judicium et quae sunt judicii.*

These texts present two different, but not mutually exclusive, aspects of the judgment. Many of them insist on the terror which will overcome the sinners, as if they were the only ones who have to appear. This is the idea of judgment as punishment, a transposition of the day of Yahweh, leading to the extermination of the enemies of God and Israel. Such a conception is nationalistic and particularistic. But there is also a clearly universalist understanding of judgment. It foresees a truly legal act involving all men, sinners and righteous alike, through which their eternal fate is to be determined. It is in this sense that *4 Ezra* (vii, 113) writes: *Dies judicii erit finis temporis hujus et initium futuri immortalis temporis, in quo per transiit corruptela, soluta est intemperantia, abscissa est incredulitas, crevit autem justitia, orta est veritas.* In this we see the passing from one world to another.

Since the rabbis taught at a time when these conceptions had already become stabilized, they affirm the universal and truly legal character of the judgment. But even with them we find traces of earlier popular opinions: the belief in a judgment which would affect only the nations (Ab. Zarah 2b); the idea that judgment is above all the manifestation of divine vengeance, from which the righteous will be delivered (R. Eliezer, *Mekilta on Exod.*, 16:25); and the tradition according to which three kings, four individuals, and certain generations, who are especially guilty, will have no share in the world to come. They will not even appear at the judgment (Sanh. xi, 3-4), and not because of leniency. In the same sense Enoch is told that several souls will not leave their resting places at the time of the resurrection, because they have already been chastised "by being killed in the days of sinners" (*The Book of Enoch*, xxii, 12 ff.).

Post-biblical literature describes the nature of the judgment in different ways. We shall quote only a few significant features.

Judgment belongs to God alone, since he is the Creator. This statement by R. Eleazar Hakkappar reflects the common opinion. Therefore, it is especially strange to see that in *4 Ezra* and *2 Baruch*, and to some extent in *The Book of the Secrets of Enoch*, judgment is exercised by the Messiah in an eschatological perspective. This clearly shows the transcendent dignity of that Messiah.

The judgment is also described in the terrifying framework of the day of Yahweh, seen appearing in the midst of thunder, accompanied by thousands of the heavenly host. At the same time the event is described as a court session, with all the legal proceedings of human tribunals.

We should point out, however, that in *The Book of the Secrets of Enoch* (lxi, 5), the Messiah separates the righteous from the wicked at the resurrection, which seems to be interchangeable with the judgment.

Men are judged by their deeds, and this may be done in two ways. Our good deeds may be changed into merits, gathered by God and kept in his treasury to reward the righteous *ex propriis operibus* (*4 Ezra*, vii, 33). With this thought in mind King Monbaz is happy to have given to the poor the wealth his forefathers had amassed:

My forefathers amassed wealth for this world, whereas I have gathered treasures for the world to come, as it says (Ps. 85:12), "Truth shall spring out of the earth, and justice shall look down from heaven." My fathers have gathered treasures which can be seized, whereas I have amassed treasures which cannot be seized, as it says (Ps. 89:15), "Justice and judgment are the foundations of your throne." My fathers have gathered wealth which bears no fruit, whereas I have gathered wealth which will bear fruit, as it says (Isa. 3:10), "Happy the just, for it will be well with them, the fruit of their works they will eat." My fathers have amassed material goods, and I have amassed spiritual goods, as it says (Prov. 11:30), "The fruit of virtue is a tree of life." My fathers have amassed for others, and I have amassed for myself, as it says (Deut. 24:13), "It will be a good deed of yours." My fathers have amassed treasures for this world, but I have gathered them for the world to come, as it says (Isa. 58:8), "Your vindication will go before you, and the glory of the Lord shall be your rear guard."

Tosefta Peah, iv, 8

Another concept, a widely spread one, is that of a book, either one in which the individual's deeds are inscribed, or the book of the living containing the names of the righteous. Such notions are based on biblical precedent. R. Akiba had the first type of book in mind: "Everything is given as a pledge, and a net is spread out over all who live. The bank is open, and the teller lends out money. The ledger lends out money, and the hand writes. Anybody can come and take out a loan. But the collectors walk around continuously and demand payment, whether the debtors know it or not; their claims are justified. The judgment is one of truth, and everything is prepared for the banquet [of the righteous]" (Ab. iii, 16).

The Book of Enoch, on the other hand, presents the book of the living, which is open for judgment (xlvii, 3), and which may be identical with the book of life, from which the names of the sinners have been erased (cviii, 3; cf. Exod.

32:32, Isa. 4:3). As in a regular court session, there are witnesses for both prosecution and defense. We have already
heard that R. Eleazar Hakkappar refers to God as both judge
and witness (Ab. iv, 22). Jewish imagination can visualize
many witnesses who would testify: "Perhaps you might say,
'Who will be able to testify against me?' The stones and the
beams of the house will testify against you, as well as two
angels of the service, your body and your soul" (Taan. 11a).

Attorneys for the prosecution and for the defense inter-
vene, but only in a spiritual way. "He who fulfills a commandment acquires a defender, but he who commits a
transgression acquires an accuser" (R. Eliezer ben Jacob,
Ab. iv, 11).

The mathematical correctness of the examination given
by the judge, and of the sentence he pronounces, is expressed
in the classical image of scales. This means that merits and
demerits are weighed. As one dead fly spoils the most
precious oil, so one wrong deed in excess is enough to lose
the benefit of good works (R. Akiba and R. ben Azzai,
Eccles. Rabbah, 10:1).

If we hold to this principle, we must conclude that the
divine judgment is very severe. This feature is underlined
in the Apocrypha. The time for mercy and patience is gone,
prayers and supplications will not help, and even penitence
is of no avail (*4 Ezra* vii, 33, 74, 102-111). Others assure
us that God will be merciful and indulgent, at least toward
the Israelites. *4 Ezra* also expresses the hope that *annuant-
iabitur justitia et bonitas tua, Domine, cum misertus fueris
eis qui non habent substantiam bonorum operum* (viii, 36).
Here is a dialogue between two rabbis who lived at the end
of the first century:

R. Eliezer said: "The scales are in perfect balance. On one
side are the sins, on the other, the merits. God makes the side

with the merits go down. This is indicated in the phrase 'full of mercy' (Num. 14:18), because he inclines toward mercy."

R. Joshua ben Hananiah: "The scales are in perfect balance . . . then God lightens the side of the sins, and the merits carry the day. This is indicated by the phrase, 'He takes away sins.' "

Pesikta de Rav Kahana, 167a

We have seen that according to certain descriptions the day of judgment is one of terror and confusion for sinners. It is a day of destruction, since it inaugurates the time of punishment. Punishment is sometimes shown to begin on the very same day. It is pointed out that God judges the world through fire—meaning either a penetrating examination from which no one can escape (*The Book of the Secrets of Enoch*, xlvi, 3), or some form of chastisement, whether by sword or fire (*The Book of Jubilees*, ix, 15). The happiness of the righteous is often mentioned; they are glad to see the wicked tortured or are even authorized to judge and to execute them (*The Book of Enoch*, xcv, 3; xcvi, 1-2).

The judgment will also put an end to mingling with sinners, from which the righteous suffer. The two categories will be definitively separated, the one going to a place of reward, the other being hurled to the place of punishment.

Eternal Reward and Punishment

The righteous are sustained by hope in such a reward. R. Tarfon said: "The day is short, and the task is great. The workers are lazy, but the reward is large, and the master urges us on. It is not for you to finish the work, but you do not have the right to shirk your duty. If you have studied the Torah well, you will receive a great reward. Your employer may be relied on to recompense you for your work.

But remember that the righteous are to receive their reward in the world to come" (Ab. ii, 15).

The word for reward used in the above statements, is "mercies" (*4 Ezra*). This conforms with the principle of retribution, so dear to the Jewish soul. But at other times the accent is rather on divine mercy. In one of *The Psalms of Solomon* it says: "On that day God will be merciful to those who fear Him, and they will live by the grace of their God, whereas the sinners will perish forever" (xv, 15). Those two ideas—outright payment or voluntary reward according to mercy—find corresponding expression: "to merit life eternal" (R. Eliezer, Ber. 28b); "to be predestined for life in the world to come." This last phrase suggests the thought that only those who are predestined for that favor will receive the eternal reward. In the same sense, *4 Ezra* speaks of reward *quae anteposita eis* (vii, 42).

As for the place of the eschatological reward, the classical doctrine is expressed in *4 Ezra*; the righteous will enter *paradisus jucunditatis* when the corrupt world will give way to an age of incorruption. We find the same idea in the Apocrypha and in rabbinic writings. That place is the Garden of Eden, the first dwelling place of humanity. One must also remember the prophecies, according to which God will create a new heaven and a new earth (Isa. 51:6; 65:17).

This led to the common belief that God will destroy this world and create a new one (*Kaddish* prayer; *Mekilta on Exod.*, 16:25; *Sifre on Deut.*, 11:21). But it was attachment to the Holy Land, especially, and the instinctive confusion between messianism and eschatology which led to the belief that the righteous will taste definite happiness in a miraculously transfigured Palestine. *The Book of Enoch* reports that the angels will prepare for the righteous a place in heaven, and also that the Temple and Palestine will be restored:

> And after this the Righteous and Elect One shall cause the house of his congregation to appear: Henceforth they shall be no more hindered in the name of the Lord of Spirits.
> And these mountains shall not stand as the earth before his righteousness,
> But the hills shall be as a fountain of water,
> And the righteous shall have rest from the oppression of sinners.
>
> *The Book of Enoch,* liii, 6-7

In the first part of *The Book of Enoch,* in *Jubilees,* and in the third of *The Sibylline Oracles,* we find the renewed Palestine as the seat of the final reward. *The Assumption of Moses* sends Israel to heaven (x, 3-9); the last part of *The Book of Enoch* does the same for the saints (civ, 2; cviii, 12). Otherwise, all those documents which do not place the final reward in the renewed Palestine put the happy in Paradise or the Garden of Eden.

That Garden of Eden is more or less clearly identified with the abode of Adam. Some texts (*The Book of the Secrets of Enoch,* viii; xlii, 3), however, place it in the third heaven, which is not God's dwelling place. Most commonly it is believed that it is on earth. Numerous rabbinic statements describe this place, which is already in existence and full of delight for the benefit of the elect. There are endless variations on this theme.

The reward includes material goods. Various rabbinic statements of the third century (e.g., *Gen. Rabbah,* 12:5) assure us that six gifts forfeited by Adam will be given back to man: brilliance, high stature, the fruits of the earth and of the trees, the stars, and life.

This last benefit, more important than all the others, is

mentioned in various forms: the life of the ages, endless life, uncounted days, the end of death. This precision indicates that mortal man especially savors that *fructus immortalitatis,* that *thesaurus immortalitatis (4 Ezra,* vii, 13; viii, 54).

According to the biblical image, the gift of true life is symbolized in the tree of life. It will be given to the righteous who will live in its shade and enjoy its fruit (R. Joshua, *Tanhuma Noah,* 2; R. Judah ben Illai, *Cant. Rabbah,* 6: 9). *The Book of Enoch* develops the image at some length:

And as for this fragrant tree no mortal is permitted to touch it till the great judgment, when He shall take vengeance on all and bring [everything] to its consummation forever. It shall then be given to the righteous and holy. Its fruit shall be for food to the elect: it shall be transplanted to the holy place, to the temple of the Lord, the Eternal King.
Then shall they rejoice with joy and be glad,
And into the holy place shall they enter,
And its fragrance shall be in their bones
And they shall live a long life on earth,
Such as their fathers lived:
And in their days shall no sorrow or plague
Or torment or calamity touch them.
The Book of Enoch, xxv, 4-6

But in spite of the material aspect of this text, such happiness had to appear insufficient to those who were greatly attached to earthly joys. Therefore, we have a long list of bodily enjoyments reserved for the blessed. There will be no more infirmities, because of waters and healing trees available (*4 Ezra,* vii, 123). There will be no childless women, since, as *2 Baruch* predicts (xxiii, 7), they will bear children without pain. R. Gamaliel goes so far as to predict that they will give birth every day (Shab. 30a). In *The Book of Enoch* (x, 17) it is stated that one thousand children will be born daily; according to R. Eliezer ben Yose the number is, rather, six hundred thousand. He bases his teaching on Psalm 45:17, "The place of your fathers your sons shall have" *(Mekilta on Exod., 19:6).*

Outstanding meals represent an even more material pleasure. In fact, the eschatological reward is sometimes called "the banquet" (Ab. iii, 16; iv, 16; Luke 14:15-24). Our whole literature is full of details about the food and drink which have been prepared for this occasion ever since the days of the creation. Then one will eat of the Leviathan and the Behemoth.

Among the more spiritual delights, there is first the light of glory, which will surround the righteous in various degrees:

Of what character will future bliss be? This sentence of Rab is often quoted: "The world to come will not be like this one; there there will be neither eating nor drinking, neither sexual enjoyment nor trade, no envy, hatred or quarreling. But the righteous will sit with their crowns on their heads and bask in the light of the Shekinah, as it says (Exod. 24:14), 'After gazing on God they could still eat and drink.' "

Berakot 17a

And when the Righteous One shall appear before the eyes of
the righteous. . . .
And light shall appear to the righteous and the elect who
dwell on the earth,
Where then will be the dwelling of the sinners? . . .
From that time those that possess the earth shall no longer be
powerful and exalted:
And they shall not be able to behold the face of the holy,
For the Lord of Spirits has caused His light to appear
On the face of the holy, righteous, and elect. . . .
Be hopeful; for aforetime ye were put to shame

Through ill and affliction; but now ye shall shine as the lights
of heaven.

The Book of Enoch, xxxviii, 2-4; civ, 2

"You are now as numerous as the stars in the sky" (Deut.
1:10). This teaches us that in the Garden of Eden there will
be seven groups of righteous, arranged one above the other.
The first is designated by citing Psalm 140:14, "Surely the just
shall give thanks to your name; the upright shall dwell in
your presence."

Sifre on Deuteronomy, 1:10

A more inward happiness is joy, a participation in a
divine attribute (John 15:11; 17:13). Seven kinds of joy are
due to vision: the sun, the moon, the firmament, the stars,
lightning, lilies, and the candelabra of the Temple (R.
Simeon ben Yohai; *Sifre on Deut.,* 1:10). There is also a
joy which is similar to peace (*The Book of Jubilees,* xxiii,
29).

Another joy is derived from the possession of God. All
of the Apocrypha state that God will dwell in the midst of
men. We read in *The Book of Jubilees* (i, 17,26) that God
promises to dwell forever in his sanctuary in Jerusalem.
The Sibylline Oracles (iii, 785 ff.) makes the same prediction: "Rejoice, O Virgin, and be happy; for the Creator
of heaven and earth has given you eternal joy. He will
dwell with you, and you will have an immortal light."

The rabbis affirm that God will make his Shekinah reside
over Israel. R. Simeon ben Yohai declares that he who observes the law of the fringes deserves to see the Shekinah
(Men. 43b). God will act as familiarly with man as he did
before in the Garden of Eden: "Ever present in your midst,
I will be your God" (Lev. 26:12). There is a parable based
on this text: "There was a king who wanted to take a walk
in his garden, accompanied by his farmer. When the latter

wanted to draw back from his presence, the king said to him: Why should you draw back? Are we not alike? In like manner God will invite the righteous to walk with him in the Garden of Eden. And when they appear to be afraid of him, he will say: Why are you afraid of me? Here I am your fellow" (*Sifra on Lev.*, 26:12).

Since God will dwell with the righteous, he will give them his spirit. (R. Ishmael, 135, *Gen. Rabbah*, 26:6). He will purify them and remove their evil nature, the cause of their sins. R. Judah offers this commentary on Zach. 12:11 ("And the land shall mourn, each family apart"):

> The Holy One blessed be He, will take evil nature and kill it in the presence of both the righteous and the wicked. To the righteous it will look like a high mountain, and to the wicked like a hair. Both groups will weep. The righteous will say, "How could we trample on such a high mountain?" The wicked will say, "Why could we not cross such a thin hair?" And God himself will be as surprised as they are, as it says (Zach. 8:6): "If this should seem impossible in the eyes of the remnant of this people, shall it in those days be impossible in my eyes also?"
>
> Sukkah 52a

After their purification the righteous will be full of virtues and observe all the laws. They will have plenty of time to study the Torah, which is both a pleasure and a merit. "There are sixty queens (Cant. 6:8)—R. Judah ben Illai related this phrase to the tree of life in the Garden of Eden. The sixty queens are the sixty groups of righteous men who will sit under the tree of life in the Garden of Eden and study the Torah" (*Cant. Rabbah*, 6:14).

What makes the reward priceless is that it is eternal. This incorruptible world will be without end, as opposed to earthly life which lasts only for one hour (Betzah 15b; *The Book of Enoch*, x, 16, 22; xlvi, 3).

Justice would not be satisfied unless the pain of the wicked corresponded to the eternal bliss of the righteous. It has two forms: the eternal punishments of Gehenna, and temporary punishment.

The Gehenna is the place of chastisement for the wicked, either immediately after their death, or in the eternity which follows the resurrection and the judgment. The word and the notion are frequent in the first century, as indicated by numerous references both in our literature and in the Gospels. Two elements are combined in this conception: the Sheol (Hades), which becomes more and more a place reserved for the wicked; and the inextinguishable fire which consumes the corpses of those who had revolted against God (Isa. 66:24). The word itself originally meant the valley of Hinnom near Jerusalem, where disloyal Jews sacrificed their children to the Moloch, and which consequently became the city dump.

Rabbinical literature has much to say about this hell, but we shall limit ourselves to essentials. The Gehenna has been created by God (R. Meier, Hag. 15a). It is the place of the divine wrath which is manifest in all the punishments he afflicts on mankind, as it says (Deut. 32:22: "By my wrath a fire is enkindled that shall rage to the depths of the nether world." This immense fire is sixty times as big as the Garden of Eden, itself sixty times larger than the world (R. Judah ben Ilai, *Cant. Rabbah*, together with Pes. 94a).

According to an opinion found in the Apocrypha as well as in rabbinic literature, the wicked will be delivered to cruel angels in order to be tortured:

When God takes the soul of the righteous, he does so gently. This may be compared to an honest man who lived in a certain city, and all the people entrusted him with their goods.

When one of them came to reclaim his property, he would go and get it, for the other man could tell him where it was. But when someone sent a son or servant or a messenger, he would have to search a long time, for he did not know where he kept it. Likewise, when God takes the soul of the righteous, he does so gently. But when he is about to take the soul of a wicked man, he delivers it to evil and cruel angels. Therefore it says (Prov. 17:11), "A merciless messenger will be sent against him."

Sifre on Deuteronomy, 34:15

The pains of the Gehenna affect the body as well as the soul. We have mentioned the parable of the blind and the lame. Above all, sufferings of a spiritual order are described in the Apocrypha; there is neither peace nor rest, but lamentations and curses, and the banquet where the righteous are seated is visualized and, in general, the painfully felt absence of the delights granted to the righteous.

The main bodily torture is that of fire, mentioned in nearly all the descriptions. Fire and Gehenna were inseparable and even identical. There are numerous statements dealing with this subject, one showing how firmly such opinions were based on the Scriptures:

Ordinary fire differs from Gehenna fire, for whereas the former was created on Sabbath eve, the latter was created the day before. Some say that it was even created before the universe, as it says (Isa. 30:33), "The pyre has long been ready." R. Yose said, "The fire which was created on the second day of the week never goes out, as it says (Isa. 66:24), 'They shall go out and see the corpses of the men who revolted against me; their worms shall not die, nor their fire be extinguished.' " R. Banaa ben Ulla said, "Why does it not say 'It was good' in connection with the second day of Creation? Because then the fire of the Gehanna was created." But R. Eleazar declared that it is included in the statement of approval on the sixth day: "All he had made was very good."

Pesahim 54a

Side by side with the classical concept of an eternal Gehenna, there are two other forms of chastisement for the wicked. One is extermination at the moment of the judgment. Here is a rabbinical reference:

The Lord said, "My spirit shall not remain in men forever" (Gen. 6.3). R. Ishmael said: "I shall not put my spirit into them at the time when I shall reward the righteous." This is in accordance with what R. Jannai [ca. 225] and R. Simeon ben Lakish [ca. 250] had said, "There is no Gehenna, but a day which will burn up the wicked." This is proven by Malachias 3:19: "That day that is coming will set them on fire." But the rabbis said, "There is a Gehenna, but a fire will come from the bodies of the wicked and burn them, as it says (Isa. 33:11), 'You conceive dry grass, bring forth stubble; my spirit shall consume you like fire.' "

Genesis Rabbah, xxvi, on 6:3

This strange statement, quite in contradiction to classical opinions, is nevertheless in accordance with various concepts found in the Apocrypha. We have already met the cruel angels who receive the souls of the wicked and destroy them. *The Book of Jubilees* (ix, 15; xxxvi, 10) describes the judgment by sword and fire. *The Psalms of Solomon* (xv,13) states that "on the day of judgment the sinners will perish forever." Does this mean a terrible pain or a real destruction? Some texts mention the disappearance of the sinners or omit the Gehenna, and seem to understand it in that way. Perhaps this concept is based on the feeling which reserves resurrection and eternal life to the righteous and thus neglects the wicked. They disappear from the horizon or undergo some kind of rapid torture in order to satisfy the demands of justice.

There is also the idea of a temporary Gehenna:

For the school of Shammai said there would be three categories at the judgment: one will be granted eternal life; eternal shame and disgrace will be given to the completely wicked. Those who are mediocre, half righteous and half sinful, will go down to Gehenna in order to be purified. Then they will be cured, as it says (Zach. 13:9), "I will bring the one third through fire, and I will refine them as silver is refined, and I will test them as gold is tested. They shall call upon my name, and I will hear them." Anna had these in mind when she said (1 Kings [Sam.] 2:6), "The Lord killeth and maketh alive, he bringeth down to hell and bringeth back again." But the school of Hillel quoted the dictum, "He is full of mercy" (Num. 14:8); he inclines toward mercy, and David said of them (Ps. 116:1): "I love the Lord because he has heard my voice in supplication." That whole section speaks of them.

The Israelites and the Gentiles who have sinned with their bodies go down to the Gehenna and are punished there for twelve months. Then their souls disappear, their bodies are burned, and the Gehenna vomits them. They change into ashes and the wind carries them under the feet of the righteous, as it says (Mal. 3:21): "You will . . . tread down the wicked; they will become ashes under the soles of your feet, on the day I take action, says the Lord of Hosts."

But the heretics and the apostates, the traitors and the Epicureans, those who have rejected the Torah and those who have separated themselves from the community, those who have denied the resurrection, and—like Jeroboam and Achab —caused others to sin, those who have terrified the earth of the living and stretched out their hands against God's jurisdiction, over them the Gehenna will close and they will be judged from generation to generation, as it says (Isa. 66:24), "They shall go out and see the corpses of the men who rebelled against me." Sheol will cease, but they will not, as it says (Ps. 49:15): "Their shadow will be consumed in Sheol."

Tosefta Sanhedrin, xiii, 3ff.

This is an interesting text. It reserves Gehenna to the worst sinners, destroys all others, and imagines a kind of purgatory for those in between. This must be explained by the tendency to let God's mercy triumph over his justice, and by the belief and hope that those Israelites who are not totally wicked will not be deprived of eternal bliss. According to a statement attributed to R. Simeon ben Yohai, Isaac, one of the "seven shepherds" of Micheas (5:4), goes to the gates of the Gehenna to deliver his children from judgment (*Cant. Rabbah*, 8:10, and other texts in a similar vein).

Chapter Eleven
Conclusion

How shall we judge the Judaism which we have described, that intermediate space, the bridge between the two Testaments? We cannot determine to what degree it benefits from the divine assistance reserved to the true religion, guardian and instrument of the unique revelation. In the eyes of a Christian, after the economy of Law had been replaced by the economy of Faith, ancient Judaism had become more and more Pharisaic, and could not lay claim to divine assistance which would save it from error and deviation, sustain it with grace, and assure it of constant progress. Nevertheless, since it was deeply rooted in Scriptures and loyal to religious institutions established by God, it continued to be substantially and richly nourished. But it was not safe from every distortion.

This is the only point which should be investigated, and only in this respect, if at all, can Judaism be reproached.

We cannot really accuse Judaism of not having been enlightened by the Christian revelation which it had rejected.

But do we not have a right to blame Judaism for having
rejected Christ and his message? We Christians believe that
the Old Testament intended to pave the way for Christianity. Therefore, when the physical heirs of ancient Israel did
not recognize the one who was the expected and authentic
blossoming of their religion, this means that they were
disloyal to the mission which God had entrusted to them.
The statement of this basic infidelity encourages us to in-
vestigate whether it is not the consequence of another
more secret and prolonged infidelity, an infidelity to the
spirit, or even to the letter, of the revelation of which Israel
was the trustee and the missionary.

How, and through what paradoxical irony was this possible? This people, which as a whole—and especially their
leaders, most of whom were rabbis and Pharisees—spends
its time in studying the Scriptures, and makes no new statement without basing it on a sacred oracle—how could
they, consciously or unconsciously, forsake or betray the
deposit of revelation?

We sincerely believe that one should not accuse Judaism
of fundamental disloyalty but only of a distortion which was
gradual and not realized for a long time. There was a deep
and instinctive tendency, a matter of feeling, but intellec-
tually well defined, which inevitably led to the rejection of
Jesus Christ's claim to be the Messiah, and also gave a
new direction for Judaism, a mentality which would im-
mobilize it in greater and greater rigidity.

We deliberately say distortion, not gross deviation and
obvious disloyalty. Let it also be added that to a certain
extent this distortion had been forced upon Israel because
it was obliged to defend itself. For centuries the Israelites
had been compelled to be on the alert against invasion or

contagion by the heathens around them. They protected themselves by a rigorous separatism. At the time of the Christian era the dangers of corruption in the form of a Hellenism which had conquered all of Alexander's ancient empire had increased in quantity and quality. Through Antiochus Epiphanes it had more or less successfully tried to take roots in Palestine and even in Jerusalem and in the Temple. Although it had been defeated politically, it had seized the spirit of the victors, the Hasmonean princes, and continued to move into the cultured milieus and to infiltrate every area of life and religion.

The Pharisees went to work to repulse this insidious invasion. They used the tactics of every society, especially a spiritual one, which feels itself menaced: They took up defense positions and tightened the static elements in a protective conservatism meant to slow down external dynamic factors. When a city is besieged, one does not have time to listen to mystics, and a man like Jeremias is thrown into jail.

This type of conservatism, in which the accent is on laws rather than mysticism, on Torah rather than on the Prophets, comes more and more to define Judaism. But it does not exclude progress—for example, in the belief in a beyond and in a more spiritual synagogue service.

This conservatism acts rigorously to strengthen separatism and particularism. It tries to reinforce the hedges which it had planted around the Torah. This is the origin of the deficiencies pointed out in this book—the strict and hostile particularism, the rejection of mysticism and of supernatural concepts or operations, an anthropocentrism which leads to the exaggeration of the dignity of man and of the inviolability of his essence in relation to divine grace, a preference for the material and the sensible in religion, and finally, the tendency to make ethics a department of law.

What consequences did these tendencies have in the different chapters of Jewish theology?

In theodicy we find the essential biblical doctrine which can be reduced to this formula: God is One, Father and King. But there are slight changes: We see the tendency to exalt mercy, especially in Israel's favor; there are limits to God's pleasure and to his total predestination, for we must respect human liberty and the principles of a just retribution; God is relegated to a certain inaccessible transcendence by being given dry and abstract attributes, holding back the biblical trend to a theology of hypostases. This whole movement, however, is somewhat compensated by an overflow of the fabulous, and we find an attempt to satisfy the need for the mystical with speculations, often esoteric, about the mystery of creation, the angels, and heaven. These changes leave intact the great lines of biblical monotheism, but may have been a contributing factor in shutting out the revelation of the Trinity.

These tendencies within the realm of theodicy influenced religion as a whole. There is still loyalty to the biblical spirit. We find the constant need to worship, the love of prayer, a painful awareness of man's infirmity and sinfulness, combined with an absolute confidence in the One who hears prayers and a jealous attachment to the traditional worship, an attachment which may lead to martyrdom. The legalistic tendencies are the source of some stiffening and distortion, especially a predominance of ritualism, encouraging belief in the absolute value of rites and symbols (sometimes dangerously close to superstition). The central importance attributed to observances changes customs imposed by religious law into ethnic signs. It is for this reason that Judaism could not expand, as its fundamental universalism would have demanded. This is also the origin of the hostility to Jesus, who tried to reduce that ritualism and to make people realize that true purity is within man and that he must get rid of laws regarding external purity. "Nothing that enters into man can defile him." Nevertheless, Judaism remains on a very high level, since the rabbis do not forget what the Prophets had said concerning an excessive trust in the efficacy of sacrifices, and they satisfy the aspirations of the mind for a more interior worship, which deeply influenced personal prayer and religious instruction.

As far as eschatology is concerned, the deviations are less clearly felt. Pharisaic Judaism clings to the new teaching concerning the resurrection of the dead, the life beyond the grave, and retribution. One may only regret that at least the popular teachers gave themselves the appearance of being too well informed about otherworldly mysteries, too indulgent toward Israel, and correspondingly too severe to the other nations.

Judaism seems to be less loyal to the biblical teaching on messianism. It preserved the hope which guaranteed vitality and survival, but did not always follow the prophetic doctrine. The concern for the national restoration tends to prevail over that of the Kingdom of God; universalist aspects become less important, and the nations are either altogether excluded from the renewed world or they are reduced to the state of slaves or serfs. Above all, the figure of the Messiah becomes vague and loses color and form. He plays a secondary role in the events of the last days; he is deprived of nearly all the supernatural traits which the inspired writers had granted him. The signs of a suffering and dying Messiah are forgotten or misinterpreted. This, too, shuts out universalism and Christianity.

Let us come to the areas in which particularism and legalism had the most disastrous effects.

We cannot blame Israel for clinging so tenaciously to its

clearly revealed national dogma, that of its divine election. We can even understand the consequences of such deep conviction. Since that great and noble nation who occupied the center of the earth believed itself indispensable to God, it had to scorn other nations as the enemies of God and his people. This in turn led to a more and more rigid separatism. The Jews withdrew into themselves and practiced unlimited charity toward one another. This went so far that outsiders like Tacitus received the impression that they nourished hatred for all non-Jews. We do not have to emphasize that such an isolation violated Israel's very mission; how could they expand if one expected proselytes to leave their fatherland in order to become Jews religiously and nationally?

Judaism's instinctive tendencies proved to be most unfortunate in the field of ethics. But we must begin by admitting that the Jews' general loyalty to the divine Law provided them with a way of life far superior to that of other nations and religions. If we point out faults it is not to write off the moral excellence of Israel. The absolute confidence in the value of human liberty was an obstacle to divine grace and a prelude to certain heresies. The supreme importance assigned to the Torah and its study made scholars look down on those who had not applied themselves to it and could therefore lay no claim to justice, piety, and saintliness. The legalistic tendencies which sprang from this attitude clothed ethics with a juridical aspect, so that ceremonial laws were placed on the same rank as those of justice and charity, and precepts, continually increased, became a burden. The inevitable result was a formalism which was interested only in the outward fulfillment of the commandments, and became accustomed to legal fictions in order to twist the laws. This is the border line of hypocrisy, and the rabbis as well as Jesus scolded the Pharisees on this point. Moreover, the insistence on the principle of retribution makes people believe they have a claim to divine rewards. This is the opposite of the gratuitousness of grace, the only attitude the Creator can have toward his creatures. We can well understand St. Paul's stubborn opposition to Judaism. He was not only afraid of repelling the gentiles by forcing them to submit to circumcision, but he felt that the insistence on the Law and on the reward which man could claim for its observance destroyed Christ's message and the whole supernatural aspect underlying the idea of grace.

Let us sum up. Clearly the effect of the distortions we have pointed out is to exclude many Jewish souls from Christianity, which must appear to them as an attack on the monotheism of the Torah, putting an end to the separation of Israel and its privileges. Another effect is blocking the spread of Judaism, putting obstacles in the way of proselytism and even bringing the making of converts to an end. The Chief Rabbi of Paris, Julien Weill, writes: "The idea of a formal mission of conversion to integral Judaism is, as a matter of principle, foreign to Judaism."[1] Is this not a renunciation of the mission which God has assigned to his servant Isaias? (49:6) "It is too little . . . for you to be my servant, to raise up the tribes of Jacob, and to restore the survivors of Israel; I will make you a light to the nations, that my salvation may reach to the ends of the earth." The chosen people cannot shirk that duty. To reject it means a betrayal of office or, at least, disloyalty, and is a consequence of the distortions we have mentioned.

In spite of all this—and this, too, is one of our conclusions —Judaism, as the possessor of biblical revelation, still owns a rich substance with which to nourish pious souls. Not only rabbis, but simple and pious laymen, find nourishment for

[1] Julien Weill, *Le Judaisme* (Paris, 1931), p. 203.

their faith in the devout reading of their Bible; they observe all the laws exactly and joyfully, and practice scrupulous justice and charity even with gentiles. Such souls delight in synagogue worship and privately recite the Psalms and songs of the holy books with the piety in which they were written.

Because of tendencies we have mentioned, exaggerating man's dignity and rights, eliminating the sense of mystery and man's supernatural dimension, many Jews have forsaken traditional beliefs and practices. Others have tried to preserve some elements of their ancient religion but in a naturalized way: the dogma of the resurrection has been replaced by theories concerning the immortality of the soul; messianism becomes "the belief in the coming of an epoch where all men will be united by the same worship, by the same feeling of love and adoration of the One God, the God of justice and charity."[2] Those who read the Bible accept it as a human book, eliminating the miracles which would offend the modern mind. Finally, in the Torah is seen only the most perfect type of a natural religion, the product of the experiences and of the moral conscience of the Jewish people. What, then, remains of a positive and divinely revealed religion?

What is kept is the national dogma of the election of Israel, its eternity and the importance of its role in the world. The twin creation, religion-nation, shaped by God himself, has been separated under the onslaught of an excessive humanism. The element "nation" remains with the undertone of "religion," but restricted to a mystical nationalism. This is especially so with the Zionists, and only a little less so with many young Jewish nationalists who proclaim Israel's rights and duties as a spiritual family, with a view

[2] Julien Weill, *ibid.*, p. 124, quoting M. Mayer, *Instructions morales et religieuses* (Paris, 1885), p. 33. On the liquidation of messianism, see our *Sur les ruines du Temple* (Paris, 1928), pp. 179, 188, 190.

to maintaining and developing their own culture, retaining their identity in the midst of other nations with which they do not wish to become assimilated. Although they are religiously indifferent, they still read and respect the Bible, but as the most representative monument of their national genius, just as they consider the national cult as an heirloom. While they do not frequent the synagogue, they excommunicate those who forsake it in order to join Christ. Nevertheless, these converts declare that only then have they discovered true Judaism, the Israel they had not previously known. For the figures of Christ and of the Church assume their proper significance only in the light of the divine realities already present in Palestinian Judaism.

Selected Bibliography

ABBREVIATIONS

HCA   Hebrew College Annual
JTS   Journal of Theological Studies
MGWJ   Monatsschrift für Geschichte und Wissenschaft des Judentums
RB   Revue Biblique
REJ   Revue des Études Juives
RSPT   Revue des Sciences Philosophiques et Theologiques
JQR   Jewish Quarterly Review

Apocrypha

SOURCES

The Apochypha and Pseudepigrapha of the Old Testament. Translated into English, with Introduction and notes to the several books. Edited by R. H. Charles in conjunction with many scholars. 2 vols. Vol. I: *Apocrypha.* Vol. II: *Pseudepigrapha.* Oxford, 1913.

Ascension d'Isaïe. Translation of the Ethiopian version by E. Tisserant. Paris, 1908.

The Book of The Secrets of Enoch. Translated from the Slavonic by W. R. Morfill. Edited by R. H. Charles. Oxford, 1896.

Die Damaskusschrift. Edited by L. Rost. Berlin, 1933.

3 Enoch, or: The Hebrew Book of Enoch. Edited and translated by H. Odeberg with Introduction, commentary, and critical notes. Cambridge, 1928.

The Letter of Aristeas. Edited and translated by H. G. Meecham. Manchester, 1935.

La lettera di Aristea a Filocrate. Introduction and commentary by R. Tramontano. Naples, 1931.

Liber apocalypseos Baruch filii Neriae. Edited and translated by

M. Kmosko. (*Patrologia syriaca,* edited by R. Graffin, Vol. II.) Paris, 1938.
Le livre d'Henoch. Translated according to the Ethiopian text by F. Martin. Paris, 1906.
Les Psaumes de Salomon. With Greek text. Translated and Introduction by J. Viteau. Paris, 1911.

LITERATURE

FREY, P. *Dictionnaire de la Bible. Supplement.* Vol. I. Col. 354-360.

Philo

SOURCES

PHILO JUDAEUS. *Philo.* ("Philosophica Judaica.") Edited by Hans Lewy. Oxford, 1946.
———. *Philonis alexandrini opera quae supersunt.* Edited by L. Cohn and P. Wendland. Berlin, 1896-1915.

LITERATURE

BRÉHIER, É. *Les idées philosophiques et religieuses de Philon.* Paris, 1928.
DRUMMOND, J. *Philo Judaeus; or the Jewish-Alexandrian.* 2 vols. London, 1888.
HEINEMANN, J. *Philons griechische und jüdische Bildung.* Breslau, 1932.
STEIN, E. *Philo und der Midrasch.* Giessen, 1931.
WOLFSON, H. A. *Philo, Foundations of Religious Philosophy in Judaism, Christianity, and Islam.* Cambridge (Mass.), 1947.

Josephus

SOURCES

JOSEPHUS, FLAVIUS. *Complete Works.* 8 vols. Cambridge: Harvard University Press, 1926-63.
———. *La guerra giudaica.* Translated with commentary by G. Ricciotti. 4 vols. Torino, 1937.
———. *Jewish Wars.* Translated by G. A. Williamson. Baltimore: Penguin Books, 1959.

———. *Josephus*. Critical edition. Edited by Niese. Berlin, 1887-1905. French translation under the general editorship of Theodore Reinach. Paris, 1900-1932.

LITERATURE

GUTTMANN, H. *Die Darstellung der jüdischen Religion bei Flavius Josephus*. Breslau, 1928.
LAQUEUR, R. *Der jüdische Historiker Flavius Josephus*. Berlin, 1920.
RAPPAPORT, S. *Agada und Exegese bei Flavius Josephus*. Frankfurt a. M., 1930.
THACKERAY, H. ST. J. *Josephus, the Man and the Historian*. New York, 1929.

Rabbinical Literature

SOURCES

The Babylonian Talmud. Translated into English under the general editorship of I. Epstein. 38 vols. London, 1938-1947.
Der babylonische Talmud. Edited and translated by Goldschmidt. 9 vols. Berlin and Leipzig, 1897 and 1929.
Bereschit Rabba. With critical notes and commentary by Theodor Albeck. Berlin, 1930-1931.
The Fathers according to Rabbi Nathan (Abot de-R. Nathan). Translated by Judah Goldin. New Haven, 1955.
Mekilta [on Exodus]. Edited by H. S. Horovitz. ("Corpus tannaiticum.") Frankfurt a. M., 1921.
Michilta de Rabbi Simon ben Jochai. Edited by D. Hoffmann. Frankfurt a. M., 1906.
Michna. Schocken Edition. (Hebrew text.) Berlin, 1937.
Midrach [on Psalms]. Edited by S. Buber. Vilna, 1919.
The Midrash on Psalms. Edited by William G. Braude. 2 vols. New Haven, 1959.
Midrach Tanhuma [on the Pentateuch]. Edited by S. Buber. Vilna, 1913.
Midraschim qetannim. Edited by S. Buber. Vilna, 1925.
Midrash Rabba [on the Pentateuch and the Megillot]. Vilna, 1896.
Die Mischna. Text, translation, and explanatory notes by G. Beer *et. al.* Giessen, 1912-33.
The Mishnah. Translated from the Hebrew, with introduction and brief explanatory notes by H. Danby. Oxford, 1933.

Osar midrashim. Bibliotheca Midrashica. A library of two hundred minor midraschim. Edited by J. D. Eisenstein. New York, 1915.
Pesiqta de Rab Kahana. Edited by S. Buber. Lyck, 1868.
Pesiqta Rabbathi. Edited by Friedmann. Vienna, 1880.
Saying of the Jewish Fathers (Pirke Abot). Translated with commentary by C. Taylor. Cambridge, 1897.
Seder Eliahu Rabba et Seder Eliahu zutta. Vienna, 1902.
Seder Olam Rabba (Die grosse Weltchronik). Edited by Ratner. Vilna, 1897.
"Shemoneh Esreh, Kaddish," etc. Appendices. Dalman, *Die Worte Jesu.* Leipzig, 1898.
Siphra [on Leviticus]. Edited by I. H. Weiss. Vienna, 1862.
Siphre [on Deuteronomy]. Edited by Friedmann. Vienna, 1864.
Siphre [on Numbers]. Edited by H. S. Horovitz. Leipzig, 1917.
Talmud Babli. Vilna, 1896.
Talmud Yerushalmi. Krotoshin Edition. 1866.
Tosephta. Edited by M. S. Zuckermandel. Pasewalk, 1880.
Yalkut Shimoni. Warsaw, 1876.

LEGENDS AND LITERATURE

ALBECK, C. *Untersuchungen über die Redaktion der Mischna.* Berlin, 1936.
BACHER, W. *Die Agada der babylonischen Amoräer.* Budapest, 1878.
———. *Die Agada der palästinensischen Amoräer,* 3 vols. Strasbourg, 1892, 1896, 1899.
———. *Die Agada der Tannaiten.* Strasbourg, 1890, 1903.
———. *Die exegetische Terminologie der jüdischen Traditionsliteratur.* Vol I: *Tannaiten.* Vol. II: *Amoräer.* Leipzig, 1899.
———. *Tradition und Tradenten in den Schulen Palästinas und Babyloniens.* Leipzig, 1914.
BONSIRVEN, J. *Exégèse rabbinique. Exégèse paulinienne.* Paris, 1928.
DALMAN, G. *Grammatik des jüdisch-palästinischen Aramäisch.* Leipzig, 1905.
FINKELSTEIN, L. *Akiba: Scholar, Saint, and Martyr.* New York, 1961.
FREY, J. B. *Corpus inscriptionum judaicarum.* Rome, 1936.
GINZBERG, L. *The Legends of the Jews.* 7 vols. Philadelphia, 1928.
GLATZER, N. N. *Untersuchungen zur Geschichtslehre der Tannaiten.* Berlin, 1933.
JASTROW, M. J. *A Dictionary of the Talmud Babli and Yerushalmi and the Midrashic Literature.* New York, 1926.
KADUSHIN, M. *Organic Thinking: A Study in Rabbinic Theology.* New York, 1938.
———. *The Rabbinic Mind.* New York, 1952.
KOHUT, A. *Aruch completum.* Vienna, 1926.

LAUTERBACH, J. Z. *Rabbinic Essays.* Cincinnati, 1951.
LÉVY, J. *Neuhebräisches und chaldäisches Wörterbuch über die Talmudim und Midraschim.* Leipzig, 1932.
MIELZINGER, M. *Introduction to the Talmud.* New York, 1935.
MONTEFIORE, G. G., and H. LOEWE. *A Rabbinic Anthology.* New York, 1938, 1959.
SPANIER, A. *Die Toseftaperiode in der Tannait Literatur.* Berlin, 1936.
STEWART, ROY A. *Rabbinic Theology.* Edinburgh and London, 1961.
STRACK, H. *Introduction to the Talmud and Midrash.* Philadelphia, 1945.

General Works

ABRAHAMS, I. *The Legacy of Israel.* Oxford, 1927.
———. *Studies in Pharisaism and the Gospels.* Cambridge, 1917.
BERGMANN, J. *Jüdische Apologetik im neutestamentlichen Zeitalter.* Berlin, 1908.
BLUMENKRANZ, BERNHARD. *Die Judenpredigt Augustins, ein Beitrag zur Geschichte der jüdischchristlichen Beziehungen in den Ersten Jahrhunderten.* Basel, 1946.
BOKSER, BEN ZION. *Pharisaic Judaism in Transition.* New York, 1935.
BONSIRVEN, J. *Le judaïsme palestinien au temps de Jésus-Christ, sa theologie.* 2 vols. Paris, 1935.
BOUSSET, W. *Die Religion des Judentums in Späthellenistischen Zeitalter.* Edited by H. Gressmann. Tübingen, 1926.
BROWNE, L. E. *Early Judaism.* Cambridge, 1929.
BUBER, MARTIN. *Two Types of Faith.* London, 1951.
CHARLES, R. H. *Religious Development Between the Old and New Testaments.* New York: Home University Library of Modern Knowledge, No. 88, n.d.
DAUBE, DAVID. *The New Testament and Rabbinic Judaism.* London, 1956.
DAVIES, W. D. *Christian Origins and Judaism.* Philadelphia, 1962.
———. *Paul and Rabbinic Judaism.* London, 1948.
EFROS, ISRAEL. *Ha-Pilosofia Ha-Yehudit Ha-Atikah.* Jerusalem, 1959.
FINKELSTEIN, L. *The Pharisees.* Philadelphia, 3rd Rev. Ed., 1962.
FRIEDLÄNDER, M. *Geschichte der jüdischen Apologetik als Vorgeschichte des Christentums.* Zürich, 1903.
GLATZER, N. N. *Geschichte der talmudischen Zeit.* Berlin, 1937.
———. *Hillel the Elder: The Emergence of Classical Judaism.* New York, 1956.
GOLDSTEIN, MORRIS. *Jesus in Jewish Tradition.* New York, 1950.
GRANT, FREDERICK C. *The Earliest Gospel.* Nashville, 1943.
GUEDEMANN, M. *Jüdische Apologetik.* Glogau, 1906.

266   **Selected Bibliography**

HERFORD, T. *Judaism in the N. T. Period.* London, 1928.

HURST, G. L. *The Literary Background of the New Testament.* New York, 1928.

ISAAC, JULES. *Jésus et Israel.* Paris, 1959.

JEREMIAS, JOACHIM. *Jerusalem zur Zeit Jesu. Kulturgeschichtliche Untersuchung zur N. T. Zeitgeschichte.* 3 vols. Leipzig, 1923, 1924, 1929.

KLAUSNER, J. *Jesus of Nazareth, His Time, His Life, His Doctrine.* New York, 1925.

KOHLER, K. *Jewish Theology, Systematically and Historically Considered.* New York, 1928.

———. *The Origins of the Synagogue and the Church.* New York, 1929.

LIEBERMAN, SAUL. *Greek in Jewish Palestine.* New York, 1942.

———. *Hellenism in Jewish Palestine.* New York, 1950.

MEYER, E. *Ursprung and Anfänge des Christentums.* Stuttgart, 1921.

MONTEFIORE, C. G. *Rabbinic Literature and Gospel Teachings.* London, 1930.

MOORE, C. F. *Judaism in the First Centuries of the Christian Era.* Vol. III. *The Age of the Tannaim.* Harvard, 1927.

PARKES, JAMES W. *The Foundations of Judaism and Christianity.* London, 1960.

———. *Judaism and Christianity.* Chicago, 1948.

RADIN, M. *The Jews Among the Greeks and Romans.* Philadelphia, 1915.

SCHECHTER, S. *Some Aspects of Rabbinical Theology.* London, 1909.

SCHLATTER, D. A. *Geschichte Israels von Alexander dem Grossen bis Hadrian.* Stuttgart, 1925.

SCHOEPS, HANS J. *Aus Frühchristlicher Zeit.* Tübingen, 1950.

———. *Paul.* Philadelphia, 1961.

SCHÜRER, E. *A History of the Jewish People in the Time of Jesus.* Edited and introduction by N. N. Glatzer. New York, 1961.

SIMON, MARCEL. *Verus Israel. Étude sur les Relations entre Chrétiens et Juifs dans l'Empire Romain (134-425).* Paris, 1945.

STRACK, H., and P. BILLERBECK. *Kommentar zum Neuen Testament, aus Talmud und Midrasch,* 4 vols. Munich, 1922-28.

WEBER, F. *Jüdische Theologie auf Grund des Talmud und verwandter Schriften, gameinfasslich dargestellt.* Leipzig, 1897.

God, the Heavens, and the Angels

ABELSON, J. *The Immanence of God.* London, 1912.
ABRAHAMS, I. *The Glory of God.* Oxford, 1925.

BOX, G. H. "The Idea of Immediation in Jewish Theology," *JQR*, XXIII (1932), pp. 415-437.

CONYBEARE, F. C. "Christian Demonology," *JQR*, VIII, pp. 59-114, 576-608; IX, pp. 444-470, 581-603.

FREY, J. "L'angélologie juive au temps de Jésus-Christ," *RSPT* (1911), pp. 75-110.

————. "Dieu et le monde d'après les conceptions juives au temps de Jésus-Christ," *RB* (1916), pp. 33-53.

JUNG, L. *Fallen Angels in Jewish, Christian and Mohammedan Literature.* Philadelphia, 1926.

MARMORSTEIN, A. *The Old Rabbinic Doctrine of God.* Vol. I: *The Names and Attributes of God.* Vol. II: *Essays in Anthropomorphism.* Oxford, 1927, 1937.

MAYBAUM, S. *Die Anthropomorphien und Anthropopathien bei Onkelos.* Breslau, 1870.

PARZEN, H. "The Ruah Hakodesch in Tannaic Literature," *JQR*, XX (1929), pp. 51-76.

SCHOLEM, G. *Jewish Gnosticism, Merkabah Mysticism, and Talmudic Tradition.* New York, 1962.

WICKS, H. J. *The Doctrine of God in the Jewish Apocryphal and Apocalyptic Literature.* London, 1915.

Israel and the Nations

ABRAHAMS, I. "How Did the Jews Baptize?" *JTS*, XII, pp. 609-612.

APTOWITZER, V. *Parteipolitik der Hasmonderzeit im rabbinischen und pseudepigraphischen Schrifttum.* New York, 1927.

BAECK, L. *Die Pharisäer.* Berlin, 1934.

BAER, Y. *Yisrael ba-amim: eeyoonim b'toledot y'mai ha-bayit ha-sheni oo-t'koofat ha-mishna ha-halaka v'ha-emunah.* Jerusalem, 1947.

BAMBERGER, BERNARD J. *Proselytism in the Talmudic Period.* Cincinnati, 1959.

BIALOBLOCKI, S. *Die Beziehungen des Judentums zu Proselyten und Proselytentum.* Berlin, 1930.

BLOCH, J. S. *Israel und die Völker.* Berlin, 1902.

BURKITT, F. C. "Jesus and the Pharisees," *JTS* (1928), pp. 392-397.

DEISSMANN, A. *Die Hellenisierung des semitischen Monotheismus.* Leipzig, 1903.

DIX, GREGORY. *Jew and Greek in the Primitive Church.* London, 1953.

ELBOGEN, J. *Die Religionsanschauungen der Pharisäer.* Berlin, 1904.

FINKELSTEIN, L. *The Pharisees, the Sociological Background of Their Faith.* Philadelphia, 1938.

HELFGOTT, BENJAMIN W. *The Doctrine of Election in Tannaitic Literature.* New York, 1954.
HERFORD, T. *The Pharisees.* London, 1912.
LAUTERBACH, J. Z. "The Pharisees and Their Teachings," *HCA* (1929), pp. 75 ff.
LIGHTLEY, J. W. *Jewish Sects and Parties in the Time of Christ.* London, 1925.
MINKIN, J. S. *Herod, King of the Jews.* New York, 1936.
REINACH, T. *Textes d'auteurs grecs et romains relatifs au judaïsme.* Paris, 1895.
RIDDLE, D. W. *Jesus and the Pharisees.* Chicago, 1928.
ROWLEY, H. H. *The Biblical Doctrine of Election.* London, 1950.
WELLHAUSEN, J. *Die Pharisäer und die Sadducäer.* Hanover, 1924.
ZEITLIN, S. *The Sadducees and Pharisees.* New York, 1936.

The Torah

AICHER, G. *Das Alte Testament in der Mischna.* Fribourg, 1906.
BLANK, S. H. "The LXX Renderings of Old Testament Terms of Law," *HCA* (1930), pp. 259-283.
ENELOW, H. G. *The Mishna of Rabbi Eliezer or the Midrash of Thirty-Two Hermeneutic Rules.* New York, 1933.
FREY, J. B. "La Révélation d'après les conceptions juives au temps de Jésus-Christ," *RB* (1916), pp. 472-510.
HEINEMANN, J. "Die Lehre vom ungeschriebenen Gesetz im jüdischen Schrifttum," *HCA* (1927).
HERZOG, I. *The Main Institutions of Jewish Law.* London, 1936.
MARMORSTEIN, A. "Religionsgeschichtliche Studien." (*Die Schriftgelehrten,* Vol. II.) Skotschau, 1912.
ZEITLIN, S. *An Historical Study of the Canonization of the Hebrew Scriptures.* Philadelphia, 1922.

Ethics

AMRAM, D. W. "Retaliation and Compensation," *JQR* (1911), pp. 191-211.
ARENDZEN, J. P. *Men and Manners in the Days of Christ.* London, 1928.
BAMBERGER, B. J. "Fear and Love of God in the Old Testament," *HCA* (1929), pp. 39-52.
BLAU, L. *Die jüdische Ehescheidung und der jüdische Scheidebrief.* Strasbourg, 1911.

BENAMOZEGH, E. *Morale juive et morale chrétienne.* Florence, 1925.

BLOCH, M. *Der Vertrag nach mosaisch-talmudischem Recht.* Budapest, 1893.

BÜCHLER, A. "The Levitical Impurity of the Gentiles in Palestine Before 70," *JQR* 1926), pp. 1-81.

——. *Studies in Sin and Atonement in the Rabbinic Literature of the First Century.* Oxford, 1928.

——. *Das Synedrium in Jerusalem.* . . . Vienna, 1902.

COHEN, H. *Der Nächste.* . . . Berlin, 1935.

DALMAN, G. *Die richterliche Gerechtigkeit im Alten Testament.* Berlin, 1897.

EHRENFELD, A. *Der Pflichtbegriff in der Ethik des Judentums.* Bratislava.

EJGES, S. *Das Geld im Talmud.* Vilna, 1930.

EPSTEIN, L. M. *The Jewish Marriage Contract.* New York, 1927.

FREY, J. B. "Le péché originel dans les anciennes sources juives," *RSPT* (1911), pp. 507-545.

HUGHES, H. M. *The Ethics of Jewish Apocryphal Literature.* London.

ISSERMAN, F. M. *Rebels and Saints. The Social Message of the Prophets of Israel.* St. Louis, 1933.

JELLINEK, A. *Das Weib in Israel.* Vienna, 1866.

KATZ, M. *The Protection of the Weak in the Talmud.* New York, 1925.

LAZARUS, M. *The Ethics of Judaism.* Philadelphia, 1900-1901.

MARCUS, R. *Law in the Apocrypha.* New York, 1927.

MARMORSTEIN, A. *The Doctrine of Merits in Old Rabbinical Literature.* London, 1920.

MEYEROWITZ, A. *Social Ethics of the Jews.* New York, 1935.

RAPPAPORT, W. *Das religiöse Recht.* . . . Berlin, 1913.

SANDER, R. *Furcht und Liebe im palästinischen Judentum.* Berlin, 1935.

SCHLATTER, D. A. *Der Glaube im N. T.* Stuttgart, 1927.

SIMON, O. J. "The Position of Faith in the Jewish Religion," *JQR* (1889-90), pp. 53-61.

STAERK, W. *Sünde und Gnade nach der Vorstellungen des älteren Judentums.* Tübingen, 1905.

WEILL, E. *La femme juive, sa condition légale d'après la Bible et le Talmud.* Paris, 1907.

YAHUDA, J. *Law and Life According to Hebrew Thought.* Oxford, 1932.

ZIEGLER, J. *Die sittliche Welt des Judentums.* Leipzig, 1928.

ZUCKROW, S. *Adjustment of Law to Life in Rabbinic Literature.* Boston, 1928.

270 Selected Bibliography

Religious Life

ABELSON, J. *Jewish Mysticism.* London, 1913.

AUCLER, P. "Le Temple de Jérusalem au temps de N.-S. J.-C.," *RB* (1898), pp. 193-206.

BAECK, L. *Ursprung und Anfänge der jüdischen Mystik.* Giessen, 1927.

BÜCHLER, A. *Die Priester und der Cultus im letzten Jahrzehnt des jerusalemischen Tempels.* Vienna, 1895.

EDERSHEIM, A. *The Temple, Its Ministry and Services at the Time of Jesus Christ.* London, 1874.

ELBOGEN, J. *Der jüdische Gottesdienst in seiner geschichtlichen Entwicklung.* Frankfurt a. M., 1924.

JEREMIAS, A. *Jüdische Frömmigkeit.* Leipzig, 1929.

KLOSTERMANN, A. *Schulwesen im alten Israel.* Leipzig, 1908.

LOEB, I. "Les dix-huit bénédictions," *REJ*, XIX (1889), pp. 17-40.

MEINHOLD, J. *Sabbas und Woche im A. T.* Göttingen, 1905.

SCHAUSS, H. *The Jewish Festivals. From the Beginnings to Our Own Day.* Cincinnati, 1938.

SCHOLEM, G. *Major Trends in Jewish Mysticism.* New York, 1941, 1946, 1955.

WENDEL, A. *Das israelitisch-jüdische Gelübde.* Berlin, 1931.

ZOBEL, M. *Das Jahr des Juden in Brauch und Liturgie.* Berlin, 1936.

ZUNZ, L. *Die gottesdienstlichen Vorträge der Juden, historisch entwickelt.* Frankfurt a. M., 1892.

Messianism and Eschatology

BAECK, L. "Der Menschensohn," *MGWJ* (1937), pp. 12 ff.

BERTHOLET, A. *Das religionsgeschichtliche Problem des Spätjudentums.* Tübingen, 1909.

BRIERRE-NARBONNE, J. *Les prophéties messianiques de l'A. T., dans la littérature juive. . . .* Paris, 1933.

CHARLES, R. H. *A Critical History of the Doctrine of a Future Life in Israel, in Judaism, and in Christianity.* London, 1899.

CHEYNE, T. K. *Jewish Religious Life After the Exile.* New York, 1898.

DALMAN, G. *Der leidende und der sterbende Messias der Synagogue im ersten nachchristlichen Jahrtausend.* Berlin, 1888.

ESHKOLI, AARON ZEV. *Ha-Tenuot Ha-Meschichit B'Yisrael.* Jerusalem, 1956.

GOLLANCZ, H. *Tophet and Eden (Hell and Paradise).* London, 1921.

GREENSTONE, J. H. *The Messiah Idea in Jewish History.* Philadelphia, 1906.

GRESSMANN, H. *Der Messias.* Göttingen, 1929.

GRY, L. *Les Paraboles d'Henoch et leur messianisme.* Paris, 1906.

KLAUSNER, JOSEPH. *The Messianic Idea in Israel.* New York, 1955.

———. *Die messianischen Vorstellungen des jüdischen Volkes im Zeitalter der Tannaiten.* Berlin, 1904.

LAGRANGE, M. J. *Le messianisme chez les Juifs (150 av. J.-C. à 200 ap. J.-C.).* Paris, 1909.

LÉVI, I. "L'avènement de l'ère messianique," *REJ,* LXIX (1919), pp. 122-128.

OESTERLEY, W. O. E. *The Doctrine of the Last Things, Jewish and Christian.* London, 1908.

RABINSOHN, M. *Le messianisme dans le Talmud et les Midraschim.* Paris, 1907.

SILVER, A. H. *A History of Messianic Speculation in Israel.* New York, 1927.

SPIRA, S. *Die Eschatologie der Juden nach Talmud und Midrasch.* Halle, 1889.

STANTON, V. H. *The Jewish and the Christian Messiah.* Edinburgh, 1886.

VOLZ, P. *Jüdische Eschatologie von Daniel bis Akiba.* Tübingen, 1936.

WISCHNITZER, RACHEL. *The Messianic Theme in the Paintings of the Dura Synagogue.* Chicago, 1948.

WÜNSCHE, A. *Die Leiden des Messias in ihrer Uebereinstimmung mit der Lehre des A. T. und den Aussprüchen der Rabbiner in den Talmuden, Midraschim und andern alten rabbinischen Schriften.* Leipzig, 1870.